Learner Choice, Learner Voice

Learner Choice, Learner Voice offers fresh, forward-thinking supports for teachers creating an empowered, student-centered classroom. Learner agency is a major topic in today's schools, but what does it mean in practice, and how do these practices give students skills and opportunities they will need to thrive as citizens, parents, and workers in our ever-shifting climate? Showcasing authentic activities and classrooms, this book is full of diverse instructional experiences that will motivate your students to take an agile, adaptable role in their own learning. This wealth of pedagogical ideas – from specific to open-ended, low-tech to digital, self-expressive to collaborative, creative to critical – will help you discover the transformative effects of providing students with ownership, agency, and choice in their learning journeys.

Ryan L. Schaaf is Associate Professor of Educational Technology at Notre Dame of Maryland University and a graduate faculty member in the Johns Hopkins School of Education at Johns Hopkins University, USA.

Becky Zayas is a middle school teacher at Forsyth Country Day School in Winston-Salem, North Carolina, USA.

Ian Jukes is Founder of the InfoSavvy Group, an international educational leadership consulting firm based in Canada and New Zealand.

Other Eye On Education Books
Available From Routledge
(www.routledge.com/k-12)

**Supporting Student Mental Health:
Essentials for Teachers**
Michael Hass and Amy Ardell

**The K-12 Educator's Data Guidebook:
Reimagining Practical Data Use in Schools**
Ryan A. Estrellado

**Teaching as Protest:
Emancipating Classrooms Through Racial Consciousness**
Robert S. Harvey and Susan Gonzowitz

**Teaching in the Game-Based Classroom:
Practical Strategies for Grades 6–12**
David Seelow

**The Brain-Based Classroom:
Accessing Every Child's Potential Through
Educational Neuroscience**
Kieran O'Mahony

**The Media-Savvy Middle School Classroom:
Strategies for Teaching Against Disinformation**
Susan Brooks-Young

Learner Choice, Learner Voice

A Teacher's Guide to Promoting Agency in the Classroom

Ryan L. Schaaf, Becky Zayas, and Ian Jukes

Cover image: iStock/DrAfter123

First published 2022
by Routledge
605 Third Avenue, New York, NY 10158

and by Routledge
4 Park Square, Milton Park, Abingdon, Oxon, OX14 4RN

Routledge is an imprint of the Taylor & Francis Group, an informa business

© 2022 Ryan L. Schaaf, Becky Zayas, and Ian Jukes

The right of Ryan L. Schaaf, Becky Zayas, and Ian Jukes to be identified as authors of this work has been asserted in accordance with sections 77 and 78 of the Copyright, Designs and Patents Act 1988.

All rights reserved. No part of this book may be reprinted or reproduced or utilised in any form or by any electronic, mechanical, or other means, now known or hereafter invented, including photocopying and recording, or in any information storage or retrieval system, without permission in writing from the publishers.

Trademark notice: Product or corporate names may be trademarks or registered trademarks, and are used only for identification and explanation without intent to infringe.

Library of Congress Cataloging-in-Publication Data
Names: Schaaf, Ryan L., author. | Zayas, Becky, author. | Jukes, Ian, author.
Title: Learner choice, learning voice : a teacher's guide to promoting agency in the classroom / Ryan L. Schaaf, Becky Zayas, and Ian Jukes.
Description: New York, NY : Routledge, 2022. | Series: Eye on education | Includes bibliographical references.
Identifiers: LCCN 2021058844 (print) | LCCN 2021058845 (ebook) | ISBN 9780367567910 (hardback) | ISBN 9780367610340 (paperback) | ISBN 9781003102984 (ebook)
Subjects: LCSH: Student–centered learning. | Motivation in education. | Classroom environment. | Agent (Philosophy)
Classification: LCC LB1027.23 .S35 2022 (print) | LCC LB1027.23 (ebook) | DDC 371.39/4—dc23/eng/20220106
LC record available at https://lccn.loc.gov/2021058844
LC ebook record available at https://lccn.loc.gov/2021058845

ISBN: 9780367567910 (hbk)
ISBN: 9780367610340 (pbk)
ISBN: 9781003102984 (ebk)

DOI: 10.4324/9781003102984

Typeset in Palatino
by Apex CoVantage, LLC

I want to dedicate this book to my family. Rachel, Connor, and Ben, you are my life. To my wonderful mother, Susan, and my sister, Kristy – thank you for the love and support. I also would like to thank the faculty, staff, and students at both Notre Dame of Maryland University and Johns Hopkins University for allowing me to fulfill my passion for teaching the teachers of today and tomorrow.

– Ryan L. Schaaf

I want to dedicate this book to my parents, who always promoted the value of a strong education. From installing my pretend classroom in our basement and pretending to be my first students to encouraging me throughout college and graduate school, I am forever grateful. To my husband, Nick, thank you for being my first editor and always allowing me to bounce ideas off of you. We are a team. Thank you for always supporting me. Ian and Ryan, thank you for this unbelievable opportunity and all that you have taught me throughout this experience.

– Becky Zayas

This book is intended to celebrate the exceptional dedication and courage educators have exhibited and to acknowledge their demonstrated capacity to adapt and innovate in extraordinarily challenging and uncertain conditions. Now is the time for us to recognize the exceptional role they play and to empower them with the training, professional development, support, and working conditions needed to effectively deploy their talents. For the education system to recover from the COVID-19 pandemic requires sustained investment in the well-being, training, professional development, and working conditions of the world's 71 million educators. Education recovery will only be successful if it is conducted hand in hand with teachers, giving them both voice and agency to participate in the critical change process.

– Ian Jukes

The authors together would like to dedicate this book to the loving memory of Dr. Jason Ohler. He was an amazing educator, writer, and storyteller. His friendship and commitment to his students and family will never be forgotten.

Contents

Meet the Authors ix
Foreword xiii

Introduction: The Need for Teacher and Learner
Agency in Pandemic Times 1

1   What is Learner Agency? 15

2   The Empowerers of Empowerment 31

3   The Digital Generations and the Great
    Disconnect With Our Schools 45

4   Rise of the Creative Class 59

5   Modern Learners, Modern Skills 81

6   The List 93

7   Authentic Assessment for Authentic Learning 245

8   The Best of Both Worlds: Providing Learner
    Empowerment in the Age of High-Stakes
    Learning 267

Meet the Authors

Ryan L. Schaaf is Associate Professor of Educational Technology at Notre Dame of Maryland University and a graduate faculty member in the Johns Hopkins School of Education at John Hopkins University. Before entering higher education, Ryan was a public school teacher, instructional leader, curriculum designer, and technology integration specialist in Maryland. In 2007, he was nominated as Maryland Teacher of the Year. Ryan enjoys presenting sessions and workshops about the potential for gaming in the classroom, the characteristics of modern-day learning, and emerging technologies and trends in education.

Ryan has published several research articles related to the use of digital games as an effective instructional strategy in the classroom in *New Horizons for Learning* and the *Canadian Journal of Action Research*. His published books include *Making School a Game Worth Playing: Digital Games in the Classroom*, *Using Digital Games as Assessment and Instruction Tools*, *Reinventing Learning for the Always-On Generation: Strategies and Apps That Work*, *Game On: Using Digital Games to Transform Teaching, Learning, and Assessment*, *A Brief History of the Future of Education: Learning in the Age of Disruption*, and *Literacy Is Still Not Enough: Modern Fluencies for Teaching, Learning, and Assessment*.

To learn more about Ryan's work, follow @RyanLSchaaf on Twitter.

Becky Zayas From her early years pretending to be a teacher in her basement "classroom" to discovering her passion for effective teaching in college, Becky was always destined to become an educator. Becky is currently a middle school math teacher at Forsyth Country Day School in Winston-Salem, North Carolina, where she teaches fifth-grade math and seventh-grade pre-algebra. She previously taught language arts, social studies, science, and math to fourth and fifth graders at an arts-integrated charter school. Becky earned her BA in elementary education with minors in dance and communication at Wake Forest University. She went on to earn her Academically and Intellectually Gifted Certification and then completed her MS in education focused on technology for educators at Johns Hopkins University. While student teaching, she was honored with Wake Forest University's Jerry A. Hall Award for Excellence in Student Teaching. In 2013, she was awarded the National Science Teaching Association's Maitland P. Simmons Memorial Award for New Teachers.

Becky is passionate about effective instruction based on student agency through the integration of technology, the arts, and authentic learning experiences. She has presented at several regional conferences on subjects including communication technologies, arts integration, and inquiry in the classroom. She has also published blog posts on both the North Carolina Association of Elementary Educators' (NCAEE) and Solution Tree's Blog. Becky enjoys developing inquiry-based classroom experiences that make learning fun, exciting, and memorable for students.

To learn more about Becky's work, follow @BeckyZayas413 on Twitter.

Ian Jukes He is the founder of the InfoSavvy Group, an international educational leadership consulting firm based in Canada and New Zealand. Professionally, Ian has been a classroom teacher, teaching every grade from kindergarten to grade 12; a school, district, and ministry leader; a university professor; a keynote speaker; and an international consultant. He has worked with clients in more than 80 countries and made more than 12,000 presentations.

Ian has written or cowritten 23 books and developed nine educational series. His most recent books include the award-winning *Reinventing Learning for the Always-On Generation*, *A Brief History of the Future of Education*, *LeaderShift 2020*, and *Literacy Is Still Not Enough*.

Outside of education, he has worked with a wide range of government agencies; the banking, medical, entertainment, and insurance industries; and organizations and communities that wish to explore possibilities for preferred economic futures.

First and foremost, however, Ian is a passionate educational evangelist. His focus continues to be on the compelling need to restructure our educational institutions so that they become relevant to the current and future needs of the digital generations – and to prepare learners for their future and not just society's past.

To learn more about Ian's work, follow @ijukes on Twitter.

Foreword

Voices give choices – when we give students voice, we give them choice. Integrating student voice into the learning process transforms the entire learning experience. When learners are provided with opportunities to access voice and agency, we unleash their inner silence and creativity, which turn into language and action.

Since at least the time of renowned educational reformer John Dewey, the importance of providing opportunities for student voice and agency has been identified as a critical part of the educational process. Dewey wrote extensively about the essential need to integrate learner experience and perspective into the daily curriculum. In *Democracy and Education* (1916), Dewey summarized his beliefs about the centrality of voice and agency when he wrote:

> *The essence of the demand for freedom is the need for conditions that will enable an individual to make his own special contribution to group interest and to partake of its activities in such ways that social guidance shall be a matter of his own mental attitude and not a mere authoritative dictation of his acts.*
>
> (John Dewey, 1916)

Today, both an interest in and a recognized need for an increased focus on learner voice and agency are being reinforced by a growing body of literature that identifies voice and agency as necessary throughout the entire educational process.

Encouraging learners to be decision-makers as an everyday part of daily life is about cultivating personal responsibility for their education. It is something that is done by systematically supporting learners as they make choices about schooling, learning, and the education system in areas ranging from what affects them personally to what affects an entire student body to what affects the entire school system.

That's why *Learner Choice, Learner Voice: A Teacher's Guide to Promoting Agency in the Classroom* is timely, practical, and much needed. Designed by teachers for teachers, this is exactly the right book at exactly the right time. The book goes beyond voice as just token consultations to looking at student voice as forming a partnership that enables learners to become meaningfully involved in their learning. Think about your students – what are the opportunities you provide for them to offer personal views about their learning? And if you do, how do you use this information? And most importantly, does it change your daily teaching, learning, and assessment practices?

Authors Schaaf, Zayas, and Jukes develop a logical and practical progression that begins with a brief overview of what student agency is and what it isn't. The book then examines the thoughts of great educational thinkers about the place for student voice in the learning process. It then considers the great challenges faced by educators working with today's learners and identifies the essential modern skills needed by modern learners. It concludes by considering the role of authentic assessment for modern learning and how to provide opportunities for student empowerment in an age of high-stakes testing and learning.

What sets this book apart from others addressing the same topic is the complete absence of rhetoric, buzzwords, and teacher talk. Readers will find clear, concise, and practical advice not just about what *must* be done or *why* it should be done but by providing a step-by-step guide about *how* to do it.

With more than 100 tried and tested hands-on activities suitable for learners at all levels, together with hundreds of free and readily accessible resources that support and extend the activities, this book is a must-have guide for every educator, regardless of who their learners are or where in the world they live.

As an educator, you will find this book both inspirational and practical. *Learner Choice, Learner Voice: A Teacher's Guide to Promoting Agency in the Classroom* is a lifeline for teachers dealing with all the pressures of the modern classroom. It's a book you will want to refer to again and again for quick and practical ideas and activities that will help prepare your students for life.

But beyond that, the book acts as a catalyst for inspiration that helps educators reimagine what education can be in a time of global transformation – because not only has the world changed but so has education. Enjoy!

Dr. Nicky Mohan

Introduction

The Need for Teacher and Learner Agency in Pandemic Times

The global pandemic has had a profound effect on traditional learning processes. Remote learning has created opportunities for learners to turn down the volume on their teachers or even turn them off completely. This ability to tune out is transforming many of our traditional assumptions about teaching and learning. Even if conventional compliance-focused approaches may have previously worked in engaging learners, these same techniques increasingly won't be as effective – particularly in a time where we will almost certainly continue to experience accelerated rates of disruptive change in our world – change caused, in large part, by the pandemic. The short- and long-term implications of this emerging reality are substantial. They require educators to reassess our relationship with learners carefully and fundamentally rethink how we approach teaching, learning, and assessment in the modern world.

Amid pandemic times, educators and educational leaders struggle with a wide range of technical and adaptive challenges. While many of these problems are technical, overwhelmingly, the most significant challenges are adaptive. Moreover, adaptive challenges reflect issues for which there are no quickly discernible answers. Thus, adaptive challenges cannot be instantly solved by external experts. Nor can solutions be implemented by mandate. Instead, solving adaptive challenges requires experimentation by those directly experiencing the problem.

In earlier times, most of the challenges educators faced were technical, and the nature of work primarily required teachers to conform to long-established practices, routines, and protocols. This approach was the foundation of the process-based, factory mindset design exhibited by the traditional education system.

However, even before the appearance of COVID-19, there had been a dramatic shift to a post-industrial, global digital world and economy, which led to additional changes to long-held values, expectations, and assumptions. As a result, we often sought technical solutions to solve adaptive challenges in our schools – something COVID-19 has further accelerated. Moving forward (hopefully) post-pandemic, the primary challenges facing educators will be more adaptive than technical.

With today's COVID-19 learners, we are increasingly facing dropout, tune-out issues. In a world full of accelerating levels of distraction and choice, there are a number of alternatives to engaging in school – many of which have been further amplified by the effects of the pandemic. More and more sophisticated, compelling distractors are competing for our learners' attention – and in the process, absorbing an increasing amount of learners' cognitive capacity and potential. For some, this distraction comes in the form of the daily stress that results from poverty, constant uncertainty, and fear, which draws students' focus away from learning. For others, it's the ever-present presence of digital technology in the form of gaming, social media, connection to peers, and constant exposure to the ever-present YouTube and TikTok culture.

The US Department of Health and Human Services (www.hhs.gov/web/social-media/index.html) estimates that American children spend more than seven and a half hours a day in front of screen media – a statistic that does not factor in the time learners also spent exposed to screens for school and homework. Thus, the pandemic has simultaneously compounded the inequalities that already exist between those who have and those who do not have access – while at the same time expanding the use of digital technology and increasing our dependence on digital devices and services.

Once we finally get beyond COVID-19, it is highly unlikely that schools will deny the intrusion of these powerful societal forces and the changes they are imposing upon us because neither factor is well aligned to a compliance-driven solution for education.

As we move forward, education will need to compete for learner attention in a time of ongoing uncertainty and instability on the one hand and instant access to digital entertainment and learning experiences, anytime, anywhere, on the other.

As we move forward, the reality we must acknowledge is that educators never really had control over learning in the first place – they simply had influence; control has only been an illusion.

In traditional learning environments, students were gathered in designated locations, so rules and expectations related to the way learners conducted themselves could more easily be established and enforced. Effective classroom management could, in some cases, create environments where at least outwardly, it appeared that students were relatively engaged. However, the pandemic has exposed the extent to which what we thought was "control" and "engagement" was more or less an illusion or facade.

Throughout time, both individually and collectively, educators have exerted influence over learners. But, despite the outward appearance of control manifested and often assumed in the classroom, the reality is that we are all effectively interacting with other individuals and groups who also have agency.

When COVID-19 compelled traditional learning to switch to a remote or hybrid model, the digital prototype used to maintain a semblance of control and order no longer worked as effectively as the in-person model. Many learners have long complained that schools have lost their purpose and relevance.

COVID-19 has, in new and very different ways, further exposed the degree of disengagement that has long existed, though not acknowledged. Now, as a direct result of the virus, the horse is out of the barn. It's hard to conceive that traditional, pre-pandemic educational systems will *ever* be able to fully reestablish even a peripheral level of control when in-person learning is once again the norm.

Today, we live in profoundly uncertain and unstable times. Both personally and professionally, we are dealing with complex adaptive challenges. Already disillusioned, disoriented, and disconnected, learners have even more reason to turn down the volume and tune us out while simultaneously having access to multiple means of doing just that, and as we are now beginning to realize, we as educators never really had the control we assumed we had.

So what does this all signify? It means we must immediately begin to rethink teaching and learning by creating conditions that encourage our learners to become self-motivated thinkers and doers, not just regurgitators of tired and stale information. To do this, we must take the time to know each learner on a personal level so we can understand and address the many reasons they're choosing to (or being forced to) utilize alternative learning options. We must leverage digital technologies as a critical element of the learning process and use their transformative potential while simultaneously minimizing its risk factors. And more than anything else, we must enthusiastically accept (rather than dismiss) learner and teacher agency and move beyond our previously held traditional institutional assumptions about teaching and learning.

And finally, as educators, we must apply the remaining authority we have post-pandemic to promote even greater levels of teacher and learner agency in our schools, communities, and society. Rather than continuing to focus on compliance, we must work to make certain our shared values can serve the individuals in our communities and ensure they are aligned around the greater good.

Facilitating this fundamental reset of our relationships with students as partners in their learning can, should, and will challenge some of our most basic assumptions about traditional teaching and learning.

Storytime

Before we started writing this book, we spent a great deal of time contemplating learner agency and empowerment. Before we proceed any further, it is vital to understand our motives in writing our research and real-world experiences learning and teaching in schools. What follows is a brief trip down memory lane that shows where we were and where we are now. Each section is written in the author's very own words from their points of view.

Becky

When I think back to my childhood experiences, I hated going to school. I became a teacher because I wanted to change the experience for *my* students. The transition from my Montessori-based preschool distinctively revolving around student choice to a traditional classroom was tough. My parents still have a worksheet I completed in kindergarten that had a bird to color in blue and lines to practice writing uppercase and lowercase *b*'s. I remember this worksheet because it has tear stains on it. I spent my earliest days at school, wishing I was anywhere else than school. Now, I often wonder if I had been given a choice as to how I practiced my letter *b*'s, would that have changed my perspective about school? I could have practiced writing my letters by writing a postcard, drawing them in the sand, or even creating pictures out of the letters. Having a choice may have turned the tables, provided me with a voice in the classroom, and allowed me to recognize the power I can have in my education rather than feeling trapped there completing meaningless worksheets. My experiences as a student informed my practices as an educator.

I have had the privilege to teach both fourth and fifth grades at an arts-integrated charter school and an independent middle school in North Carolina. I am fortunate enough to be given the freedom to teach creatively as we are encouraged to utilize the arts as a foundation for students to gain understanding and demonstrate newfound knowledge. However, I am still responsible for preparing students to be successful on state-mandated standardized tests. It has been my personal experience that many teachers fear that giving students a choice in creative learning opportunities will negatively impact students' test scores. Many of my colleagues felt pressured into "teaching to the test" and focused on multiple-choice questions rather than authentic learning opportunities where students have a powerful voice in their learning experiences. However, I have found that "teaching to the talent" of the students is more effective. As an educator, I have discovered the joy of learning based on students' talents, strengths, and passions.

These experiences allow students to be successful in learning academic standards, as well as to develop lifelong skills, such as critical thinking, problem-solving, collaboration, creativity, communication, and global citizenship. In this way, students develop a love of learning while strengthening critical literacies.

One of my favorite memories involving student choice, creativity, and critical thinking happened just last year. As we had planned in advance, a colleague rushed into my classroom holding a sealed envelope. Inside the envelope was a letter from Broadway producers interested in turning the novel *Tuck Everlasting* into a Broadway musical. The letter asked students to decide whether they wanted to become a choreographer, lyricist, playwright, set designer, costume designer, or casting director. After making their choice, students read the book from the perspective of their roles before they developed their final projects.

If you had entered my classroom as students were working on their final challenge, you would have seen dancers developing choreographic movements in the corner; while a quieter student sat under a table writing her script, several students developing Google Slides with their final casting decisions and piles of craft supplies for students who were designing costumes and sets. My job was to serve as a motivator and facilitator during this blissful time of productivity. This included answering questions, providing supplies, and giving support when needed. The students worked entirely independently as they completed their projects.

In the past, students did not always develop buy-in with classroom projects because I did not always provide them with the opportunity to choose their learning process and product. When I took a step back, I noticed that all my students were not only engaged and but also excited and invested in their creative pursuits. They would beg and beg me for more time to work on their *Tuck Everlasting* projects.

For me, what stands out the most about this experience is the wide variety of projects and the diversity of thinking involved in creating them. At the same time, students were able to meet their learning goals through a medium of their choosing. Student choice cultivated a strong sense of ownership and investment in their learning. This experience was incredibly fulfilling for both the learners and me. As a practitioner, seeing my students' successes in using their strengths and talents to create, construct, and deliver their self-selected projects was incredibly rewarding. Students were successful in demonstrating their learning based on the academic goals, while at the same time, they worked collaboratively, solved problems, thought critically, demonstrated creativity and innovation, and communicated using a wide variety of digital and non-digital tools – all skills that will stick with them long past their year as a fifth grader.

Ryan

In my previous life, before teaching in higher education, I was a third-grade teacher in Howard County Public Schools – an affluent suburban school district in the Baltimore-Washington metropolitan area. Although I was saddled with preparing my young learners for high-stakes testing and the constant paperwork, duties, and other tasks associated with today's classroom teachers, I loved teaching new things in new ways to my eager young scholars. One instructional unit sticks out in my mind the most – public service announcements.

Most of today's educators should be able to recall some form of public service announcement – Smokey the Bear taught us to prevent forest fires, a hot skillet with an egg frying in it taught us that drugs were bad for our brains, and McGruff the Crime Dog convinced kids to stay safe and obey the law. Public service announcements were intended to convey an important message in a short time with the main goal of being remembered.

My students loved learning, but they truly thrived in situations where they could express themselves in unique ways where they had choices and options. Instead of mandating that all of my students create a public service announcement poster, I provided them with the opportunity to pick the topic and select the medium they wished to create it in. Working in collaborative teams, some groups decided to create a video, while others created audio ads, pamphlets, or posters. And their freedom did not stop there. They were also provided with a list of 20 to 30 issues they might want to use to create a public service announcement. Some topics and issues included recycling, stopping pollution, drug prevention, anti-cheating, eating healthy, anti-bullying, and stranger danger. If students preferred to work independently or if they wanted to switch groups to explore a different topic, then I tried to accommodate their requests.

The students performed remarkably well throughout the unit. For the videos and audio ads, learners conducted their research, created scripts, rehearsed together, and produced their projects. For the posters and pamphlets, the groups conducted their research, brainstormed content and design aspects, and developed their creative projects. No matter what the topic was or the artifact they created, students loved the public service announcements. They enjoyed the freedom to select the topic they wanted to explore and how they demonstrated their new knowledge. My learner's curriculum goals were fulfilled. The cross-curricular nature of these projects allowed my learners to fulfill numerous standards from various subjects, such as English/Language Arts, Health, and Science. They were provided with many powerful choices. My students got to have their cake and eat it too!

Ian

I am an educator by choice – it's a job I love. I passionately believe that I was put on this earth to be a teacher. My calling in life is to work with children and young adults as they move through life and make their transition to adulthood. I do this by demonstrating my concern for them, passing on any wisdom I might have, and guiding them through the development of the practical and essential skills and knowledge they will need to enable them to be successful in their future lives.

I studied and worked to become a teacher with the best of intentions to try and make a positive difference in the lives of each one of my students. As a student-teacher, I was provided with lots of support and encouragement about how to plan lessons and how to design assignments and activities that reinforced the learning. However, very little time in my courses was spent on how to give instruction. That's why, when I stood in front of a class, I decided to just mimic the techniques that had been modeled to me when I was a student. I did this by talking. I didn't plan to teach this way – it was just something that happened automatically and unconsciously.

When I started teaching by talking, then testing what I had talked about, my university professors, faculty advisors, and sponsor teachers encouraged me and told me that I was on the right track. When I became a fully certified teacher, I started working through the curriculum guides that had been developed for my courses. I soon discovered that the more content I was expected to teach, the more I tended to depend on talking, then testing. Watching my students echo back to me the content that I had presented to them or that was contained in their textbook was an exhilarating experience. Teaching followed by testing was something that just seemed to be more reliable evidence and confirmation of my effectiveness as a teacher than anything else I could think of. And the more I talked with and watched my colleagues in action, the more comfortable I became teaching and testing. It was the way things had always been done. There seemed no reason to question what I was doing because it was clear that teaching and testing was just the way you did things.

Having found my comfort zone, I committed myself to my teaching career with energy and enthusiasm. I was completely confident that I was achieving my goal of preparing my students for their future lives.

However, after I had been using the teaching-then-testing method for several years, I started to notice that, in reality, the effect my instruction had on my learners was much less than I had hoped for. It all began with students – even my very best students – forgetting the material I had taught them – even though the stuff they had forgotten involved them answering the same questions they had correctly answered the questions on my tests just a few days previously.

I also began to realize that my students were unable to consistently and effectively transfer and apply the skills I had taught them to new or even slightly different activities. They seemed to be largely dependent on me to help them by suggesting strategies as to how to solve new problems, and they quickly became lost or discouraged when they ran into problems that were even slightly different from those I had given them previously. However, the biggest jolt to my system came when I suddenly realized that I was not engaging them with my teaching style – that they were becoming disinterested with what I had to say and disengaged from me and the content of my lessons.

Even with my very best intentions to do what was right for my learners, I was unconsciously and unintentionally doing to my students the same thing that had been done to me when I was a student. I wanted to teach my students in a way that was relevant and interesting so I could help them prepare for life beyond school. Instead, I realized, to my absolute shock and horror, I was simply repeating the same types of learning experience I had experienced when I was a student – a style of teaching that had been neither engaging nor helpful for me.

In reality, my teaching then testing was simply equipping my students with school skills, not the real-world skills I had hoped to impart. School skills are skills like how to effectively cram for an exam or how to discard or ignore material that didn't count because it wouldn't be on a test – the skills that help students progress further through the school system but won't be of help to them when they leave.

When I realized what I had been unconsciously doing, I was shocked and disillusioned. As I struggled with the reality of my lack of effectiveness as a teacher, I began to search for alternatives to the traditional teaching-then-testing approach. I realized I had to completely rethink things – I needed to develop a new model for instruction – a model that reflected the realities of the modern world we are living in – a model that would both engage and motivate modern digital learners. That's what this book is about.

A Starting Point

What follows represents our individual and collective experiences about how to make this happen. Our approaches are neither complete nor perfect. Given the rapidly changing nature of the world we live in, and considering the disruptions currently occurring in education due to the ongoing nature of the pandemic, this book has been designed to challenge you to continuously reexamine the ways we teach and the way learners learn – and to keep working to make it better. This book is targeted at educators of all levels who are faced with the task of teaching content-laden courses to modern students of the digital generations.

So where do we begin? We're going to draw on the insights of a carpenter to determine our starting point. A carpenter would state that the key to building a structurally sound house is to start by properly building the foundation. The home will have all kinds of problems if you don't get the base of the house on a solid and square footing. We think this wisdom applies equally as well to our task of building a new approach to teaching. As educators, we have to start with the foundation of our thinking and make sure it's solid, square, and true. So the starting point is to ask, what can we use as the base for our teaching? Are there any attributes of teaching that stand the test of time, and which will provide us with a rock-solid and squared foundation for a new approach to instruction? We believe there are three.

1. Engagement

As we have researched the art and science of teaching and talked with educators around the globe about what makes for good teaching, one attribute of effective instruction that has emerged that towers over all the others is engagement. Regardless of the subject being taught or the age of the students in the class, engagement is what effective teachers create. They know that catching students' attention is the key to opening the door to their minds. Effective teachers take the course content in the curriculum guide and develop learning activities that spark interest in the minds of their students.

2. Relevance

Effective teaching is more than just creating interest. To be of lasting value to learners, instruction must also be relevant to the world that they will enter upon graduation. Relevance in instruction goes to the very heart of our mandate to educate our learners for future success when they leave us. Relevance is also an important factor in creating engagement because learners are much more likely to "buy in" to instruction that they can see relates to the real world.

3. Support for Learning

However, simply providing engaging, relevant instruction is still not enough to ensure that students will learn what they need to learn. Effective educators provide support to learners to help them acquire the skills and knowledge they need to succeed, especially those learners who do not catch on to new teaching right away. Effective teachers provide constructive feedback to students to assist them with their learning. These teachers also employ strategies to get feedback from their students to see how well the teacher's instruction is being understood.

These three attributes of engagement, relevance, and support for learning are timeless and universal aspects of effective instruction. Teaching based on a foundation of these characteristics will serve our students well. The question now becomes, how do you ensure that your instruction has these attributes in the modern world? More importantly, how do you – how do we – promote learner agency, learner choice, learner voice, and learner empowerment while still preparing today's generations of learners for the next test, the next unit, the next grade, and their futures outside of schools? That's what we want to explore in the rest of this book.

1

What is Learner Agency?

Writer Kathleen McClaskey said, "A learner with agency is a learner that is future-ready!" (2017, para. 10). But this sentiment wasn't always the case. Ancient cultures practiced many different forms of schooling. Egypt, Japan, Mesopotamia, and Greece saw the advantage of having an intellectual class that could read and write. Over time, more and more children began entering places we would loosely describe as schools. In these settings, mentors, wise men, clergy, parents, tutors, and teachers would impart their knowledge or teach trades to their young charges. In most instances, the teacher was the ultimate source of information and font of all knowledge, acting as the primary gateway to learning for all of their students.

In examining this dynamic, the learners provided fertile, malleable minds and imaginations for their teachers. This was the perfect medium to shape the next generations of academics and scholars in their societies. In return, the teachers, tutors, or mentors required disciplined, obedient, and passive learners who were willing to immerse themselves in the lessons. In the hearts and minds of learners, teachers were simultaneously the engineers and gatekeepers of their tomorrows.

Over time, as more children and young adults were provided with the opportunity for an education, schools evolved into the versions we experienced and in which many of us now teach. Many of us experienced the 2 × 4 × 6 model of learning – information contained within two covers of a textbook, taught within four walls of a classroom, and separated into six evenly spaced instructional periods a day.

When schools had to produce individuals who would grow up to become the farmers, factory workers, or other routine cognitive workers needed for the 20th-century economy, this system worked exceptionally well. This model taught students to obey the rules, listen closely, follow directions, never question authority, be on time, meet deadlines, complete work, answer questions when called upon, and only speak when spoken to.

In the predictable, stable, and slowly evolving world of yesterday, schools produced the ideal student. The challenge is that this predictable, stable, and slowly evolving world of yesterday is *not* the world we live in today. Today's world is unpredictable, unstable, and volatile. Disruptive factors, such as the evolution of technological systems, and the emergence of artificial intelligence have created a world filled with fundamental uncertainty. This has only been amplified by the arrival of COVID-19, which has sent education into a giant tailspin.

If the educators of today want to prepare their students for living, working, and learning in a rapidly evolving world; if the educators of today want to help their learners solve the problems that will confront the next generations of humanity; if the educators of today want to motivate their learners so they can flourish in the uncertain times that await us all; if the educators of today believe their primary mission is to prepare their learners for their tomorrows and not just our yesterdays, then we must empower them to work and live independently because, after all, once they leave our schools, they are on their own – sink, swim, or soar.

Student or Learner?

As we move forward, we must appreciate that students are *not* just students – they are also learners. Some educators may see this differentiation as the proverbial splitting of hairs. After all, "student" is a term all teachers have come to use without much thought of its origin. In fact, the word "student" comes from the Latin *studeium*, which translates as "painstaking application."

Educators commonly use the terms "student" and "learner" interchangeably. The problem with this practice is that the term "student" is anchored in a traditional educational mindset. According to Wikipedia, a *student* is defined as a person enrolled in a school or other educational institution with the goal of acquiring knowledge. Using this definition, the student is a product of the place in which they learn.

By comparison, *Merriam-Webster* identifies a *learner* as an individual gaining knowledge or understanding of or skill by study, instruction, or experience. Although the student/learner distinction may seem little more than a matter of semantics, the difference is substantial – it's a matter of mindset. By shifting the emphasis and power structure from schools to learners, we, as educators, begin to discover opportunities to change the focus of education to empower learners to become independent, divergent thinkers and doers. Let's drill a little deeper into our differentiation between (see Figure 1.1) students and learners.

Student Versus Learner Mindset

In differentiating between student and learner, we are *not* criticizing or demeaning schools, educators, or the term "students." Every day a great deal of hard work and encouraging practice goes on in schools. The authors are all advocates, fans, and even cheerleaders for the hard work being undertaken. Our goal in writing this book is to encourage individuals both inside and outside of education to seriously consider how we can empower

STUDENT MINDSET	LEARNER MINDSET
Students learn in a classroom during fixed-time class periods.	Learners can learn anytime, anywhere, and at any pace.
Students are instructed by a teacher.	Learners can learn from any source of information – teacher, parent, peer, video, or any other resource. They can also learn through tinkering, experimentation, or exploration.
Students learn from a set curriculum.	Learners can let their passions and interests drive their learning experiences.
Students are motivated by grades, academic promotion, or a degree.	Learners are motivated by the pursuit of new knowledge, the next challenge, or the mastery of a skill.
Students succeed by listening and following directions.	Learners identify their own goals.
Students are someone attending a school or learning institution.	Learners can be anyone, at any age, learning any subject or skill.

FIGURE 1.1 Student vs. learner mindset

learners rather than just restricting them. Educational philosopher Robert Hutchins said it best, "The object of education is to prepare the young to educate themselves throughout their lives" (Bush, 1992). Learners must become the primary agents of their learning.

How Do Others Define Learner Agency?

There is no broad consensus related to the definition of learner agency. However, there appears to be a great deal of overlap between each and every viewpoint. Holdsworth (2018) defines learner agency as "the active and purposeful learning by students that builds their capacity to take action" (para. 3). Jennifer Poon, Fellow at the Center for Innovation in Education, suggests there are four components of learner agency: setting advantageous goals, initiating action toward those goals, reflecting on or regulating progress toward those goals, and actively pursuing self-efficacy (learner's belief in his or her ability to succeed in a particular situation) (Poon, 2018).

Perhaps the most influential voice in this scholarly pursuit is Margaret Vaughn, an associate professor at the University of Idaho. She simplifies learner agency as a "student's desire, ability, and power to determine their course of action" (Vaughn, 2018, p. 63). The framework we adapted (see Figure 1.2) helps to categorize the educational community's three dimensions of learner agency.

The first dimension targets dispositions, which are the attitudes, tendencies, and character traits displayed by learners. Ideally, learners should demonstrate their ability to be creative,

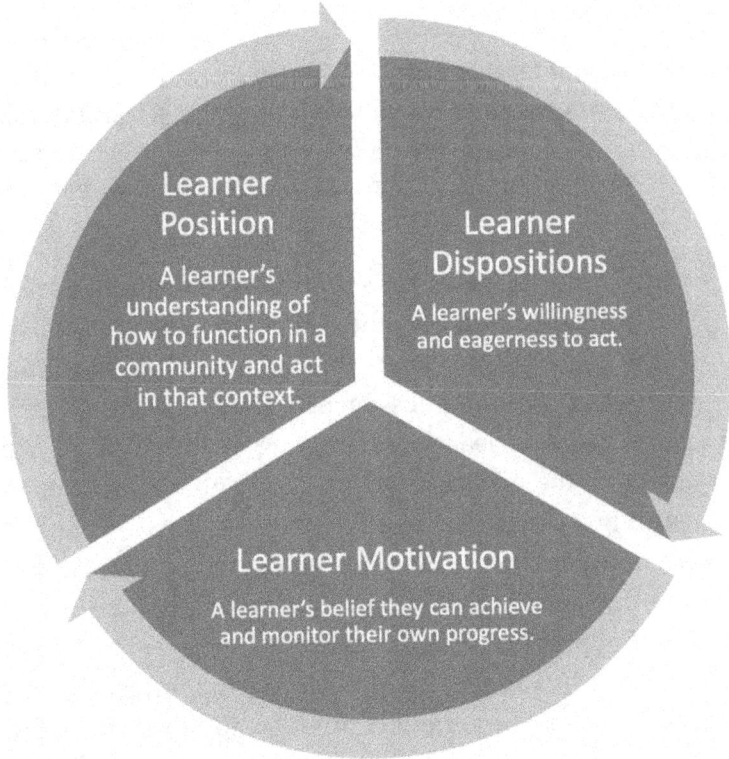

FIGURE 1.2 Dimensions of learner agency (adapted from Vaughn, 2018)

take risks, and be goal-driven. The next dimension focuses on motivation, which involves a learner's belief in his or her ability to be successful and monitor their own progress toward a goal. Finally, the third dimension involves how learners use their historical, cultural, and social understanding to interact and engage with people and groups.

Learner Agency: Our Definitions

If we distill the main concepts from the various definitions and frameworks that have been identified from the annals of progressive education literature, learner agency comes down to a **learner's attitude, motivation, and empowerment within a learning context.**

> **Our definition of learner agency refers to the attitudes, motivations, and empowerment individuals have within a learning context** as exhibited in the learner's ability to select a learning environment, a content or subject area, a learning approach, and a learning pace.

- **Learner choice** is the process of turning over more decision-making to learners, so they develop a greater sense of ownership over the ways their interests, passions, backgrounds, and preferences blend together.
- **Learner voice** is learners involving themselves as active agents in the genesis, delivery, and enhancement of their learning journey.
- **Learner engagement** refers to the degree of interest, attention, curiosity, and passion that learners exhibit during the learning process.
- **Learner motivation** is the process during which the learners' attention becomes focused on fulfilling their goals, during which their efforts are directed toward achieving their objective. These efforts are categorized into two

types – intrinsic and extrinsic. The main goal is for learners to be intrinsically motivated to learn.
- **Learner ownership** is the level of investment and empowerment learners have in the topics they explore, the environment they choose, and the process they use during learning.
- **Learner self-efficacy**, according to Bandura (1997), is based on a learner's belief in their ability and capacity to learn. It represents the ability for learners to exude control over one's motivation.

Learner Agency: A Paradigm Shift

In this book, our goal is to support educators in their quest to transform the roles and responsibilities of learners in the instructional process. In a traditional model of school, learners are expected to be compliant, pliable, and obedient. The problem is that if this is the only way they experience learning, they will not be equipped for what lies ahead of them beyond their school experience as they move on into their careers and lives.

> The goal of education and blueprint for learners should be for them to develop into self-directed, self-regulated, creative, independent, divergent thinkers and doers.

Although there are no perfect instructional manuals or teacher guides to help in this transition from a teacher-powered to a learner-empowered environment, this book will offer valuable opportunities and pathways to start the process.

Unlike many of the superficial workbooks or guides that follow the practice of ready, fire, aim (or ready, aim, backfire), this book begins by first laying a strong foundation. After all, if a house is built upon a weak or incomplete foundation, in due course the dwelling will almost inevitably falter, wash away, or collapse.

To establish a solid foundation, we will begin by examining the learning theorists and thought leaders who are influential in the research and practices of learner agency. Then, we will examine today's generation of learners and consider why we affectionately call them the digital generations and the reasons why they require (and demand) more say and control of their learning.

We will then explore the external factors in the modern world that require today's learners to develop tomorrow's next-generation skills.

And finally, we will provide the juicy stuff – the instructional strategies, teaching ideas, and potential learning products that will encourage learners to explore their voice, choice, and ownership of learning to cultivate these vital skills. This succulent mega-section is lovingly referred to as the List. It is custom-created to provide a treasure trove of inspiration for educators that want to empower their learners to become independent thinkers, doers, and reflectors.

Assessing Your Existing Instructional Approach

Teaching is a very complex task. You must, of course, have the essential content knowledge of the subject(s) you are teaching. However, there's much more to effective instruction than knowing the Pythagorean theorem, or the capital of each country, or the steps in the scientific method.

You must understand the developmental psychology of the learners you are teaching.

You must develop a wide range of strategies for how to convey key concepts and information to the young minds of your learners.

This pursuit is never over, which requires educators to become lifelong learners in the art of teaching, assessment, and self-reflection.

As we continue to teach the hearts and minds of our learners, the longer the list of what we still need to learn about effective teaching seems to grow. But despite this never-ending pursuit, each educator must have the same goal – to be a more effective teacher.

Think of this goal as your destination, and think of this book as a road map to help you to get there. The journey toward effective instruction is almost ready to begin, but every adventure needs a beginning – a starting point. Before you can plot your course to where you want your teaching to be, you must first determine where your teaching is now. Here is a brief self-assessment exercise we hope will help you get a picture of where you are as a teacher.

What Is Your Educational Paradigm?

Take a few minutes to consider how many of the following statements about teaching and learning apply to you. The first set relates to when you were a "student" in school. The second set relates to your current teaching practices. The third set relates to teaching in the future. The purpose of this exercise is for you to evaluate the current state of your teaching style and practice. For this reason, it is critical for you to honestly assess how many of these statements apply to you. More importantly, remember there is no shame in admitting you have room to grow as a professional educator. Personal growth should be your goal for your learners' sake.

Your Student Learning Experience

What was learning like when you were a student? What kinds of teaching did you experience? Add one to your score for each statement that applies to you.

1. I learned in a classroom that had rows of desks.
2. A bell rang and I moved to a different class.
3. Mainly, the teacher talked and I listened.
4. My teachers primarily taught content and theory without its application to life.
5. My teachers were the experts in the classroom.

6. The teacher taught a lesson, then I answered questions that were written on the board, or in the textbook, or on a photocopied worksheet.
7. I copied the notes my teacher wrote on the chalkboard, whiteboard, or overhead projector.
8. I was too nervous or embarrassed to ask questions when I didn't understand what the teacher said.
9. I completed a lot of multiple-choice and fill-in-the-blank tests.
10. I or other students I knew made cheat sheets to prepare for tests.
11. I often answered test questions correctly without really knowing what the answers meant.
12. Memorization of the course content was more important to me than forming opinions.
13. Regardless of what my teacher said, what mattered in a course was determined by what was on the test.
14. I saw learning as the memorization of facts and procedures.
15. All assessment of my learning was done by my teachers.
16. My teachers selected all the instructional materials we used in class.
17. Most of the time, the school schedule stayed the same.
18. My teachers never asked for student input or ideas.
19. If I talked to my neighbors during class, I would be corrected or punished.
20. Other than physical education class, recess and lunch were the only times I was ever active.

Your Current Teaching Practice

If you could watch a video of your current planning, teaching, and assessment process, what would you see? How many of the following statements would be true? Add one to your score for each statement that applies to you – and remember, try to be honest in responding.

1. The first thing I think about when planning a new lesson is how to explain the content to students.
2. The last thing I do when planning a new lesson/unit is to create the test.
3. I do most of the talking in the classroom.
4. I expect students to sit and listen when I'm teaching.
5. I primarily teach the material in the textbook or mandated curriculum.
6. I write notes on the chalkboard, whiteboard, or overhead projector.
7. I expect students to take notes when I'm teaching.
8. My questions to students in class primarily focus on content recall.
9. After I have finished teaching, students do learning activities to reinforce what I have taught them.
10. I assume that my students learn the same way I learn.
11. I see smartphones as a major distraction to student learning.
12. At least half of my assessment of learning is done with written tests.
13. My main teaching goal is to cover the content that will be on the test.
14. I use reports, labs, essays, and tests for the majority of my assessment of learning.
15. A large proportion of the tests I give to students are in a multiple-choice or fill-in-the-blank format.
16. I assume students understand my instructions if they don't ask questions.
17. I do all or almost all the assessments of student learning.
18. The feedback I give my students mainly consists of the score I write on their tests and assignments.

19. My teaching and assessment are largely the same as I experienced when I was a student.
20. I'm not aware of a substantially different way to teach and assess other than the way I teach now.

Teaching With the Future in Mind

Would you like to transform your practices? If so, what teaching and learning processes would you like to use in the future?

* Note: there's a change in scoring here – this time, add one to your score if a statement does *not* apply to you.

1. When I plan new lessons/units, I continually think about the future my students will face when they graduate from high school and beyond.
2. I ask students to create a portfolio of work that includes a variety of ways to demonstrate learning.
3. I create evaluation rubrics to assess student learning in their project work.
4. I rely more on project work to demonstrate student learning than tests.
5. I create real-world tasks for students as the main vehicle for instruction.
6. I allow students to demonstrate their learning in a variety of ways other than quizzes, tests, reports, essays, and labs.
7. I talk less in my teaching to students as the school year progresses.
8. Students take a larger role in assessing their work as the school year progresses.
9. I equip students with essential process skills that will empower them to tackle the tasks I ask them to do. *(Process skills are ways of thinking about and interacting with materials and phenomena that can lead to an understanding of new ideas and concepts. By using these skills, learners can*

gather information, test their ideas, and construct explanations of the world.)
10. I can identify at least five process skills that are essential for success in the future (other than the three Rs).
11. I have developed strategies for teaching those process skills to my students.
12. I can clearly articulate the difference between lower-level and higher-level thinking skills.
13. I have developed teaching strategies to progressively move my students into higher levels of thought.
14. I assess both content and process skill development when I evaluate student learning.
15. My goal is to teach only what my students ask me to teach them.
16. I teach students how to determine the accuracy and significance of the information they retrieve from the internet.
17. I teach students how to collaborate with both face-to-face and virtual partners.
18. I allow students to fail in their project work without it dropping their grades.
19. I build time into my schedule for work with each student to give them feedback on their work.
20. I have a plan for helping students less as the school year progresses.
21. I encourage my students to incorporate their passions and interests into their learning activities.
22. I encourage my students to use the tools and materials they are familiar with to learn.
23. Learners can choose the end product to demonstrate their new knowledge.
24. Learners can master new skills and content at their own pace
25. I facilitate instructional activities that provide learners with opportunities to assess themselves and their peers.

Analyzing Your Score

In section 1, "Your Student Learning Experience," if ten or more of these statements describe your experience in school, then you have likely been imprinted with a traditional mindset for teaching – an approach that has its roots in the late 19th and early 20th centuries.

In section 2, "Your Current Teaching Practice," if ten or more of these statements describe the way you teach, then your teaching may reflect the same traditional mindset for instruction that you experienced when in high school.

In section 3, "Teaching With the Future in Mind," if ten or more of these statements *do not apply* to the way you currently teach, you may not yet have embraced learner empowered instruction.

It is essential to keep this snapshot of your current approaches to teaching in mind as we move forward in our exploration of the possibilities for cultivating learner agency.

Summarizing the Main Points

- A *student* is defined as a person enrolled in a school with the goal of acquiring knowledge. By shifting the emphasis and power structure from schools to *learners*, we, as educators, begin to discover opportunities to change the focus of education to empower learners to become independent, divergent thinkers and doers.
- Our definition of learner agency refers to the attitudes, motivations, and empowerment individuals have within a learning context as exhibited in the learner's ability to select a learning environment, a content or subject area, a learning approach, and a learning pace.
- The goal of education and blueprint for learners should be for them to develop into self-directed, self-regulated, creative, independent, divergent thinkers and doers.

- The ultimate pursuit of providing learners with a relevant and meaningful education requires educators to become lifelong learners in the art of teaching, assessment, and self-reflection.

Essential or Extension Questions

- What are some of the clear distinctions between students and learners?
- Why are learners' motivations, dispositions, and positions in the learning environment so integral to helping learning develop more agency?

References

Bandura, A. (1997). *Self-efficacy: The exercise of control.* New York: W. H. Freeman.

Bush, G. (1992). *Statement on signing the higher education amendments of 1992.* Retrieved from https://bush41library.tamu.edu/archives/public-papers/4601

Holdsworth, R. (2018). Student voice, agency, participation. *Connect, 229.* Retrieved from https://research.acer.edu.au/connect/vol2018/iss229/

McClaskey, K. (2017). Everyone is a storyteller. *EdCircuit.* Retrieved from www.edcircuit.com/everyone-storyteller/

Poon, J. (2018). Part 1: What do you mean when you say "student agency"? *Education Reimagined.* Retrieved from https://education-reimagined.org/what-do-you-mean-when-you-say-student-agency/

Vaughn, M. (2018). Making sense of student agency in the early grades. *Phi Delta Kappan, 99,* 62–66. doi:10.1177/0031721718767864

2

The Empowerers of Empowerment

World-renowned educational advocate and mathematician Seymour Papert stated, "I am convinced that the best learning takes place when the learner takes charge" (1993, p. 25). Time is a luxury in today's relentless, ever-changing world. It is a precious resource educators never have enough of. They lack the time in their busy schedule to test unsupported fads or cyclical trends that pop up regularly in education that offer a promise without substance. What they require is a foundational, philosophical mindset to work from and strategies supported by the research and literature of the great minds of education – both past and present. This chapter offers a brief examination of the philosophies and individuals that underpin the absolute necessity for providing learners with more autonomy, agency, and empowerment. This chapter outlines the theorists' views on learning and establishes a new pedagogical profile for educators to consider during their professional pursuits.

The Factory Model

The many systems, bureaucracies, and principles present in today's schools were structured based on Frederick Winslow Taylor's principles of scientific management (1911). His factory model and mindset was considered to be the most advanced form of organizational productivity possible due in large part to its organization, uniformity, and standardization.

Coincidentally, schools were modeled using Taylor's principles based on the assembly line factories of the early 20th century. In this model, the teachers were seen as workers; the learners were considered products the schools produced, and schools themselves were seen as factories. Schools were designed to make learners into automatons doing defined tasks as accurately and rapidly as possible. In these learning environments, control, conformity, and compliance were considered "optimal" and "favorable" for success.

Unfortunately, for today's teachers and learners, schools are no longer preparing learners for a traditional workforce. The structure and instructional mindset of today's schools are meant to create the learners of the 19th and 20th centuries, not 20 and more years into the new millennium.

Again, this is not a "blame the teacher" moment; this is a "change the mindset" movement. If education wants to prepare creative, independent, and divergent thinkers and doers that are ready for whatever profession or passion life throws their way, then the system must change. We cannot expect the factory model of schools whose main benefits are uniformity and standardization to serve non-standardized learners who will work and live in a non-standardized world.

The primary purpose of today's schools and the main focus of today's education system must be on the very learners its mission is to serve. And while educational stakeholders will tell you learners are the main focus of everything being done in schools today, in reality, learners now have very little power, voice, or choice in what, when, where, why, and how they learn. From pre-K through 12th grade, learners have adults telling them what to do and for how long to do it. It is no surprise that in 2018, there were 2.1 million dropouts between the ages of 16 and 24 – a rate of 5.3% (National Center for Education Statistics, n.d.). Although this does not sound like a large population, a business in the marketplace would be considered an economic flop if this percentage of their goods or services were defective or failed to fulfill consumer expectations.

Learner agency, autonomy, and empowerment are themes present throughout the history of learning. These student-centered learning methods have been advocated for by some of the greatest educational minds of yesterday and today. Before educators develop the how to empower learners, they must understand the why. What follows is an incomplete list of some of the great minds and schools of thought associated with learner agency and empowerment. After a short introduction of each person or philosophy, we will share the attributes of their work that reflect our working definition of learner agency.

> Learner agency refers to the attitudes, motivations, and empowerment individuals have within a learning context as exhibited in the learner's ability to select a learning environment, a content or subject area, a learning approach, and a learning pace.

Johann Pestalozzi (1746–1827)

Known as the Father of Pedagogy, Swiss reformer Johann Pestalozzi led the charge for educational change in 19th-century Europe. Attempting to democratize education, Pestalozzi believed in the ability and the right for every individual, both men and women, to learn.

> He believed that empowering and ennobling every individual in this way was the only way to improve society and bring peace and security to the world. His aim was for a complete theory of education that would lead to a practical way of bringing happiness to humankind.
>
> (PestalozziWorld, n.d., para. 4)

Pestalozzi wanted to provide young learners with an education to promote freedom and independence to improve their lives. Believing in an active, child-centered education rather than a passive, teacher-centric one, Johann Pestalozzi observed the necessity for learners to have direct experiences in the world and the use of natural objects and manipulatives in cross-curricular learning experiences. Pestalozzi also believed education must emphasize how and what is taught. Eventually, Friedrich Froebel, a German pedagogue and student of Pestalozzi, established the concept of today's kindergarten.

Pestalozzi

- believed in the right for every individual human to learn,
- concluded that empowering individuals with an education was the only way to improve society, and
- prescribed an active, child-centered education rather than a passive, teacher-centric one.

Maria Montessori (1870–1952)

Maria Montessori was an Italian physician and innovative educator known for her educational methods that built on how children naturally learn. Unwilling to be limited by traditional expectations for women, Montessori opened a full-day childcare center for underserved learners in a poor district of Rome. Based on the belief in the creative potential of children and their innate drive to learn, she crafted the Montessori system. Montessori designed learning materials and environments that fostered the children's natural thirst for knowledge and provided freedom for them to choose their tools and materials to learn with. One of the core beliefs in Montessori's philosophy is to provide learners with the agency to self-select work that leads to intrinsic motivation and sustained attention (American Montessori Society, n.d.).

Montessori
- believed children have an innate drive to learn,
- designed learning materials and environments to foster how children learn, and
- provided learners with the agency to self-select work during extended work times.

John Dewey (1859–1952)

Operating on a philosophical belief in pragmatism and democratic ideologies, John Dewey was central to the progressive movement in the early 20th century. An American professor and philosopher, Dewey explored agency extensively in schools and society as a whole. He emphasized the importance of education in providing environments in which individuals' capabilities could be cultivated. Through his studies and research conducted at the University of Chicago Laboratory Schools, he concluded that people learn best through hands-on, experiential approaches.

By moving away from strictly rote learning and adopting learning-by-doing methods, learners can pursue their interests and build their methods for acquiring and applying specific knowledge. Dewey instructed teachers to observe their student's interests and helped them develop problem-solving and critical thinking skills that would serve them inside and outside of the classroom. His theories also recommended schools employ an interdisciplinary curriculum or a curriculum that focuses on connecting multiple subjects as they would be experienced in the real world.

Dewey

- emphasized learning-by-doing using methods such as hands-on projects and experiential learning,
- integrated the curriculum instead of dividing it,
- promoted problem-solving and critical thinking, and
- encouraged social responsibility and democratic ideals.

Paulo Freire (1921–1997)

In a traditional education system, learners can feel oppressed and powerless. Brazilian educational reformist Paulo Freire explored the oppressive structural conditions in education. Growing up in poverty and navigating an uncertain political climate where he was jailed for his ideals, Freire aimed to help learners develop critical consciousness, which is the first step toward liberation and social change. His (Freire, 1972) *theory of critical pedagogy* is a call for awakening. Not a direct instructional method or lesson plan, the theory attempts to advocate for students to act and assert themselves as critical agents of their learning that question long-standing assumptions and misconceptions that education is always fair for all. Freire believed traditional learning models were too authoritative and advocated that all people should be able to experience an education that helps them transform the world.

Freire

- proposed the theory of critical pedagogy,
- empowered learners and teachers to question systemic oppression in learning, and
- promoted agency so learners could become critically conscious of the world to transform it for the better.

Jean Piaget (1896–1980)

Psychologist and epistemologist Jean Piaget's theory of constructivism asserts that learning is an active process that requires a change in the child. Children cannot be viewed as empty vessels, with teachers acting as content dispensers of knowledge. Learners come to school with their ideas and mental models about the way the world works. Piaget argues that new information is constructed over existing ideas and mental constructs in learners. This change is achieved through the activities the learner engages in and the critical reflection that takes place afterward. In other words, people only deeply understand what they have mentally constructed for themselves. This deep understanding will not occur when information is passively received. In a constructivist learning environment, Tam (2000) suggests teachers and students share authority, while Brooks and Brooks (1993) encourage them to accept student autonomy and initiative. Constructivism promotes a sense of agency as students have ownership of their learning journey.

Piaget
- proposed learners constructed new knowledge to replace old mental constructs,
- valued learner experience over instruction, and
- promoted learner reflection on and about their learning experiences.

Seymour Papert (1928–2018)

Seymour Papert, a South-African-born computer scientist, mathematician, and educator and former student and colleague of Piaget, further developed Piaget's constructivist views. He advocated for coercion-free learning environments and developed the theory of constructionism, which promotes the idea that learning should be actively explored through the construction and delivery of authentic products. Constructionism emphasizes the agency of learners as active participants in the construction of their learning. As educators, the main role in Papert's vision of learning is as a facilitator guiding learners but allowing them to make decisions about the direction of their projects and learning experiences. At the center of Papert's research on instructional tools and methods of learning is the idea that children must be empowered to take charge of their thinking and learning processes rather than be forced to become passive receptacles of top-down instruction. As Martinez and Stager so succinctly state, "His [Papert] life's work has been creating tools, theories, and coercion-free learning environments that inspire children to construct powerful ideas through firsthand experiences" (2019, p. 18).

Papert
- promoted the idea that learning should be actively explored through the construction and delivery of authentic products,
- advocated that children must be empowered to take charge of their thinking and learning processes, and
- concluded that the main role of educators must be as a facilitator guiding learners and allowing them to make decisions about the direction of their projects and learning experiences.

Sir Ken Robinson (1950–2020)

British educational advocate and author Sir Ken Robinson received a knighthood in 2003 from Queen Elizabeth II for his services to the arts. He spearheaded national and international projects on creative and cultural education. Robinson's main argument was that education should foster creativity in pupils by offering a broad curriculum and encouraging individualization during the learning process. Observing that today's education system is industrialized, standardized, and built upon student conformity, Robinson articulated the flaws in the current education system that treats all students as one-size-fits-all and interchangeable. The instructional programs of today are implemented with minimal variation in course material or instructional style.

Robinson (as cited in Halimah, 2020) believed the mission of educational stakeholders is to make every unique and talented child find his or her place in the education system by urging schools to transform teaching and learning into an experience personalized for every student involved. Sir Ken also advises communities to create more learning centers that cater to a learner's passions, dreams, and talents. He also advocated for learning to be heavily supported by tools and resources, including digital technology.

Robinson

- advocated education must foster creativity in pupils by offering a broad curriculum and individualization,
- challenged stakeholders to articulate the flaws in education to take positive actions to correct them, and
- advocated for learning to be supported by resources such as digital technology.

Reggio Emilia (Developed Post–World War II)

Not a person but a place – Reggio Emilia is a Northern Italian city renowned for its philosophy in early childhood education. Developed by Malaguzzi after World War II, the Reggio Emilia approach is based on the mindset that all children are creative and full of potential with a deep-seated sense of curiosity and endless imagination capable of constructing their learning. While children follow their interests and passions, they always stay connected with others. Adults nurture their learning by providing support and a rich learning environment. Instead of utilizing a one-size-fits-all curriculum, Reggio Emilia utilizes a learner-centered approach based on project-based learning so each child develops a love for discovery. Throughout authentic, real-world projects, children naturally embody the spirit of investigators, experimenters, researchers, risk-takers, designers, and explorers.

Educators can observe and create opportunities for learning by opening up new environments, letting children raise thought-provoking questions, and inviting others to collaborate. After educators provide guidance and intervention, the learner takes back control and progresses independently until the project is completed and shared with others. Educators are not lecturers or instructors. Instead, they are learning companions participating in the learner's journey of discovery that can introduce instructional resources, provide access to new tools, or offer entirely new perspectives.

However, educators must remain mindful not to take over the constructive learning process, knowing that this limits a child's endless imagination and motivation. The children are fully in charge and develop a sense of ownership of their progress, which is foundational for lifelong learning.

Emilia Reggio

- believes all children are creative and full of potential with a deep-seated sense of curiosity and imagination;
- utilizes a learner-centered approach based on project-based learning, so each child develops a love for discovery;
- asserts that if a teacher must intervene, the learner takes back control and progresses independently until the project is finished and can be shared with others; and
- emphasizes that children be fully in charge of their learning and develop a sense of ownership.

Although this collection of advocates or philosophies only scratches the surface, it provides enough foundational knowledge for educators to construct a new, reimagined, or revamped pedagogical profile. As a reminder, learner agency refers to the attitudes, motivations, and empowerment individuals have within a learning context as exhibited in the learner's ability to select a learning environment, a content or subject area, a learning approach, and a learning pace. In the following section, we have filtered through what the theorists and philosophies acknowledged about learner agency to produce a pedagogical profile for educators. The profile will help educators nurture learner agency and empowerment practices in learning environments.

Pedagogical Profile of Learner Agency

- A belief that learning is a right of every individual
- A belief that every person has an innate drive to learn
- Promotes an active, participatory learner-centered education
- Understands that empowering individuals with a relevant education improves society
- Designs learning materials, environments, and experiences that foster *how* children learn
- Provides learners with the agency to self-select work
- Provides learners with the opportunity to conduct their work during extended work times
- Emphasizes a learning-by-doing approach to instruction
- Uses hands-on projects and experiential learning
- Integrates topics, subjects, ideas, and skills instead of dividing them
- Promotes problem-solving and critical thinking
- Encourages social and community responsibility
- Empowers learners to ask good questions and voice their informed opinions
- Promotes agency in learners to help them cultivate a critically conscious outlook of the world to transform it for the better

- Proposes learners construct new knowledge to replace old mental constructs
- Values learner experiences over traditional instruction
- Promotes learner reflection on and about their learning experiences
- Initiates learning experiences that promote the construction and delivery of authentic learner products or artifacts
- Empowers learners to take charge of their thinking and learning processes
- Facilitates and guides learners to make decisions about the direction of their projects and learning experiences
- Encourages individualization and creativity whenever possible
- Articulates the flaws in education to take positive actions to correct them
- Advocates for resources such as digital technology
- Provides opportunities for learners to select the tools and resources they use during the learning process
- Nurtures curiosity and imagination
- Utilizes learner-centered approaches based on project-based learning
- Uses discovery learning
- Intervenes only when needed (learners are encouraged to take back control and progress independently)
- Seeds opportunities for learners to take charge and develop a sense of ownership

As this chapter comes to a close, take a few minutes to reexamine the pedagogical profile. How many of the profile elements about teaching and learning apply to you? How many do you wish were already a part of your teaching arsenal? More importantly, what are some instructional ideas and strategies educators can utilize to embrace learner agency and empowerment? The next chapter, bluntly referred to as the List, will help educators answer this very question.

Summarizing Main Points

- Educators lack time to explore unsupported fads or cyclical trends in education that promise results without support.
- The many systems, bureaucracies, and principles present in schools today were structured based on a factory model in large part to its promises of organization, uniformity, and standardization.
- Educators need a foundational framework to work from and strategies supported by the great minds of education to perpetuate learner agency, advocacy, and empowerment.
- Although this list only scratches the surface, Pestalozzi, Montessori, Dewey, Freire, Piaget, Papert, Robinson, and Reggio Emilia represent the great minds and approaches in education. A common theme throughout them all is learner agency, advocacy, and empowerment.
- The "Pedagogical Profile of Learner Agency" is a curated list of approaches, strategies, and paths of practice collected and shared with educators to cultivate learner agency and empowerment practices into any learning environment.

Essential or Extension Questions

- Why won't the factory model of learning work anymore for schools?
- Which elements of each person or philosophy align with your teacher mindset?
- Which elements of each person or philosophy do you wish to incorporate into your teacher mindset?
- Is there a learning theorist or philosophy missing from this list? How do its principles or practices align with learner agency and empowerment?

References and Other Resources

American Montessori Society. (n.d.). *Five core components of Montessori education*. Retrieved from https://amshq.org/About-Montessori/What-Is-Montessori/Core-Components-of-Montessori

Brooks, J., & Brooks, M. (1993). *In search of understanding: The case for constructivist classrooms, ASCD*. NDT Resource Center Database. Retrieved from https://ocw.metu.edu.tr/pluginfile.php/9173/mod_resource/content/1/In%20Search%20of%20Understanding.pdf

Freire, P. (1972). *Pedagogy of the oppressed*. New York: Herder and Herder.

Halimah, K. (2020). Sir Ken Robinson's ideas on the transformation of schools. *Medium*. Retrieved from https://medium.com/age-of-awareness/sir-ken-robinsons-ideas-on-the-transformation-of-schools-b77317512d43

Martinez, S., & Stager, G. (2019). *Invent to learn* (2nd ed.). Torrence, CA: Constructing Modern Knowledge Press.

National Center for Education Statistics. (n.d.). *Dropout facts*. Retrieved from https://nces.ed.gov/fastfacts/display.asp?id=16

Papert, S. (1993). *The children s machine: Rethinking school in the age of the computer*. New York: Basic Books.

PestalozziWorld. (n.d.). *Johann Heinrich Pestalozzi*. Retrieved from www.jhpestalozzi.org/

Tam, M. (2000). Constructivism, instructional design, and technology: Implications for transforming distance learning. *Educational Technology and Society, 3*(2).

Taylor, F. (1911). *The principles of scientific management*. New York: Harper Bros.

3

The Digital Generations and the Great Disconnect With Our Schools

Nobel Prize–winning writer Rabindranath Tagore asserted, "We cannot limit our children's learning to our own, for (they) are born & they will live in a different time than us." Today, we live in a world that has profoundly changed and continues to change in almost unimaginable ways. As a result, we live in a society that is transforming before our very eyes. Due to increasing exposure to sophisticated technology, educators and parents are realizing they are dealing with a fundamentally different kind of child whose experiences, expectations, and assumptions about the world we live in have already begun to force us to rethink every facet of their complex and complicated lives.

Before continuing with our deep dive into the empowerment, voice, and agency of today's learners, it is crucial to provide a comprehensive profile of today's kids. They were born into a time filled with tremendous advancements in science, technology, and engineering. Human ingenuity has combated and overcome many forms of illness; built breathtaking architectural wonders; engineered intergalactic spacecraft, probes, and instruments that have ventured far beyond our solar system; and detected the first exoplanetary bodies orbiting stars thousands of light-years away. Our amazing species have cloned extinct animals, observed the subatomic realm, and created an information source so expansive and easy to access that it takes mere seconds to find the answers to most questions.

Living in such disruptive times has produced what we refer to as the digital generations: the iGeneration (born after 1995) and the post-millennial generation (born after 1997) – basically any generation born or raised during the proliferation of technological devices in combination with the exponential growth of the digital landscape (Coates, 2007). As a consequence, this generation of learners is completely different than any other previous generations.

This chapter will help readers fall in love with the digital generations as we explore the elements and experiences that have shaped them. It will provide evidence showing they cannot be taught in the same manner as previous generations. And it will help educators understand how to use these insights into the digital generations to provide them with learning experiences infused with agency and empowerment.

Previous Generations

In the past, children spent a great deal of time outside, enjoying free, unstructured play. They were outside after breakfast, made a pit stop for lunch, then cruised right back outside until either it was dinnertime or the streetlights flickered on. They played with a core group of friends so neighborhood parents could tell where they were gathered simply by looking for the collection of bikes lying outside of a neighbor's house.

Television screens and AM/FM radios were small escapes that provided enjoyment for the whole family. However, watching or listening to one of these devices for hours upon hours every day was unheard of.

In schools, the earlier generations studied their multiplication tables and practiced their cursive handwriting. Their teachers were the ultimate authorities and source of knowledge in the classroom. If a learner or teacher did not know the answer, the dictionary or a set of encyclopedias was on standby as a reference. And if you were sent to see the principal, it usually meant you were in serious trouble.

Now, before anyone levels any accusations at us about an oversimplification or narrow view of the past, we admit this picture is a bit of a cliche. In the past, not every child had the same experiences as the 1960s, '70s, or '80s kid living in an American suburb. However, no matter what the past generations experienced, life looked a lot simpler than it does today.

> The previous generations were paper and pencil trained.
> The digital generations are light and sound trained.

> The previous generations lived in stable and predictable times.
> The digital generations are growing up in increasingly unstable and unpredictable times.

> The previous generations had television, record players, tape recorders, and radios.
> The digital generations have smart TVs, computers, smartphones, tablets, satellite radios, digital assistants, and other smart, connected devices.

The digital generations spend a great deal of their time inside in front of a device with 24/7 access to anyone and anything.

The Role of Digital Devices

During the past few decades, we have witnessed amazing advancements in the sophistication of various technological devices. The ENIAC (Electronic Numerical Integrator and Computer) was the first electronic programmable computer constructed in the United States. Completed in 1945 at the University of Pennsylvania, the ENIAC was the size of a house and as heavy as two school buses. Through decades of innovation and iteration, computers have become increasingly powerful, portable, and affordable (Mobley, 2001).

Despite the existence of an ongoing digital divide and the socioeconomic struggles of some, access to technology has never been greater. As of 2019 (SCMO, n.d.), there are over two billion computers, one billion digital tablets, and five billion smartphones in the world – a number that will only increase because of the global pandemic. If we were to calculate all of the interrelated and interconnected devices with the ability to transfer data over a network without requiring human-to-human or human-to-computer interaction (affectionately referred to as the internet of things), then the number of devices would be over 20 billion – roughly three devices for every human living on earth today (SCMO, n.d.). Personal computers, laptops, smart TVs, video game consoles, digital tablets, and e-readers are just some of the current devices people use daily for work, news, entertainment, education, commerce, and communication.

Although these devices and their functionality help us in many ways, nothing compares to the evolution and the universal adoption of smartphones. Since Apple's iPhone and Google's Android devices burst onto the technology market more than a decade ago, a rapidly growing number of people have depended on them as their second brain.

If a learner needs to know how many planets are in our solar system, then a simple text-based or verbal query can find the answer in a fraction of a second. If a learner needs the formula for the Pythagorean theorem, then a quick Google search can locate the formula, display numerous visuals associated with the theorem, and retrieve a wide variety of video tutorials on how to use the formula and about six million other miscellaneous resources they can sift through. The reality is our devices have become both a blessing and a curse. If the digital generations require information on how to change a flat tire, make the perfect pancakes, create a YouTube channel, or figure out who Steve Urkel was, then a simple search can find the answers. As educators, it is important to allow the digital generations to use these as preferred tools during the learning process.

> Choice and voice lead to empowerment.

If learners can answer a question by asking Siri, or completing a Google search, then educators need to ask them new types of questions. The compulsion to focus on memorization is largely driven by the need to prepare learners for the tests teachers and their learners regularly have to face. Unfortunately, this is increasingly happening at the expense of helping learners develop the new and very different modern learning skills they will all need once they leave school – skills we will explore in a later chapter. Digital technologies engage learners in ways that are relevant to their lives, allowing them to learn by doing as they experiment with new social and cultural norms. The reason that school is boring for some learners today is that schools have not caught up with what learners can do outside of school.

The Internet in a Minute

The year is 2021. Human invention and ingenuity have created an immense array of connected global networks known as the digital landscape. Unlike people, data never sleeps! Over 4.5 billion people, or almost 60% of the world's current population, are now connected to the internet – this is a meteoric rise from three billion just six short years ago.

In an internet minute, close to 640 million gigabytes of data are transferred, 19 million texts are sent, 200,000 people send tweets, Facebook users share 150,000 messages, YouTube users upload 500 hours of video content and watch 1.3 million videos, Netflix streams over 404,000 hours of video content, Zoom hosts 208,000 participants in virtual meetings, consumers spend one million dollars during online shopping, 1.3 million video or voice calls are made, people enter two million Google searches, 204 million emails are sent, 400,000 apps are downloaded from Google Play or the App Store, Twitch welcomes 1.2 million viewers, and almost 700,000 people are scrolling through Instagram, and all these people spend countless hours both day and night staring at their devices (DOMO, 2020; Fance, n.d.; Lewis, 2020).

If these numbers haven't already shaken you, then visit www.internetlivestats.com and stare in disbelief as data metrics rapidly increase in each feed. And the data summarized here represents only a small sampling of the enormous surge in internet usage that has occurred in the past two decades.

This new digital reality has had a profound and lasting impact on the everyday perspectives, assumptions, and application of digital tools, something further amplified among the younger generations.

What's Going On and How Do We Deal With It?

In the past, children typically would play outside unsupervised for extended periods. However, there has been a gradual loss of innocence as a result of a growing awareness of child dangers, such as bullying, predators, human trafficking, drug abuse, and gang activity. Such threats have resulted in parents becoming far more reluctant to permit their children out of sight. This level of caution and vigilance has only been further stoked by a global pandemic, resulting in increased physical isolation and extended separation of our youth. As a result, today's younger generations are locked down more than ever.

When the older generations were children, one of the worst things that could ever happen was to be sent to your room because there was absolutely nothing for you to do other than to reflect on your sins. Today, the same action would probably elicit cheers because the younger generations are instantly connected to the digital landscape.

At the same time, the digital generations are frequently misrepresented in popular media. They are often accused of being antisocial beings who lack manners or even an understanding of common social conventions.

Researchers such as boyd (2014), Robinson (2015), and Downey and Gibbs (2020) say that this is not the case – that on the contrary, for the vast majority, the digital world is a far from isolating, antisocial experience. Outside of school, they're constantly immersed in a collaborative culture based on building relationships that allow them to interact not only with their classmates but also with people who aren't even geographically close. The internet has become a teen hangout – the ultimate mall where teenagers can meet and chat.

It turns out, the digital generations are very social; here's the difference – they're just not social the way older generations think of social. They live at least part of their time in digital worlds that they've created for themselves. They play Fortnite, Minecraft, Apex Legends, Call of Duty, Pokemon Go, Halo, Angry Birds, and hundreds of other games that are exciting and engaging – and they use digital apps and tools to constantly stay connected to everyone and everything – and in these virtual environments they create and control everything – they're users – they're active – there's excitement, novelty, risk, the company of peers – the new digital landscape is somewhere they can turn for advice and information.

They observe, inquire, participate, discuss, argue, play, critique, and investigate. Many young people are apathetic in the classroom because there's such a huge gap between what exists in the real world outside of school versus what they're *made* to do in classrooms.

According to Brophy, "Even in a classroom where a teacher praises (a child) once every 5 minutes, the rate of praise for the average student would be once every 2 hours" (1981, p. 10).

That might at least partially explain why there are so many learners in our classrooms today who are waiting for the video game version of school to go on sale, so they don't have to attend our traditional schools anymore.

Studies (Thomas, 2017) show that games outperform textbooks in helping learners learn fact-based subjects such as geography, history, physics, and anatomy, while also improving visual coordination, cognitive speed, and manual dexterity (Latham, Patston, & Tippett, 2013). That's the reason why so many learners become easily frustrated and disengaged because many of them have a digital life outside of school and a non-digital life in school.

There are some experts from the older generations who argue that the experiences the digital generations are having – and the skills they're developing – are worthless, time-wasting, and irrelevant – that play and games are simply preparation for work and life after school. This suggestion that games are a waste of time only holds up if you consider serious, deep learning to be a waste of time.

Increasingly the younger generation expects they demand – to be able to be in control of their world at least part of the time. The problem is that what they expect and consistently experience in the worlds outside of school with their devices and games and apps, and texting and selfies and TikToks are often completely at odds with what they experience in the classroom.

So after learners have spent hundreds of hours of their lives playing games, communicating on social media, and exploring virtual environments outside of school, they come to the classroom where almost everything is controlled by adults, and they're forced to sit silently listening in a world where things are hierarchical and unidirectional – where the teacher stands at the front of the room talking at them nonstop and telling them what to do.

> And you know what kids tell us? They say that school is boring – that they control nothing, that they have to sit passively and listen. For them, school is all about constantly being passive observers and learning endlessly deferred gratification.

We can guarantee you that it is not possible to engage young people in an educational system where the quality of experiences schools provide isn't as inviting and engaging as the quality of the experiences they can get outside the classroom. Outside of school, the modern world is a media-rich, visual environment. Between the internet, video games, apps, and 500 channels of cable, the competition for our children's attention has become intense. Unlike their school experiences, they have both voice and choice as to what they do and how and when they do it.

Have you ever noticed that you never have to remind learners to play their video games – on the contrary, it's inevitably a struggle to get them to stop playing because they always want "just another 15 minutes." Just imagine an education system that was as immersive, entertaining, and engaging as YouTube, TikTok, or a video game. Wouldn't it be wonderful to hear your learners begging to spend just another 15 minutes with math, history, or science?

If boredom is the number one cause of disengagement and truancy, then our education system needs to be beyond wildly entertaining. If we want to prepare our children for the future, then learning needs to become a lot less like school and just about as compelling as a video game or virtual reality.

In these rapidly changing times, the traditional sit-and-listen classroom is just not enough for them – our challenge is to keep up. The digital generations will never accept a traditional stand-and-deliver instructional model. They need to be in a situation where they're controlling things – and that can never happen in a traditional school environment.

So we just have to ask. Why is it that our young learners can solve the most complex problems in a video game involving executive decision-making and analytical thinking or quickly learn to use a sophisticated tool or app – yet some "educational experts" continue to profess that today's learners can't add or read or learn?

Right beneath our radar, digital learners are highly skilled. They are very much an intellectual, problem-solving, thoughtful, and very social generation. They have highly developed critical thinking, problem-solving, and social skills, and they can be highly motivated if given the right opportunities.

The problem is that their social skills and their problem-solving skills are just not the skills that we, the older generations, value – nor are these the skills that we typically test for or teach in schools today. As a result, their extraordinary cognitive and technical abilities are often simply not acknowledged or dismissed outright.

It's taken us years of study and research to understand that for today's digital generations, it has become increasingly difficult for them to distinguish between where work ends and where play begins. That's why they want their learning to be engaging, relevant, instantly useful, and fun (Jukes, Schaaf, & Mohan, 2015). But beyond this, more than anything else, when it comes to learning, the digital generations want to know the answers to three simple questions:

> Why in the world am I learning what you're trying to teach me? What possible connection does this have to me and my world? And even more importantly, how can I learn this by myself and with my peers?

Turning the Corner and Heading for Home

Now there's much more we'd like to say – but we hope this brief description explains, at least in part, why today's learners act differently, why they behave the way they do, why they respond to the world the way they do, how they learn, how they view the world, what interests and engages them, and why their expectations and assumptions are so much different from previous generations. We hope this might help explain at least in part some of the fundamental differences between their generations and ours and why.

And yet sadly, and this is what frustrates us more than anything else – even though we now have several decades of research on what works in the classroom, almost nothing of what we've learned about how our children's brains and minds function and how they learn is being applied in the classroom today – so we just have to ask this question. If learners are way ahead of teachers in developing the skills needed to succeed in the digital world of the future – and if many teachers are largely oblivious to the significance of the skills learners have acquired in this digital world – and if teachers continue to do things in the classroom that we already know don't work – because many do – then who has the learning problem? Is it the learners, or is it us?

We think there's great irony in the fact that many experienced teachers are struggling to try to become relevant to learners in the new digital and post-pandemic landscape. That's because it is a great challenge unlearning being a traditional teacher.

Summarizing the Main Points

- ♦ Living in such disruptive times has produced what we refer to as the digital generations.
- ♦ Despite the existence of an ongoing digital divide and the socioeconomic struggles of some, access to technology has never been greater.

- This new digital reality has had a profound and lasting impact on the everyday perspectives, assumptions, and application of digital tools, something further amplified among the younger generations.
- The digital generations are frequently misrepresented in popular media. They are often accused of being antisocial beings who lack manners or even an understanding of common social conventions.
- Digital learners are highly skilled. They are an intellectual, problem-solving, thoughtful, and very social generation. They have highly developed critical thinking, problem-solving, and social skills, and they can be motivated.

Essential or Extension Questions

- How has technology affected the younger generations?
- As educators, do we hold any biases toward the digital generations with how they act, communicate, or learn?
- How can educators empower members of the digital generations?
- Knowing some of these fundamental differences present in the digital generations, how can parents and educators form healthy connections with them?
- What choices can learners make outside of school? What choices can learners make inside of schools? (School lunches don't count!)

References and Resources

boyd, d. (2014). *It's complicated: The social lives of networked teens*. New Haven: Yale University Press.

Brophy, J. (1981). Teacher praise: A functional analysis. *Review of Educational Research, 51*(1), 5–32.

Coates, J. (2007). *Generational learning styles*. River Falls, WI: LERN Books.

DOMO. (2020). *Data never sleeps 8.0*. Retrieved from https://web-assets.domo.com/blog/wp-content/uploads/2020/08/20-data-never-sleeps-8-final-01-Resize.jpg

Downey, D., & Gibbs, B. (2020). Kids these days: Are face-to-face social skills among American children declining? *American Journal of Sociology, 125*(4), 1030. doi:10.1086/707985

Fance, C. (n.d.). In just a single minute, here are all that happens on the internet. *Lifehack*. Retrieved from www.lifehack.org/articles/technology/just-single-minute-here-are-all-that-happens-the-internet.html

Jukes, I., Schaaf, R., & Mohan, N. (2015). *Reinventing learning for the always-on generation: Strategies and apps that work*. Bloomington, IN: Solution Tree Press.

Latham, A. J., Patston, L. L., & Tippett, L. J. (2013). The virtual brain: 30 years of video-game play and cognitive abilities. *Frontiers in Psychology, 4*, 629. doi:10.3389/fpsyg.2013.00629

Lewis, L. (2020). *Infographic: What happens in an internet minute 2020*. Retrieved from www.allaccess.com/merge/archive/31294/infographic-what-happens-in-an-internet-minute

Mobley, B. (2001). *The ingenuity of common workmen: And the invention of the computer* (Retrospective theses and dissertations 660). Retrieved from https://lib.dr.iastate.edu/rtd/660

Robinson, K. (2015). *Creative schools: The grassroots revolution that's transforming education*. New York: Viking.

SCMO. (n.d.). *Logistics facts*. Retrieved from www.scmo.net/logistics-facts

Tagore, R. Retrieved from https://minimalistquotes.com/rabindranath-tagore-quote-83452/

Thomas, A. (2017). Digital game-based textbook vs. traditional print-based textbook: The effect of textbook format on college students' engagement with textbook content outside of the classroom. *The Turkish Online Journal of Educational Technology, 16*(4). Retrieved from https://files.eric.ed.gov/fulltext/EJ1160632.pdf

4

Rise of the Creative Class

The Challenge of Change

American writer Eric Hofner observed, "In a world of change, the learners shall inherit the earth, while the learned find themselves perfectly equipped for a world that no longer exists" (as cited in Rich, 1997, Abstract). We want to begin this chapter by talking about the change Hofner was speaking of. Change in our children, change in our families, change in our communities, and change in our world. The greatest challenge we face in times of rapid, disruptive, pandemic change is that the scope of the transformation can be both dramatic and, at the same time, subtle and sneaky. We all know something is happening, but it is often hard to pinpoint exactly what has changed and how it is changing.

In this chapter, we will briefly examine the agents of change occurring in the world today and connect this to the necessity of cultivating learner agency, empowerment, and ownership.

Disruptive Innovation

We have some important questions to ask. They are the foundation of this book. What does the future hold for our nations? What does the future hold for our citizens? What does the future hold for our children? In what kind of world will we live? And what attitudes, motivations, and abilities will our children need to be successful in an unknown future?

Christensen, Horn, and Johnson (2008) defined disruptive innovation as change that fundamentally transforms traditional ways of doing things. Innovations such as digital technology, cloud computing, big data, genetic engineering, smart materials, mobile commerce, social media, biotechnology, 3-D printing, nanotechnology, artificial intelligence, robotics, neuroscience, and in recent times, COVID-19 are just some of the big disruptors of today and tomorrow.

These disruptions are transforming how we work, how we play, how we communicate, and how we live in a rapidly changing world. What follows is a brief overview of disruptive innovation, the future of living and working in the modern world, the implications this holds for education and today's learners, and why it is so imperative to promote learner agency and empowerment.

Disruptive innovation changes everything in its path. Today, we live in a swirling vortex of revolutionary changes that are creating intense economic shifts, disorienting demographic patterns, and creating disruptive cultural transformations. Powerful new technologies and disruptive innovations are globalizing just about every aspect of our world. And these disruptions have enormous implications for our communities, families, and the future of education because they have fundamentally altered the working world to the point that it is all but unrecognizable to older generations. Let's take a look at what's happened.

For the longest time, right into the latter half of the 20th century, one of the primary drivers of the economy was the factory job and factory mindset. Back in these times, workers were judged by how many widgets they made during their shift. Acting as human robots, workers would do the same task, hour after hour, day after day – this was brutal and mind-numbingly boring work. This mindset for work and life was so prevalent in our lives that even our schools had been modeled on a factory approach to instruction and learning. However, this model and the jobs associated with the factory mindset have been disappearing from the economy for decades (Long, 2016).

Why? Because disruptive innovations have made it possible for this kind of work to be done by anybody, almost anywhere in the world. And today, where labor is the cheapest is not here – it is in countries like China and even more inexpensive places such as Vietnam, India, Bangladesh, Pakistan, and other low-wage, Third World countries (Amadeo, 2017, March 30).

Location Dependent Work

There has been one exception to this mass exodus of jobs – that is, unless the jobs involve location-dependent work. Location-dependent work includes jobs in the construction industry, carpenters, plumbers, electricians, metal fabricators, truck drivers, miners, loggers, barbers, cooks, delivery service drivers, auto technicians, restaurant workers, and cleaning staff, to name but a few.

All of these blue-collar jobs require workers to be physically on-site to do their work. While some of these jobs have been affected by the ups and downs of the global economy, there is still a high demand for location-dependent blue-collar workers. The same strong demand, however, does not apply to white-collar workers. White-collar jobs are quickly disappearing from the economy (Brown, 2016).

This is happening because powerful new software tools that replace white-collar workers are already disrupting traditional ways of doing business. Digital tools make it possible for far fewer workers to do much more work. And even when white-collar workers are not displaced by software tools, these workers are already at risk of having their jobs outsourced to workers in Third World countries. The reason these jobs can be outsourced is that many tasks done by white-collar workers today involve what is described as *routine cognitive work*.

Routine Cognitive Work

Routine cognitive work involves doing repetitive mental tasks over and over again. Routine cognitive, white-collar work includes people who do jobs such as bookkeeping, tax preparation, data entry, call center work, receptionist work, help desk, or customer support, as well as computer programmers and legal researchers.

All of these kinds of routine cognitive work involve doing the same mental tasks over and over again. This means that this kind of work not only can but has, is, and will continue to be outsourced. Today in the new digital landscape, we live in a hyperconnected, hyper-disrupted world. As a result, routine cognitive workers must not only compete with people in the next city, region, or state; they also have to compete with an extensive global labor pool of inexpensive but experienced workers.

The Global Economy

A global digital people network is rapidly transforming the nature of work. As a result, both here and elsewhere around the world, we are quickly moving from companies of hundreds or thousands of permanent workers to businesses that contract temporary remote employees. This rising phenomenon is known as the gig economy.

There has been a dramatic shift in the world of work that now includes far more part-time, freelance, e-lance, and contract employment. In the past twenty-five years, more than half of the new jobs in advanced economies around the world have been of the temporary, part-time, or self-employed variety. At the same time, there have been far fewer full-time jobs that have traditionally been the foundation of the middle class. These trends seem to indicate that we are nearing the end of many generations of guaranteed, full-time employment that supports a person at a comfortable standard of living across a lifetime.

As a result, today we live in a very different world and economy than the one in which many of us grew up. Increasingly the fundamental unit of the new workforce is no longer the corporation or company; rather, it is the individual worker. Even the location of the workplace has changed. Accelerated by the pandemic, now instead of workers coming to the work, increasingly the work comes to the workers whenever and wherever in the world they are at that moment. Disruptive innovations have made organizing, managing, and collaborating with a global workforce a simple task.

The Modern Workforce

The automation of work is another trend that must be considered when looking at the modern world. Work is not just being outsourced and offshored; it is also being automated. For example, every time you use the Amazon website to make a purchase or you drop your mortgage numbers into the Fannie Mae web form (www.fanniemae.com/portal/index.html), what you have done is unintentionally and unconsciously take away some frontline, routine cognitive worker's job. Think about legal software (www.lawyers.com), think about tax preparation (https://turbotax.intuit.com/), think about automated checkout counters – if a job or task can be reduced to a mathematical algorithm, it is easy for businesses to produce robots, microchips, and software that will do the job cheaper, faster, and oftentimes better. When that happens – poof – that segment of the job, or even the entire job itself, vanishes forever.

By way of comparison, traditional factory floors were designed for mass production. There were large numbers of workers who sat or stood in rows repeatedly doing the same thing, at the same time, by themselves. In this new, disrupted world, this is no longer the case. In the new global economy, 80% of the workers primarily manage their work and are expected to be continuously learning new processes, new concepts, and new applications (Smith, 2016). Increasingly, workers are expected to operate in temporary groupings of coworkers who collaborate on tasks that primarily require intellectual rather than physical capabilities. As a result, far more workers today need mental skills rather than just physical skills to harness the power of disruptive innovations to increase their productivity.

As artificial intelligence evolves, any task that requires the analysis of information can be done both better and faster by computers and robots. This not only includes the jobs of traditional laborers and factory workers, but it also includes the jobs of physicians, lawyers, accountants, and stockbrokers, among many, many others. This robot revolution has not only freed many employees from physical labor in the workplace – but it has also freed a lot of those same workers permanently from their jobs.

New Skills for a New World

Let's pause for a moment and reflect on the changes that we have briefly examined to this point. We acknowledge that many readers might be uncomfortable with this trend and, particularly, might not like what this means for your children. But whether you are comfortable with what is happening or not, in an increasingly global economy, this is the new reality we all have to face. Many businesses and industries, not only nationally but also internationally, believe that accessing this new global workforce is the only way to stay competitive.

These developments have not only changed the nature of the workplace, but they have also fundamentally changed the skill sets needed by the workers to operate in these new work environments. Based on current trends, in the next few years, it is likely that people who need constant managing and direction will not just be unemployed; increasingly, they will likely be unemployable.

Because of the disruptions described here, the very nature of work has fundamentally changed. Today we live in a ½ × 2 × 3 economy. There are half as many workers, getting paid twice as much money, who are expected to produce three times as much value using new digital technologies, software, and robotics while applying new skill sets that allow them to be significantly more productive than those who cannot use the power of disruptive technologies (Jukes & Schaaf, 2020). Skill development that has not been commonly a part of traditional schools and schooling.

To be clear, modern workers must have very different skill sets from those used by traditional manual workers. Modern workers are highly specialized craftspeople who have a repertoire of sophisticated new skills and regularly use their brains far more than they use their bodies. That is why the new global economy provides very few jobs for the poorly educated. The days of well-paid, unskilled, or semi-skilled work are over. So increasingly the only choice for many of today's workers is either they have high skills or they get minimum-wage jobs.

The Rise of the Creative Class

In *The Rise of the Creative Class – Revisited* (2014), author Richard Florida examines workplace trends in the modern world. Florida says we can essentially divide a nation's workforce into four basic groups. Consider the chart in Figure 4.1 (developed by Ian Jukes; Jukes & Schaaf, 2020, p. 35):

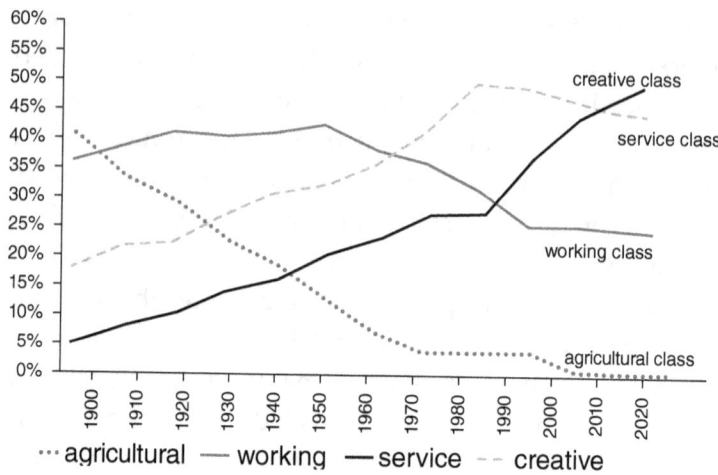

FIGURE 4.1 The four groups of the modern workforce
Developed by Ian Jukes; Jukes & Schaaf, 2020, p. 35

The Agricultural Class

The first group is the agricultural class. In 1900, more than 40% of the workforce was involved in agriculture. In 2020, automation has reduced that number down to about 1% of the workforce. This is mainly because farmers and their work animals had been automated, so what used to be done by dozens of workers and hundreds of animals can now be accomplished by one worker and machines.

The Working Class

The second group is the working class. These are the traditional manufacturing, labor, fishing, logging, and mining jobs. These are the jobs that only require basic skills to perform. The problem with only having basic skills is that as the economy has fundamentally shifted and digital technologies have replaced humans, there is far less demand for workers with only basic skills.

Location-Dependent and Service Workers

The third group is the location-dependent workers and the service workers. These are the people who do routine cognitive work. As you can see from the chart, these types of jobs peaked about 1980 and are now steadily declining.

The Creative Class

The fourth group is what Florida (2014) calls the creative class. These are the people who regularly do non-routine cognitive work and consistently apply higher-level thinking skills to their jobs.

Consider the graph in Figure 4.2. You may notice on the right that the percentage of creative class workers exceeded the percentage of service class workers in the workforce about 2008. You may also notice that since 1980, these lines are inverse trends – they are going in opposite directions. That is because, since personal computers and other digital innovations started appearing about 1980, they have had an enormous impact on the workforce.

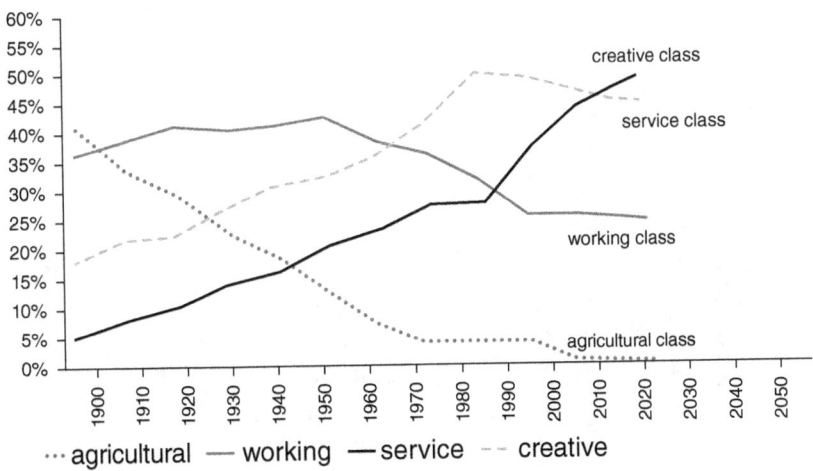

FIGURE 4.2 The four groups of the modern workforce

Developed by Ian Jukes; Jukes & Schaaf, 2020, p. 35

Here's what's happening. Service class jobs are being replaced by technologies, while creative class jobs are being facilitated by technologies. Creative class jobs require skills and expertise that cannot be replaced by disruptive technologies; they can only be augmented or enhanced.

Creative class jobs primarily require what we describe as headware skills, not just hardware skills. Headware skills are thinking skills – abilities such as critical thinking, problem-solving, adaptability, flexibility, productivity, accountability, communications, data management, leadership, creativity, innovation, citizenship, and collaboration skills. These are often described collectively as the 21st-century or modern fluencies (Mohan, Jukes, & Schaaf, 2021).

Now, if we take Florida's (2014) chart and convert the data to stacked bars (Figure 4.3), it looks like this:

You see the steady decline of agriculture work, and you see the continued growth of the creative class. If you look carefully at this data, you will understand why we face such a fundamental problem in education today and why learner agency is so vital for learners to develop.

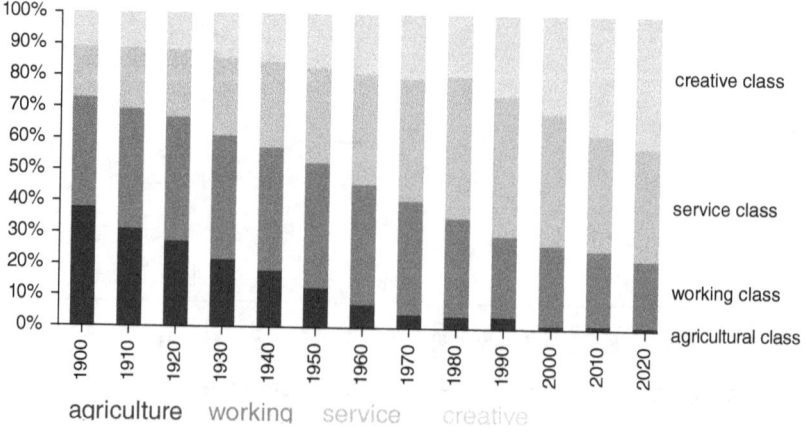

FIGURE 4.3 The four groups of the modern workforce as stacked bar graphs
Developed by Ian Jukes; Jukes & Schaaf, 2020, p. 36

Education in Modern Times

The challenge we face is that the educational model used today was designed for a time when we had a very different economy, workplace, and way of life. It was a world based on three-quarters of the workforce working in agriculture, natural resources, and manufacturing. The skills needed were basic literacy skills, the ability to memorize, the capacity to follow instructions, and in many cases, physical labor skills.

Today, we have to help learners prepare for an increasingly disrupted world and a very different economy – an economy where three-quarters of the workforce is in service class or creative class jobs. By 2020, Florida projected that creative class jobs could be as much as 50% of the workforce (Florida, 2014).

However, why stop at the year 2020? Let's apply some exponential thinking and project job prospects for Florida's (2014) four classes of workers out about 35 years into the future to the year 2050, when the students completing high school this year will be about 53 years old, and those in kindergarten will be about 40 years old. Let's see if this projection can give us any suggestions about the skills we need to focus on with our students now.

This graph represents the original numbers extended out to the year 2050. Take a moment to analyze the graph. Do you notice any trends? What are the implications? We believe this graph reveals something incredibly important for the future of this nation. Look at the projections and consider the types of skills learners need to be adequately prepared for life and work in the modern world.

What Does This All Mean?

We need to stop and consider what this picture of the future means in terms of what our learners are learning right now. Our challenge is that while many of us recognize there is a problem, for the most part, our current educational system continues to

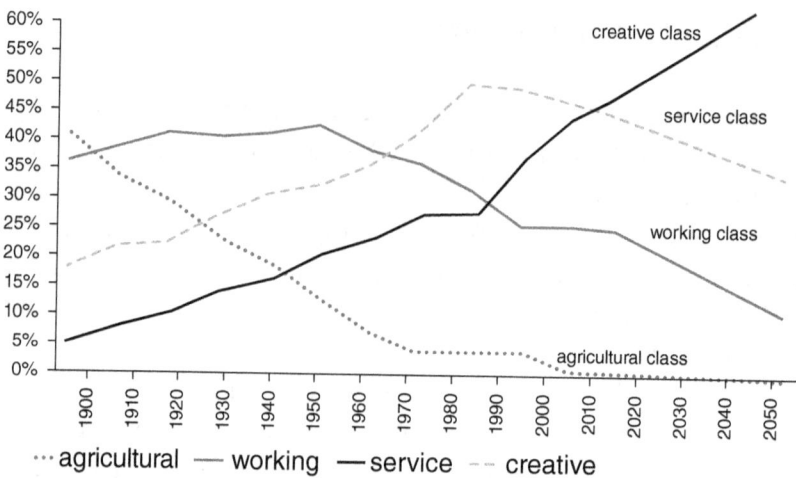

FIGURE 4.4 The four groups of the modern workforce projected to 2050
Developed by Ian Jukes; Jukes & Schaaf, 2020, p. 36

promote traditional structures, traditional organizations, traditional teaching, standardized content, and standardized testing. An approach that is widely viewed as the only means with which to assess standardized learning for learners – many of whom, because they were born into the new digital landscape, have non-standardized brains. And this is happening at the very same time that the global economy is rapidly eliminating traditional, repetitive, standardized jobs.

With this traditional mindset of learning, what we continue to do is take every learner's uniqueness and shove it into a one-size-fits-all funnel of traditional education, where we stuff them full of information, then expect them to regurgitate back a series of single, right answers.

Moreover, we are not being truthful to either our learners or their parents when we assure them that if they master the existing curriculum, if they memorize the content, if they do well on the standardized tests, then this is all they will ever need to be prepared for the rest of their lives. This perspective is particularly disconcerting when Richard Elmore's (2006) research indicates that between 80 and 85% of the work that students do in classrooms today continues to focus on factual recall and low-level procedural thinking. In other words, 80 to 85% of classroom work is focused on routine cognitive work – the work that is increasingly being cloud-sourced, outsourced, offshored, and automated – and consequently disappearing forever from the economy. This trend is a serious problem.

The Challenge of Change

The challenge is that the subjects and skills that are the easiest to teach and easiest to test are now also the skills that are the easiest to automate, digitize, and outsource. We need to stop thinking about success for our children only in terms of traditional test scores that rely heavily on teaching to a single correct answer – and that primarily only measure convergent and not divergent thinking. When we take this approach, learners may complete their education with certificates and credentials, but many of them will still lack the essential competencies needed to be thoughtful, engaged, and empowered citizens – and in addition, get and maintain good jobs in a rapidly changing economy where a worker's value is no longer exclusively based on what they know but rather the speed at which they can learn, unlearn, adapt, relearn, and apply.

The Case for Learner Agency

We hear talk all the time from politicians and employers about the importance of individualism, autonomy, and initiative. We admire creativity, ingenuity, and resourcefulness. We praise the self-made, the independent thinker, the school dropouts who make good. We know that capitalizing on individual skills and differences is essential for successful adaptation to disruptive change. But in the same breath, education continues to cling to a traditional curriculum from another century that is designed to standardize learning. It is a system that marginalizes and diminishes those who do not buy into the traditional ways of doing things.

What we have done is take an Industrial Age mindset behind the design of the traditional classroom and traditional learning and carry, it forward into the 21st century. The current Industrial Age model for teaching, learning, and assessment is working well if what you need is 25% of students with skills and 75% who are unskilled and simply expected to follow instructions. The problem is that this is not the reality of today's world and workplace.

For this to happen, we need to start concentrating on cultivating in all of our learners the essential skills, knowledge, and habits of mind necessary to survive and thrive in the modern world. We must do this, and we must do this now. The gap between the learning that our students currently do and what is required to survive in the modern world grows wider and deeper every day. To put it bluntly, if we continue down our current path, we will be educating both our youth and our nations into unemployment and irrelevance.

Short-Life Versus Long-Life Skills

Historically, the focus of schools has primarily been on short-life skills. These are the skills related to the memorization of specific content or learning how to use discrete procedures. Today, decades on, we live in an educational world that is increasingly driven by content standards, learning objectives, curriculum, texts, and pacing guides. We have a worksheet culture – we have high-stakes standardized tests, benchmark exams, and other assessments that drive instruction. These are all short-life skills – skills that quickly cease to be relevant or useful, particularly when you live in an age of constant disruption.

Today, in both life and the workplace, there is far more demand for long-life skills. Long-life skills are the modern fluencies that were described previously – including critical thinking, problem-solving, communications, information management, leadership, creativity, innovation, citizenship, and collaboration. These are skills that are not only valid now but will remain valid 30 years from now when the students we have today are retiring from their careers. Long-life skills have no expiration date, so they will be as useful 30 years from now as they are today. We will more carefully examine modern learning skills in the next chapter.

Houston, We Have a Problem!

It is the writers' observations that many students today have disengaged from school and have either dropped out physically or mentally. Although the numbers have improved slightly in the past ten years, in the US and Canada, there are still places where 10, 20, 30, or even as many as 50% of students drop out before they complete high school – and for some people, that's acceptable. Even if that's not your kids that are dropping out, that's not acceptable! As we commented previously, if we ran a business and 10, 20, 30, or as many as 50% of our products were defective, we wouldn't stay in business very long.

And we want to be very clear – our learners are not just dropping out of high school. High dropout rates also apply to the students we see as our successes, the ones who go on to post-secondary studies. Almost half of post-secondary students drop out before completing a degree (Weissmann, 2012 March 29). In fact, in some cases, dropout rates from post-secondary institutions are as bad, if not worse, than dropout rates from high schools. What's wrong with this picture?

Students are leaving both high school and post-secondary education in completely unacceptable numbers. Why? Because many students today increasingly sense the absolute disconnect between our continued focus on traditional content, traditional instruction, and standardized assessment – and the constantly changing realities of living, working, and learning in the modern world.

The New Pandemic-Driven Economy

Today, we live in a pandemic-driven economy where it's increasingly everyone for themselves, where the rules of survival are always changing, and where fundamental uncertainty and functional instability are the orders of the day. Our parents lived in a world where what you learned once in your youth was expected to sustain you for a lifetime and a single career. Today, the idea of the "40-year employee" who spends his or her entire career working for one company and in one career is a complete novelty. The cradle-to-grave security of the old company model is just a faint memory for most people. Increasingly, the message people get from both companies and employees is that if they want long-term loyalty, they should buy a dog.

Many of us have likely heard the prediction that students today should anticipate that they will have somewhere between four and seven careers in their lifetime. This estimate is more than 20 years out of date. In the new digital landscape, the new estimate is that today's generations of students should anticipate having 10 to 17 or more careers (not jobs working in the same industry, but distinct careers) – and all this by the time they are 38 years old (US Bureau of Labor Statistics, 2017, October 20). The average length of stay in any job today for the digital generations is typically only about 1.5 to 3 years (Carter, 2016). Something the current pandemic has only amplified.

The challenge is that having 10 to 17 or more careers will require learners to replace almost their entire bodies of knowledge several times during their working lives. Having 10 to 17 (or more) careers means that the idea of cultivating a finite body of knowledge learned once in your youth, which is sustained for a lifetime as previous generations experienced, will just not work anymore.

It is also important to stress that having 10 to 17 or more careers by the time someone is 38 years old is not a sign of failure, lack of commitment, or lack of self-discipline on the part of modern workers. What this reflects is the new economy and the new lifelong employment reality that all of our students are facing. A reality where they will have to be constantly managing their careers and always be thinking – what is going to happen next?

In light of the new global digital economy, educational leaders face the monumental challenge of bringing our schools into line with the realities of the modern world. No longer can we expect students to get everything they will need for their entire lives by attending school once in their youth. We are now in a new age where people must be learners for a life of constant learning and relearning, where they will not have a teacher telling them what to do or how to do it. They must become independent, creative, self-directed learners. A modern-day education filled with learner agency, empowerment, and independence will be required to flourish.

The Ripples of Change

One thing we can predict with absolute certainty about today's learners is that a decade or two from now, they will not all be doing the same thing – and they certainly will not be depending on the same body of knowledge they are today. The problem is that powerful and disruptive change agents like the pandemic are constantly and dramatically changing the working world. This has taken many educators and educational leaders by surprise.

The ripples of change are causing fundamental shifts in the necessary work and life skills – and this is happening at an incredible speed. According to a Merrill Lynch report (2000), 50% of an employee's skills become outdated within three to five years – a trend that means learning today must become an essential, year-round activity. For our students, lifelong learning is mandatory. It is the only insurance policy individuals and groups have against being blindsided by disruptive changes.

The New Digital Divide

For many years, there has been commentary about a digital divide, which was once seen as a factor of wealth. The digital divide was about the gap between the have and have-nots. Today, the digital divide is increasingly regarded as a factor of education – about the difference between the knows and know-nots.

It is becoming increasingly clear that the skills learners need to be successful in school are a fundamentally different set of competencies and, in many ways, a lesser set of skills than those skills essential for success in life and work. While traditional schooling is necessary, it is no longer sufficient preparation for success as a citizen, parent, or employee.

The Purpose of Education in Modern Times

So what does this all mean for education? If education is going to stay relevant in the digital world, if education is going to fulfill our mandate of preparing learners for their future and not just our past, if education is going to provide our students with both the short-life and long-life skills, they will need to operate in the world beyond school both now, and in the future, education must be about more than just developing in students the school skills required to pass the next test, the next course, or the next level.

We need to begin to introduce students to the long-life skills and learning opportunities they will need to thrive as citizens, parents, and workers in the culture of the 21st century. However, to do this, we must make fundamental changes – and we need to make those changes now. Without significant change, the future of education – an institution increasingly disconnected from the needs of its clients – is very bleak, to say the least.

At this juncture, it is important to emphasize that the purpose of education is about much more than just getting young people prepared to enter the workforce. The purpose of education is also about the social, academic, cultural, and intellectual development needed so that today's generations can grow up to be engaged, independent, and contributing citizens. However, it is not, as some people believe, a matter of either-or, us-or-them, our way or the highway. Education must prepare young people equally for life, work, and citizenship.

The bottom line is that we cannot just continue to teach facts that we hope and expect learners to regurgitate back to us because, in a hyper-accelerated world, facts change too quickly. Increasingly, the world just does not care what you know or what you have memorized – because almost everything is instantly available on Google if you have effective search skills.

Increasingly, the world only cares and will only pay people for what they can do with what they know. We cannot continue to use yesterday's skills, tools, ideas, business models, or technologies to address the coming changes. Today, a nation's most critical assets are no longer agricultural products, minerals, wood, paper, steel, or other traditional goods. Today our nation's most significant assets are a highly educated, technologically literate workforce of lifelong, independent thinkers and learners who are equipped with modern skills they can apply again and again throughout their entire lives. This must be the goal of learner agency, empowerment, and choice.

The Future of Nations

For the longest time, our nations have been known for their resources – now we must become known for our resourcefulness. If we are going to succeed in uncovering the full intellectual and creative genius of all of our nations' learners, it is educators that are going to make it happen. Educators have the most challenging of jobs today.

Educators are the learning facilitators for millions of young children in the Knowledge Age. Modern education stands in the gap between their present and their future – between their failure and their fulfillment. It is the collective energy, passion, creativity, commitment, and hard work of educators – every day – that builds a bridge that enables our children to cross the gap from the present to the future.

Summarizing the Main Points

- According to author Clayton Christensen, disruptive innovation is change that transforms the traditional ways of doing things. Innovations in digital technology, cloud computing, big data, genetic engineering, smart materials, mobile commerce, social media, biotechnology, 3-D printing, nanotechnology, artificial intelligence, robotics, and neuroscience are disrupting how people work, communicate, and produce goods and services.
- Disruptive innovations have made it possible for many kinds of work to be done by anybody, almost anywhere in the world. These types of jobs tend to be routine cognitive work or work that involves doing repetitive mental tasks over and over again, such as data entry, tax preparation, and bookkeeping.
- The education offered today was designed for a time when we had a very different economy, workplace, and way of life. It was during a time of predictability. Now, thanks to disruptive innovation, educators must concentrate on cultivating the essential skills, knowledge, and habits of mind necessary to survive and thrive in the modern world in their students.
- Many schools today focus on short-life skills, which focus on memorization of specific content knowledge or discrete procedural learning. Long-life skills are the modern learning skills that are valid now and will remain valid 50 years from now.
- If education is going to stay relevant in the new digital landscape, if education is going to fulfill our mandate of preparing students for their future, then schools must

make fundamental changes. They will need to begin to introduce students to the skills and learning opportunities they will need to thrive as citizens, parents, and workers in the culture of the 21st century.

Essential or Extension Questions

- Can you brainstorm several instances of companies or products that became obsolete thanks in part to a disruptive innovation that changed a market or affected the quality of human life?
- According to Richard Florida, what are the types of jobs that are increasing in number? What is the forecast for these types of jobs in the future? Why must educators be cognizant of these trends in the modern-day workforce?
- Why are headware skills so important for the modern (and the future) workforce?
- What are the differences between short-life and long-life skills?
- How would older generations view a person that possessed 10 to 17 careers in their lifetimes? How has this mindset changed over time?

References

Amadeo, K. (2017, March 30). *How outsourcing jobs affects the U.S. economy*. Retrieved from www.thebalance.com/how-outsourcing-jobs-affects-the-u-s-economy-3306279

Brown, G. C. (2016, April 13). *By 2020 5 million white collar office jobs will disappear*. Retrieved from www.linkedin.com/pulse/2020-5-million-white-collar-office-jobs-disappear-world-gary-brown

Carter, D. (2016, July 6). *Goodbye, linear factory model of schooling: Why learning is irregular*. Retrieved from www.edsurge.com/news/2016-07-06-goodbye-linear-factory-model-of-schooling-why-learning-is-irregular

Christensen, C. M., Horn, M. B., & Johnson, C. W. (2008). *Disrupting class: How disruptive innovation will change the way the world learns.* New York: McGraw-Hill.

Elmore, R. (2006). *Education leadership as the practice of improvement* [Audio recording]. Retrieved from www.scottmcleod.org/2006UCEAElmore.mp3

Florida, R. (2014). *The rise of the creative class – revisited.* New York: Basic Books.

Jukes, I., & Schaaf, R. (2020). *A brief history of the future of education: Learning in the age of disruption.* Thousand Oaks, CA: Corwin.

Long, H. (2016, March 29). *The U.S. has lost 5 million manufacturing jobs since 2000.* Retrieved from http://money.cnn.com/2016/03/29/news/economy/us-manufacturing-jobs

Merrill Lynch. (2000). *The knowledge web.* Retrieved from https://faculty.darden.virginia.edu/Ebusiness/E-Learning/the%20knowledge%20web.pdf

Mohan, N., Jukes, I., & Schaaf, R. (2021). *Literacy is still not enough: Modern fluencies for teaching, learning, and assessment.* Thousand Oaks, CA: Corwin.

Rich, J. C. (1997). In times of change learners inherit the earth: The 1997 presidential address. *Journal of Neurosurgery, 87*(5), 659–666. doi:10.3171/jns.1997.87.5.0659

Smith, A. (2016, March 10). *Public predictions for the future of workforce automation.* Retrieved from www.pewinternet.org/2016/03/10/public-predictions-for-the-future-of-workforce-automation

US Bureau of Labor Statistics. (2017, October 20). *National longitudinal surveys.* Retrieved from www.bls.gov/nls/nlsfaqs.htm

Weissmann, J. (2012, March 29). Why do so many Americans drop out of college? *The Atlantic.* Retrieved September 20, 2016, from www.theatlantic.com/business/archive/2012/03/why-do-so-many-americans-drop-out-of-college/255226

5

Modern Learners, Modern Skills

Twentieth-century fiction writer E. M. Forster declared, "Spoon feeding, in the long run, teaches us nothing but the shape of the spoon" (2015). If education wants to prepare learners for the world that awaits them once they leave school, if educators want to access the full intellectual and creative potential of every learner, if educators want learners to develop the critical next-generation skills needed to survive in the modern world, then education must create a path between traditional and progressive learning. Education must move beyond pedagogies of control to facilitating learning journeys that empower the present-day and future generations.

What Is Modern Learning?

For this book, we define modern learning as the acquisition and application of knowledge and the cultivation of work habits, attitudes, and essential skills that include both traditional and digital literacies, as well as what we will describe in the following paragraphs as the modern fluencies. These skills and attributes are fundamental to both meeting the demands of the curriculum and being successful in life. It is important to emphasize that a modern learning approach is not intended to replace traditional skills but rather to build upon foundational skills, such as reading, writing, and math, to amplify student learning.

However, beyond the attributes of a traditional classroom, modern learning can also be messy, fun, flexible, agile, active, spacious, accommodating, positive, meaningful, thoughtful, fresh, relevant, lifelong, supportive, transferrable, adaptive, encouraging, happy, collaborative, connecting, engaging, personal, mobile, digital, safe, self-directed, hands-on, risky, shared, reflective, inclusive, challenging, open-ended, modeled, passion-driven, innovative, interactive, fluid, integrated, and not limited for learners and educators by the four walls of the classroom.

The old saying is "The person doing the talking is the one doing the learning." This observation carries even more weight as we seek to dismantle systems of inequity in the learning process since it translates to "The person doing the talking is the person with the power." Stop and consider the following for a moment:

Who has the power in our classrooms?
Who should have the power in our classrooms?

risky   interactive
hands-on   self-directed
accommodating   supportive
spacious   active   digital
mobile   relevant   agile
open-ended   lifelong   collaborative
connecting   flexible   engaging
challenging   thoughtful   transferrable   shared
innovative   fun
messy   safe   positive   modeled
encouraging   meaningful   personal   fluid
reflective   fresh   happy   inclusive   integrated
adaptive   passion-driven

FIGURE 5.1 What is modern learning?

What Are Modern Learners?

The gap between the learning that our current generations experience and what they need to survive in the modern world grows wider, deeper, and harder to bridge every day. So let's cut right to it – modern learners

- are independent thinkers and doers (however, they are also skilled at productively working as part of a team or group);
- can communicate written and orally using a wide variety of mediums;
- have both highly developed intrapersonal and interpersonal skills;
- are comfortable using a wide variety of digital and non-digital tools;
- can solve problems using both convergent and divergent thinking;
- prefer learning that occurs anytime, anywhere, at any pace;
- want to experience real-world, authentic, learner-centered instructional approaches;
- are leaders in their learning, are self-disciplined and self-motivated, and are driven by their passions;
- crave constant knowledge and personalized content and are exceptionally curious;
- are active, impatient, and mobile thinkers;
- question everything but also seek the answers; and
- are determined to succeed and push through challenges and are willing to take risks and learn through mistakes, tinkering, or iteration to learn.

What Are Modern Learning Environments?

Today's learning environments must create domains that promote learner agency and ownership – spaces that are filled with curiosity, creativity, innovation, exploration, collaboration, empathy, and exhilaration. In this coveted list of learning behaviors, state-of-the-art digital technologies, expensive furniture, and unlimited budgets don't need to be part of the equation. While it would be great to have unlimited resources, real-world practicality often gets in the way. Education budgets are usually the first thing to disappear when times get economically difficult. In reality, modern-day, future-ready learning environments do not require big budgets. Using a student-centric approach is a critical component when combined with inspired teaching and learning. It is not only about tools and resources – it is about heart and mindset.

The concept of "classroom learning" must be reimagined into what Mohan (2018) describes as modern learning organizations (MLOs). MLOs are flexible learning environments that align with how today's students learn, but when needed, they can also facilitate traditional teaching and learning experiences. MLOs can contain open areas utilizing breakout rooms, common areas, individual or shared spaces, learning hubs, blended learning labs, learning studios, makerspaces, and other multi-purpose learning environments that help promote student voice and learner agency. An environment such as this requires the expertise of a modern educator to facilitate the learning process.

What Is a Modern Educator?

Modern educators

- are lifelong, future-focused learners,
- know how to operate and apply new technologies,
- build positive digital footprints using social media and social media tools,
- engage in professional learning communities,
- connect and collaborate with both like-minded individuals and others who hold different points of view,

- work to cultivate both local and global perspectives on issues,
- are facilitators of learning and not just traditional sages on the stage or content lecturers,
- embrace discovery learning,
- enhance theoretical learning by broadening the perspective of the curriculum with real-world meaning (context is as important as content recall),
- elevate the level of thought from LOTS (lower-order thinking skills) to HOTS (higher-order thinking skills),
- create positive and constructive feedback loops to enhance the learning process,
- are holistic evaluators that focus on both content and process, and
- promote independent and divergent thinking so learners can construct their knowledge.

It's All About Mindsets

Learning is all about the big A – attitude. For learners and educators, classrooms cannot feel like intellectual prisons. Today and tomorrow's learning spaces must become incubators of everything compelling about learning. The starting point in this instructional metamorphosis is with the teacher! Mindsets are one of the most difficult things to change because people traditionally take the path of least resistance and tend to get stuck in their paradigms as if it was day-old oatmeal.

The foundation of learning starts with the attitude and spirit of empowered learners. The excitement and engagement level of both educators and learners must rise to 110%. After all, engagement, excitement, and curiosity must be contagious. Teachers can nurture an infectious hunger for knowledge in their students and, in doing so, build inspiring environments led by learners.

The Great Disconnect

When children enter primary school, they are completely dependent on their teachers to tell them what to do, how to do it, when to do it, where to sit when they are doing it, and even how long to sit. Their primary focus in school is mastering the content and learning through memorization in tightly controlled instructional environments.

In this world, content mastery is more important than critical thinking. Teachers tell their students what they need to know to pass the test, to pass the course, to pass the grade, to move to the next level, and finally to graduate. All the answers are prearranged, preformatted, and ready for absorption by those who are willing and able to play the game called school. These students are academically successful. They are the students who are comfortable operating in a culture of dependency – a majority are dependent on the teacher, the textbook, and the test.

Then, after spending 13 or more years in the system, our students graduate from our schools, and the educational infrastructure that has held them up for all these years is suddenly removed. Many of the students fall flat on their faces as they enter the real world, and we can't understand why – even though it is we, the educators, who are responsible for creating this culture of dependency in the first place.

Today, success in school does not guarantee success in life. Somewhere along the way, in our efforts to ensure compliance in our learners, we have lost sight of the need to develop the capacity to become independent and divergent thinkers and doers.

Becoming Redundant

If our students are to survive, let alone thrive, in the 21st-century culture of technology-driven automation, abundance, and access to global labor markets, then independent thinking and its corollary, creative thinking, hold the highest currency.

To help our learners make a successful transition from school to life, we must shift the responsibility of learning from the teacher, where it has been traditionally, to the learners, where it belongs. Our job as educators is to move from demanding that our students be compliant to making ourselves progressively redundant.

> The new and different paradigm of teaching and learning is that of progressive withdrawal. Our responsibility must be to ensure that our learners no longer need us by the time they graduate from school.

This is no different than what we do as parents. As challenging as it might be, particularly during our children's teenage years, our responsibility is still to help them become independent individuals who can stand on their own as they begin to make their way through life.

We live in the dynamic world of InfoWhelm, where content is growing exponentially in both quantity and complexity. In this shifting landscape, where digital content is readily available at our fingertips, learners must be able to move beyond mastery of content recall. They must become discerning and creative consumers of information. To do this, learners must become familiar with modern fluencies.

In the recent book, *Literacy Is Still Not Enough: Modern Fluencies for Teaching, Learning, and Assessment*, the authors (Mohan, Jukes, & Schaaf, 2021) suggest that while reading, writing, and arithmetic remain important, they are no longer enough. For learners to thrive in the culture of the 21st century, they must move beyond traditional literacies to the essential modern skills – what is described in the book as the modern fluencies.

What Are the Modern Fluencies?

The essential modern fluencies are the critical mental process skills that all learners need to acquire above and beyond an understanding of traditional content. These process skills are important now and will remain just as important fifty years from now. These are processes that are learned, adapted, and applied in the context of solving real-world problems and challenges.

The essential fluencies are solution fluency, information fluency, collaboration fluency, creativity fluency, communications fluency, and global citizenship.

Solution Fluency
Solution fluency is the ability to think creatively to solve real-world problems in real time by clearly defining the problem, designing an appropriate solution, applying the solution, then evaluating the process and the outcome.

Information Fluency
Information fluency is the ability to unconsciously and intuitively interpret information in all forms and formats to extract the essential knowledge, authenticate it, and perceive its meaning and significance.

Collaboration Fluency
Collaboration fluency is team-working proficiency that has reached the unconscious ability to work cooperatively with virtual and real partners to create original real-world and digital products.

Creativity Fluency
Creativity fluency is the process by which artistic proficiency adds meaning through design, art, and storytelling. It involves form and function and the principles of innovative design combined with a quality functioning product.

Communications Fluency
Communications fluency is the ability to communicate with text and speech in multiple multimedia formats and to communicate visually through video and imagery in the absence of text.

> **Global Citizenship**
> Becoming a global citizen is a learned process comprising a range of knowledge and skills. Global citizenship comes with responsibilities. Global citizenship involves individuals and groups developing awareness about the various issues related to religions, cultures, traditions, values, perspectives, beliefs, and situations that are faced regularly.

The Big Shift in Education

To unfold the full intellectual and creative genius of all of our children and prepare them for their futures, not our pasts – we must provide all learners with the relevant modern learning skills and experiences that can form a bridge between their world and ours – and as they cross that bridge, so do entire nations – something that happens in modern learning environments where learners use higher-level thinking to create authentic solutions to relevant, real-world problems.

Fostering street-smarts in school-smart students requires a major shift in the existing educational paradigm. This shift demands that we rethink our assumptions about instructional design, what constitutes learning, and even what it means to be intelligent. Ultimately, we must also rethink how we assess and evaluate effective instruction and learning.

To do this, we must look for alternatives to the traditional organization of schools. We need to uncover our long-standing and unexamined assumptions about teaching and learning, about what a classroom looks like, where learning takes place, and the resources needed to support it. What we need are modern learning environments!

The Learner Agency Movement

The qualities of the modern learner, the guidance of a modern educator, and the influence of the modern fluencies intertwine to make up modern learning environments. Most importantly, the bow that ties this interwoven braid together is learner agency. Learner agency is encouraged through opportunities for learners to share their thinking and connections, design and build their authentic products, select individual learning goals to monitor, and construct their understanding through self-selected learning and assessment opportunities.

Learner choice and voice promote agency and provide a platform for the empowerment of the present-day and future generations. Educators have the opportunity to shift their approaches to place learners at the center of education and never look back.

While leading a movement centered on learner agency might at first seem overwhelming, the power to transform education does not happen by trying to make massive changes in a short period. Rather, real, meaningful, sustained change comes from taking a series of baby steps – by facilitating one learner-centered experience a day and one learner-created product at a time. That's what we will explore in the next chapter.

Summarizing Main Points

- Modern learning is the acquisition and application of knowledge and the cultivation of work habits, attitudes, and essential skills that include both traditional and digital literacies, as well as what we will describe as the modern fluencies.
- Today's learning environments must create domains that promote learner agency and ownership – spaces that are filled with curiosity, creativity, innovation, exploration, collaboration, empathy, and exhilaration.
- The essential modern fluencies are the critical mental process skills that all learners need to acquire above and beyond an understanding of traditional content. The essential fluencies are solution fluency, information

fluency, collaboration fluency, creativity fluency, communications fluency, and global citizenship.
- Learner agency is encouraged through opportunities for learners to share their thinking and connections, design and build their own authentic products, select individual learning goals to monitor, and construct their understanding through self-selected learning and assessment opportunities.
- Promoting more learner agency might seem overwhelming. The power to transform education does not happen by trying to make massive changes in a short period. Rather, real, meaningful, sustained change comes from taking a series of baby steps.

Essential or Extension Questions

- Who has the power in your classroom? Who should have the power in your classroom?
- How would you define a learner-centric approach?
- How can learners demonstrate their new knowledge in ways other than a worksheet or task devoid of real-world connection?
- Which modern fluency do you feel you successfully incorporate into your academic program? Which would you like to explore further or improve in?
- Can you think of a lesson or assignment that is the perfect candidate to experiment with empowering learners with more ownership and choice?

References

Forster, E. M. (2015). Retrieved from http://lemasney.com/consulting/2015/05/21/spoon-feeding-in-the-long-run-em-forster-cc-by-lemasney/

Mohan, N. (2018). *Leaders' perception of the influence of SB21 on systemic decision making and persistence on becoming learning organizations* (Unpublished doctoral dissertation). Lamar University, Beaumont, TX.

Mohan, N., Jukes, I., & Schaaf, R. (2021). *Literacy is still not enough: Modern fluencies for teaching, learning, and assessment.* Thousand Oaks, CA: Corwin Press.

6

The List

In their wonderful book, *Empower: What Happens When Students Own Their Learning,* authors John Spencer and A. J. Juliani suggest, "If we want students to innovate in the future, we need them to own the process now" (2017, p. 97). To this point, we have attempted to make a compelling case as to the importance of learner agency, choice, and voice.

We have helped readers define what learner agency is and isn't. We shared some of today's and yesterday's kindred spirits of education that have rallied behind the ideals of empowering learners instead of controlling them. We have shared why it is imperative to nurture members of the digital generations to be creative, divergent thinkers and doers. We have even focused on the essential modern-day skills today's and tomorrow's learners must cultivate to thrive in tomorrow's world.

However, many educators are left asking: What now? Now what? Our readers may have arrived at the decision to empower their learners but still require assistance in executing this golden path. The more appropriate question for educators to be asking is *how*? How will I empower my learners while still teaching the mandated curriculum and preparing learners for the required tests they must face?

We have prepared a teacher resource for the ages! The following list is a menu of learning experiences, ideas, and products that will perpetuate the idea of "learning by doing."

There is a multitude of ways for educators to empower learners by giving them a voice in the classroom. However, we propose that the most impactful way to do this is by offering a variety of real-world learning experiences and authentic ways to demonstrate understanding. Learners want and need to make meaning and transfer understanding through a wide variety of ways. These experiences will naturally empower learners while at the same time fostering the development of future-focused skills transferable to the real world.

This menu of over 100 different experiences and student products may first appear formidable. Rather than overwhelming the reader, we hope this list is viewed as empowering. Since this book is about learner voice and choice, the way to use this treasure trove of learning experiences is inherently up to you.

However, we view this list's main goals are twofold. First, this list can be used as a way to vary learning experiences for modern-day learners. Maybe you have noticed the last several projects students have completed were all different forms of digital presentations. Well, they say variety is the spice of life. Variety spices up the level of student agency in the classroom. You can use this collection as a rich buffet offering a range of strategies learners can use to express themselves and their learning while addressing the modern fluencies. Learners will appreciate the opportunity to develop their understanding through diverse activities and products. Alternatively, teachers can present learners with options from the List, giving them the power of choice – allowing them to select *how* they want to demonstrate their understanding of a specific topic. Providing learners with the opportunity to select the product they are most excited to complete will put the *power* into em*power*ment.

Further, it's essential to understand that each of these methods can be scaffolded or adapted for a wide variety of learners and their exceptionalities. After all, as educators, we know our students and their diverse learning needs better than anyone else. Learner-centered activities provide clear opportunities to differentiate experiences based on students' strengths and challenges. The goal must be to give students agency. The methods outlined here provide a starting point for educators to adapt for the learners and the learning goals they are focusing on.

Before proceeding on this extensive journey through the List, we want to provide you with an explanation of the elements of each entry.

1. First, we name the entry (strategy, product, resource, artifact, etc.).
2. Then, we suggest grade levels and possible academic subjects we believe best connect with the type of learner expression identified. (As a reminder, these suggestions should just be considered approximations. You should feel free to adapt or modify the activities to fit your learners' needs.)
3. Next, subjectively, we rank each entry based on the preparation time, instructional time, and levels of technology required for implementation. Again, we must emphasize that these guidelines are *subjective* approximations. Feel free to use your judgment.
4. Each entry also identifies the future-focused competencies, such as problem-solving, collaboration, creativity, and research and communication skills the instructional method most naturally fosters.
5. We then provide a summary that defines the subject of the entry, shares possible curriculum connections to spark integration ideas, and suggests logistics to incorporate the strategy in the classroom.

6. Finally, we provide links to a collection of online resources, including lesson plans, blog entries, and academic articles that can be used to supplement implementation.

Now that we have provided an overview of learner empowerment and agency, suggestions on how to utilize the List, and an understanding of the structure of each list entry, we're ready to go. Without further ado, we would like to present you with the List.

1. Advertisement

One of the most difficult tasks to undertake in this life is to persuade someone to do something, anything. A powerful skill in the modern world is to combine communication, presentation, and salesmanship into a persuasive message that will move people. Advertisements have been doing this for years using different media to communicate messages. In the past, companies and big businesses used ads in newspapers, billboards, magazines, and radio broadcasts to pitch products and boost sales. Nowadays, advertisements can be distributed using many additional digital and non-digital media, such as mailers, pamphlets, television commercials, web-based videos, websites, podcasts, pop-up windows, social media messaging, spam, and telemarketer calls.

The art of persuasion must be cultivated in schools to produce graduates who are ready for the complexities of the modern world. First, learners could critically analyze the hidden meaning and messages in existing advertisements, which will facilitate the deconstruction of dominant social narratives and cultivate media literacy. Next, learners can create their own advertisements, providing an opportunity for learners to develop their persuasive skills using a variety of media.

Advertisements are a versatile method of learner expression. All ages and content areas can use some form of advertisements for persuasive communication. In social studies, learners can create printed advertisements to convince colonists to rebel against the Crown or the Southern states to abolish slavery or to attract

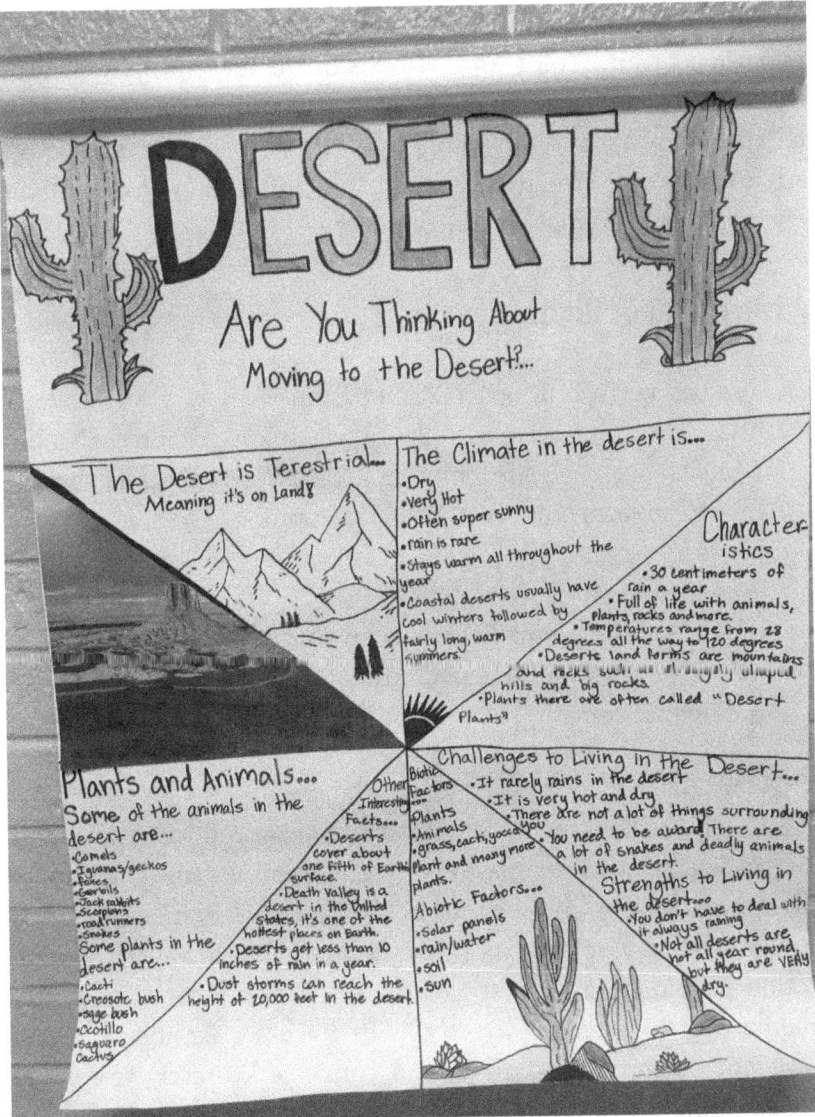

FIGURE 6.1 Image of a desert advertisement poster
Credit: Kaylie Scott, Forsyth Country Day School

visitors to a national monument. In language arts, persuasive writing and speaking is a skill of paramount importance. Learners can create digital and non-digital advertisements for books, fictional and nonfictional characters, or other persuasive artifacts.

Learners can create advertisements on paper using various materials to add color and dimension to their project. Learners can also utilize technology to create projects through digital design programs or using hyperlinks to create interactive advertisements. Finally, learners can create video-based advertisements to convince or entice observers.

Advertisement Digital Resources

Persuasive Techniques in Advertising
https://www.readwritethink.org/classroom-resources/lesson-plans/persuasive-techniques-advertising-1166.html?tab=4

Using Advertisements in the Classroom
https://ncte.org/blog/2017/01/using-advertisements-classroom/

Pictures and Slogans Persuade an Audience
https://www.scholastic.com/teachers/lesson-plans/teaching-content/pictures-and-slogans-persuade-audience/

2. Annotation

Although learners read a wide variety of texts throughout their school years, learners are rarely given the opportunity to choose how they develop connections between texts. Learners are often given tasks to respond to or questions based on content. Annotation provides a means for learners to develop positive study habits and to interact directly with the text. Annotations are notes or ideas that are made and connected directly to related text and images. Although highlighting passages or underlining important ideas is beneficial to understanding text, annotation allows learners to make choices as to how they connect with text and allows for a deeper level of interpretation.

Annotation can be used across the curriculum with any form of text or image to better comprehend and connect with content. Students can annotate using illustrations to identify moments in the text that one connected with, laughed at, or was confused about. Emojis can be used to encourage students of all grade levels to begin annotating text in a quick and familiar way. Annotations can be coded in a format that students and teachers can develop collaboratively or create annotations that can be individually designed by each student.

Annotation is typically used with printed text and images. However, there are also digital annotation tools, such as Hypothesis (https://web.hypothes.is/start/), that allow learners to interact with text virtually. Other digital tools such as NowComment (https://nowcomment.com/) allow students to collaboratively annotate, making it even easier for students to connect with peer ideas.

Annotation Resources

>More than Highlighting: Creative Annotation
>www.edutopia.org/article/more-highlighting-creative annotations
>Top Tech for Digital Annotation
>www.commonsense.org/education/top-picks/top-tech-for-digital-annotation
>Tips for Teaching Annotation in Science Class
>www.scienceandmathwithmrslau.com/2018/03/tips-teaching-annotation-science-class/

3. Audio Recording

Audio recordings are not new to the classroom. In the past, educators have used records, cassettes, and compact discs to share audio content with their learners. However, due to advancements in digital tools, both educators and learners are now able to record audio with the use of a digital device and an audio microphone (whether internal or external). Classrooms contain a diverse population of students with varied strengths and learning styles. Voice recording allows students who are not comfortable sharing their thinking in the form of writing to share orally.

Audio recordings are an extremely flexible tool in the classroom. Learners are able to use audio to take notes, demonstrate reading comprehension and fluency, memorize new words and definitions, compose music, record poetry, create audiobooks, or even produce a radio show! In science, students can create radio public service announcements or host a radio show in which they discuss a scientific phenomenon. For literacy development, students can orally interview a character from a novel or practice their grammar skills by scripting an original commercial. Students can also develop audio versions of their creative writing pieces and explore how punctuation changes the enunciation of their writing. In math, students can verbally explain the steps they would use to solve a problem or create audio word problems of their own.

Audio files (such as MP3) tend to be much smaller than video files, making them much more portable and easier to share over the web. Common software applications like Audacity (www.audacityteam.org/download/) and GarageBand (www.apple.com/mac/garageband/) make it easy to record and edit audio content on a computer. Digital devices, such as smartphones and media players, contain dozens of apps that allow a person to record just about anything, anywhere. There are also free web tools such as SpeakPipe (www.speakpipe.com/voice-recorder), 123apps Voice Recorder (https://online-voice-recorder.com/), and Vocaroo (https://vocaroo.com/) to capture audio recordings without a login requirement.

Audio Recording Resources

4 Ways Audio Recording Can Boost Classroom Learning
www.edutopia.org/discussion/4-ways-audio-recording-can-boost-classroom-learning

34 Interesting Ways to Use Audio in Your Classroom
http://taccle2.eu/wp/wp-content/uploads/2013/04/31InterestingWaystoUseAudioinyourClassroom2.pdf

Vocaroo
https://vocaroo.com/

4. Avatar

In the context of the digital world, an avatar refers to a digital graphical representation of the user in 2-D (like an emoticon) and 3-D forms (like a Mii on Nintendo). Avatars are commonly used in gaming, online communities, social networks, and web-based forums. For many of the digital generations, avatars have become a crucial part of their digital and real-world identities. Avatars allow individuals to represent themselves online in whatever way they choose. They can even be considered alter egos since users can customize their appearances in such a way that they are entirely different from their actual personas and real-world appearances.

In learning, avatars can serve multiple purposes. The use of online learning environments is a growing part of our everyday lives. In digital environments, learners can create their own avatars to represent themselves during their daily online educational activity. Avatars are a creative way to enhance digital storytelling that can be applied to any content area. For literacy development, avatars can also be used as a way for learners to create illustrations of characters in their writing passages or develop avatars of characters in novels based on text evidence. In social studies, students can create avatars to represent historical figures and recreate digital versions of famous historical events.

Creating an avatar is a wonderful introduction to digital graphic design because the finished product does not have to be a masterpiece to represent its creator. Interactive avatars can be used to enhance instructional content and develop student presentations differently and creatively.

Avatar Resources

> Voki
> www.voki.com/
> Digital You: Tech Tools to Help You Create Amazing Avatars for the Online Classroom

www.codlearningtech.org/2018/03/01/digital-you-tech-tools-to-help-you-create-amazing-avatars-for-the-online-classroom/

Teaching History: Voki

https://teachinghistory.org/digital-classroom/tech-for-teachers/24655

5. Blocking of a Scene

The theater is a creative vessel for breathing life into the classroom. "Blocking a scene" is the process by which the director sets the movements and physical interactions between the actors, the set, and props. The blocking is typically notated directly in the script using a pencil, much like an annotation. When blocking a scene, learners need to have an understanding of power dynamics between characters, how they would interact, and how they would behave around each other. Giving learners the opportunity to block a scene allows them to develop leadership skills, as they will have to guide the actors in their movement choices while also demonstrating a multilayered understanding of the content.

By blocking a scene, learners have the opportunity to demonstrate a deeper level of understanding of both the content and its real-world effects on people. Learners can easily turn fictional text into scenes or use readers' theater to bring the text to life. Learners can also use nonfiction text in science to inspire stage direction to demonstrate interactions and reactions of vocabulary such as hydrogen and oxygen, biotic and abiotic factors, or igneous and metamorphic rock. In social studies, directors can stage historical scenes reenacting integral momentous moments. Math can be integrated by having students mark the actor's blocking on a coordinate grid. Furthermore, learners can block math word problem scenes in order to develop a greater context for the mathematical situation.

Any subject that has "characters" that have a dynamic relationship can serve as the focus of a blocked scene. Learners can organize their blocking using paper and pencil on a grid, directly onto a script, or on a graphic organizer where they need to defend their reasoning for the movement choices.

Blocking of a Scene Resources

> Blocking 101: How Directors Tell Stories with Movement
> https://dramatics.org/blocking-101/
> Math + Arts: Stage Props, Blocking, and Graphs
> www.pbslearningmedia.org/resource/ket-6drama/props-blocking-graphs/

6. Blog

Depending on your interests, you likely read at least one blog daily that follows your favorite topics. A blog is a digital journal that chronicles informal writing on a given topic or connected topics. Blogs often include links to videos and other resources, written reflections, and comments. Writing blogs allows learners to demonstrate understanding or express themselves in an authentic published format. Learners can develop communication skills by responding to others' blogs by sharing opinions and asking questions.

The implementation of blogs can be adapted for use in a wide variety of subjects. Learners can work on individual blogs or a shared class blog. In literacy courses, learners can have independent blogs where they share their thoughts and opinions on a book. In science, learners may share digital lab reports or collaboratively debunk myths. For social studies, learners can discuss current events. For math, learners may discuss their strategies for solving word problems. Applicable for any subject, learners can reflect daily on what they have learned throughout the day, which serves as a formative assessment for teachers.

Digital blogs allow learners to write for an authentic audience. However, the use of graphic organizers to serve as drafts can help guide learners in enhancing the quality of blog posts. Developing a rubric will also help guide learners in writing interesting and insightful blog posts. There are a wide variety of websites designed to host students' blogs, including Edublogs and KidBlog.

Blog Resources

Edublogs
https://edublogs.org/
Writing, Journaling, and Blogging Websites for Students
www.commonsense.org/education/top-picks/
 writing-journaling-and-blogging-websites-for-students
Teaching with Blogs
www.readwritethink.org/professional-development/strat-
 egy-guides/teaching-with-blogs-30108.html

7. Board Game

Playing board games requires an understanding of how to play through the rules, comprehension of strategy, and sometimes a little bit of luck. Traditional board games include any game in which pieces are moved around based on the rules on a flat board. The elements of board games can be utilized for learners to demonstrate their understanding of content by developing their own board games.

Learners can create board games that connect to all content areas. Students develop writing skills by inventing directions and rules. In science, students can create a board game that takes players through the steps of scientific phenomena, such as the water cycle or how a volcano erupts. Learners can also further literacy understanding by creating games that demonstrate the application of grammar rules or take players through the story of a novel study. In social studies, board games can transport players into historical events, much like a game-based simulation, requiring learners to make choices as to what they would do in historical situations. Learners can also analyze probability through student-created board games or practice math

FIGURE 6.2 Image of a student-generated board game

Credit: Rebecca Craps, Maya Barrier, Kole Pemberton, Jazmin Guardo, Eliot Caty, Forsyth Country Day School

computation by developing board games that require players to solve math problems by advancing through the board.

Although board games do not require any technology to be created, students may want to use Google Slides or any design program as a way to develop the board, board game pieces, or cards used in gameplay. The Noun Project (https://thenounproject.com/) is a great resource for basic images that students could incorporate into their board games.

Board Game Resources

More than a "Design Your Own Board Game" Project
www.teachingabovethetest.com/2017/12/more-than-design-your-own-board-game.html
How to Help Students Design Educational Board Games
www.classtools.net/blog/get-students-designing-educational-board-games/
Social Studies Board Games
www.lessonplanet.com/article/social-studies/social-studies-board-games

8. Book Bento Box

A bento box is a meal that is organized into portions of food divided by sections in a box. Bento boxes are a Japanese tradition that highlights the organization and plating of the food as much as the tastes. Some teachers are using the concept of bento boxes as a way for learners to organize and demonstrate understanding. Students can develop book bento boxes, which involve organizing objects that are related to symbols, characters, themes, or plots of novels in a creative and pleasing composition. These educational compositions are then photographed by the teacher, combining the Asian tradition with higher-level thinking skills and the beauty of visual compositions in photography. Teachers often display the images on social media with the hashtag #bookbento.

Although teachers typically utilize bento boxes as a way for learners to demonstrate their connections to literature, book bento boxes can be adapted to fit other content areas as well. In science or social studies, learners can develop boxes based on a time period or the cause and effects of historical events, demonstrate the steps of scientific processes, or depict vocabulary terms. Learners can also create big idea bento boxes based on conceptual themes for subjects such as interconnectedness, relationships, or innovation. In addition, learners can design bento boxes about math concept areas, such as geometry terms or the classification of irrational and rational numbers, or develop a coordinate grid to organize their objects.

The depth of understanding demonstrated by book bento boxes can be amplified by integrating digital tools. Learners can create basic digital book bento boxes by using images organized virtually on the computer. Learners can find examples of digital book bento boxes and share theirs using the hashtag #digibookbento. Digital tools make bento boxes interactive with the inclusion of media, audio, and hyperlinks.

Book Bento Box Resources

> Our 4th Grade #BookBento Project
> https://vanmeterlibraryvoice.blogspot.com/2019/05/our-4th-grade-bookbento-project.html
> Building Beautiful Blog Bentos
> http://blogs.slj.com/neverendingsearch/2019/05/04/building-beautiful-book-bentos/
> Thinglink
> www.thinglink.com/

9. Book Jacket/Cover

Although one should not judge a book by its cover, teachers can certainly assess understanding through a student-designed book cover. Book covers include a book's title, pertinent information about the book, and an image that depicts the storyline and catches the readers' eyes. Developing book covers and book jackets provides an integrative format for learners to demonstrate understanding while developing and analyzing the main ideas of the subject matter. First of all, learners need to solidify the main idea or theme into a few words to develop the title. Then, learners creatively depict the main idea or theme as a drawing, graphic design, or photograph. In order to develop an effective and creative book jacket, learners need to evaluate the information that is essential and then incorporate it in a creative manner.

Learners can create book jackets focused on a wide variety of subjects. Using a book jacket as a lens to study literature helps students use symbols in the book to help determine the theme. Beginning a novel study by looking at various editions of books with different covers allows learners to compare and contrast the content in the images, which helps unearth possible symbols in the book and serves as a gateway to determine possible themes. After completing the novel, students can use what they have learned to create their own book cover design. For example, after completing a social studies lesson on the causes of World War II, they can develop a title for a book cover that demonstrates their big takeaway. After completing a science experiment, learners can construct a title that represents their scientific conclusions. Then students can select or create images to illustrate the book cover. The pictures learners include will make connections to the main themes explored in the book. Developing book covers requires students to analyze and synthesize content effectively. Both of which are skills that can be applied to limitless tasks.

When creating book covers, learners can decide whether to create one using pencil and paper or a wide variety of publishing software such as Microsoft Word and PowerPoint. There are also many online tools that allow students to easily format book covers, such as Book Cover Creator, Google Slides, and Canva.

Book Jacket/Cover Resources

Book Cover Creator
www.readwritethink.org/classroom-resources/student-interactives/book-cover-creator-30058.html
Storyboard That

www.storyboardthat.com/create/worksheet-templates-book-jackets
Canva
www.canva.com/create/book-covers/

10. Brochure

Known for their mixture of visuals and text, the format of brochures offers students the opportunity to create versatile learning artifacts. Brochures can share a lot of information about a particular topic in small spaces that are easy to read. This makes them a perfect way to present a project for school. If learners can fold a piece of paper into thirds and write content concisely while adding pictures, charts, maps, or other design features, then they can make an informative brochure.

Some of the steps for creating a brochure include planning the topic and layout, researching the topic being conveyed, creating the brochure, and sharing it with an authentic audience. Some potential brochure ideas include creating book reviews, travel guides, history informationals, public service announcements, and advertisements. There is really no limit on the range of topics learners can explore through the development of an informative or persuasive brochure.

Brochures can be created either physically with paper or virtually with publishing software, such as Google Docs, Slides, or Canva. Many teacher-created templates for Google Docs exist, which help students to develop their projects using a digital format. Although paper-created pamphlets are effective ways to demonstrate information, digital brochures allow learners to integrate media through hyperlinks that enhance the ability to communicate ideas.

Brochure Resources

Make a Brochure for a School Project
www.wikihow.com/Make-a-Brochure-for-a-School-Project

Adobe Spark Pamphlet Maker
https://spark.adobe.com/make/pamphlet-maker/
Canva's Brochure Maker
www.canva.com/create/brochures/

11. Bulletin Board

The learning environment should be rich, visually appealing, and supportive for learners. For years, educators have used bulletin boards to convey academic themes, provide visual learning aids, and share news and events. However, bulletin boards can take on a new role as a student-generated learning masterpiece. Although "good work" boards are fairly common and share exemplary work with the learners, they can also eliminate some students' work due to a lack of space for display.

A well-designed bulletin board can become part of a learner's instructional environment and enhance student learning. The primary purpose of participatory bulletin boards is for students to demonstrate their grasp of the knowledge or skill they were trying to achieve. Interactive bulletin boards can be easily created using a giant graphic organizer, such as a T-chart or Venn diagram. Learners can then add ideas to the interactive bulletin board using sticky notes or index cards. In social studies, classes can create timelines, maps, and visuals related to content topics. In math, learners can create interactive charts, graphs, or a definition display. In reading, learners are able to track reading progress, share ideas, or design a mural. In science, bulletin boards may take the form of brainstorming charts, experiment logs, or vocabulary word walls.

Although no technology is required for learners to create bulletin board displays, digital tools such as Canva and the Noun Project can be used as a way for learners to develop certain elements of the displays.

Bulletin Board Resources

81 Back-to-School Bulletin Board Ideas from Creative Teachers
www.weareteachers.com/back-to-school-bulletin-board-ideas/

Pinterest
www.pinterest.com/
Use *#bulletinboard* to search other social networks such as Twitter and Instagram for the perfect bulletin board ideas.

12. Cartoon

After school, many kids rush home to sit on the couch to watch cartoons. Wouldn't it be great to have this same level of engagement in the classroom? Teachers can utilize cartoons' colorful and exaggerated characters to serve as a platform for learners to creatively demonstrate understanding in a variety of ways.

Utilizing two-dimensional cartoons serves as learner-led experiences and encourages creativity. Cartoons have a natural connection to literacy through writing skill development. Learners can also create cartoons based on a chapter of a book or as a way to demonstrate literary themes. In math, learners can create cartoons based on word problem situations or as a way to identify the steps in a mathematical computation. Learners can also personify math vocabulary to demonstrate understanding creatively. What might an isosceles triangle say to an equilateral triangle in a cartoon? In science, learners can create cartoons based on any scientific phenomenon or as a method to explain a vocabulary word.

In social studies, political cartoons serve as primary sources to guide discussions related to opinions and the complexity of historical events. Political cartoons infuse historical facts into pop culture and art. Learners can ultimately create their own political cartoons based on current events or a past historical debate. Encourage learners to create political cartoons from both perspectives of an argument to critically analyze.

Although learners can create cartoons using traditional art supplies, there are several online resources that allow learners to animate their cartoon characters. Powtoons and Toondoo allow learners to transform one-dimensional informational presentations into creative animated products that they can be proud of. Learners can present information in an engaging and fun format allowing them to make choices about the characters, movements, and dialogue. The limitless variations of cartoon products provide learners with a set of unique tools to demonstrate their new concepts.

Cartoon Resources

Cartoons in the Classroom
https://natlib.govt.nz/blog/posts/cartoons-in-the-classroom
Powtoons
www.powtoon.com/home/?
The Association of American Editorial Cartoonists
https://nieonline.com/aaec/cftc.cfm

13. Choice Board

A well-designed choice board, sometimes referred to as a learning menu, is the ultimate activity that promotes student choice in the classroom. A choice board provides students with a buffet of options, putting the power of choosing how to express understanding in their hands. A choice board is an organized template of activities for learners to complete. They are often organized in a grid, similar to a bingo board. Some teachers may encourage learners to complete three activities in a row or complete a certain number of activities. However, being creative in the design and implementation of a choice board is crucial. A choice board can be organized into categories where students are asked to earn a certain number of points based on their activity choices.

Choice boards can be implemented in any subject area. To develop a quality choice board, the activities should all focus on a topic or learning goal but also provide various perspectives on the topic. Students can conduct research in one activity, create an advertisement in another, or share their opinion in an audio recording as still another. A variety of choice board activities can be based on different learning styles, levels of Bloom's taxonomy, or learning modality. Choice boards are self-differentiated because learners are able to select activities that they will be successful with and that appeal to personal interests. Choice boards truly give learners the power of selecting the format to demonstrate learning.

Not only can teachers create choice boards as a way to give students choice, but learners can also practice finding resources related to topics by creating their own choice boards. Choice boards can be created on paper or digitally using a multitude of digital tools such as Google Docs or Google Slides.

Choice Board Resources

https://blog.tcea.org/choice-boards-2/
Creating a Choice Board for Your Classroom
https://blog.tcea.org/creating-a-choice-board/
How I Use Choice Boards to Increase Student Engagement
www.weareteachers.com/choice-boards/

14. Cereal Box

Cereal boxes are colorful and often include funny cartoon characters that result in children in shopping carts begging their parents to purchase sugary cereals. The elements that make cereal boxes stand out are the same ones that can serve as a fun and creative project. Within a cereal box, learners can creatively come up with a title, a character to advertise the cereal, a cute story that introduces the cereal, and a list of ingredients. Students can then add fun games, such as word searches, crossword puzzles, or mazes.

Cereal boxes are a way for learners to demonstrate their thinking in any subject area. In social studies, learners can create a cereal box for any time period or based on any historical theme. What "ingredients" were a part of World War II? What would a cereal based on Greek gods and goddesses be named? In science, learners can create cereal boxes that depict the cause and effect of scientific experiments (creating a cereal box based

FIGURE 6.3

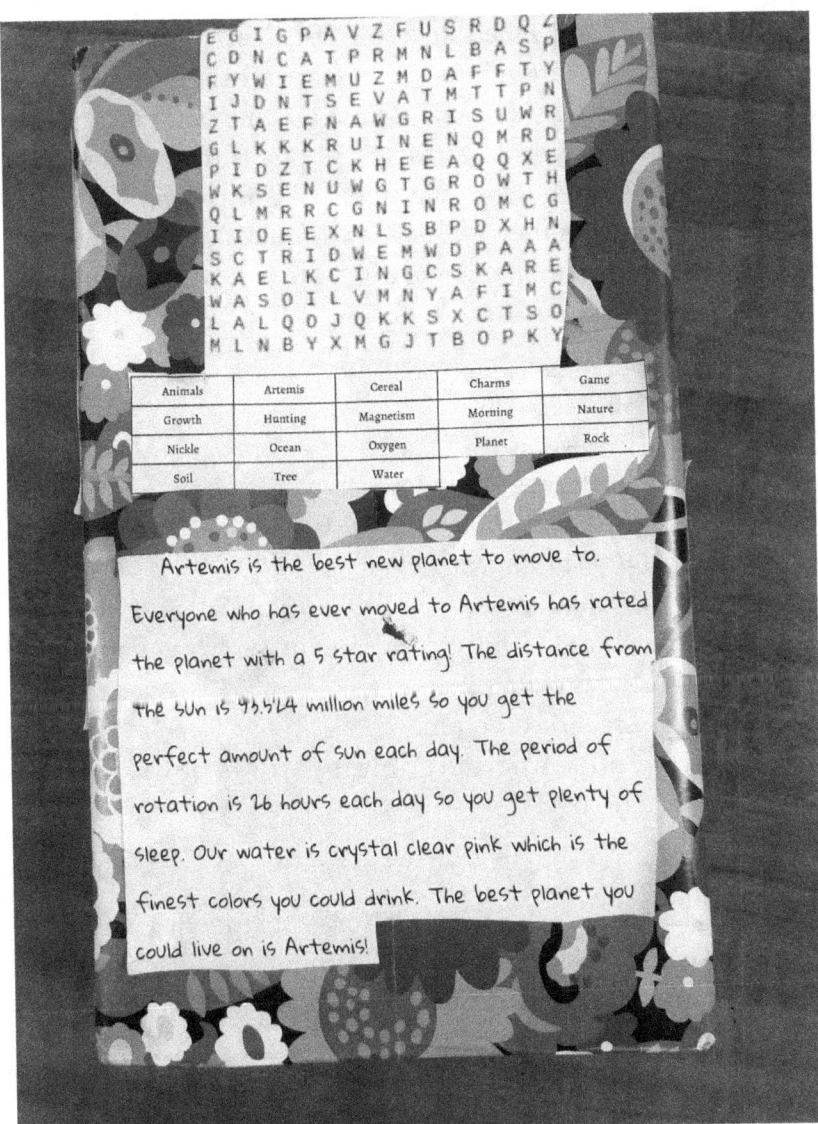

FIGURES 6.3 & 6.4 Images of the front and back of a student-generated cereal box

Credit: Alysha Christian, sixth-grade teacher at the Arts Based School. Anderson McGowan

on chemical changes called Reactant-Os). Learners can integrate math applications through nutrition facts, which include calorie information, serving size, and vitamin and mineral percentages.

Paper glued on top of a real cereal box is the simplest way for learners to design their own cereals. Learners can use pencil and paper to design their own boxes or publish a cover with all the product information using a digital tool to print and adhere to their box.

Cereal Box Resources

Cereal Box Autobiography Project
www.youtube.com/watch?v=_W4KV0Gnwc0&ab_channel=PencilsandMagicWands
Cereal Box Book Report
www.lakeshorelearning.com/resources/free-resources/crafts/cerealBoxBookReport/
Design a Cereal Box: Volume
https://goopennc.oercommons.org/courseware/lesson/216/overview

15. Class Books

Creating class books is a versatile form of student expression. They are ideal projects for young learners since each child in the class can create a single page or book section. The combined efforts of the class can all be included and bound into an authentic artifact of learning. Young learners feel a sense of ownership when the book is finished, and it is often a favorite selection when students visit the classroom library to borrow a book during independent reading time.

Book topics can include a beginning-of-the-year all-about-me book that shares interesting information about each learner. In science, learners can generate collaborative books about experiments and observations or about topics such as space, the ocean, or animals. In reading, learners can write their reactions to a story, share their favorite book, or create their very own classroom ABC book. In social studies, learners can write about their favorite president or prime minister, a book sharing their individual cultural traditions, or a class fact book about whatever time period, place, or event is the current focus in the curriculum. There are really no limits to the types of class books learners can create. As an added bonus, have the class include a small "About the Author" section or a photo to celebrate their written contributions.

Class books can be created using paper and pencil, either using blank pieces of paper or with teacher-created templates that help the uniformity of design. There are also a wide variety of websites such as Storyjumper and Studentreasures Publishing that provide digital tools in order to turn learner ideas into professionally bound books.

Class Book Resources

> DIY Classroom Books
> www.pinterest.com/kellimae04/diy-classroom-books/
> Storyjumper
> www.storyjumper.com/
> Studentreasures Publishing
> https://studentreasures.com/

16. Coding

Coding allows learners to create projects using programming languages to develop projects using specific digital instructions. Not only does coding lead to the development of next-generation skills, it provides learners the opportunity to connect digital literacy with various content areas.

Coding's relevance to algebraic properties provides a natural connection to math through the development of pattern recognition and abstract reasoning. Coding can also be used to create a wide variety of projects that can connect to any curriculum area. Many coding programs allow learners to develop games, digital stories, comics, and applications. In literacy, classes can use coding to bring their writing to life through coded animation or by creating a version of a choose your own adventure story. In social studies and science, learners can develop their own game that requires players to answer questions related to the content or immerses players in specific scientific or historical scenarios.

There are a wide variety of online programs available for learners to create coding projects, such as Code.org (http://Code.org), Code for Life (www.codeforlife.education/), and Scratch (https://scratch.mit.edu/). Although coding is authentically completed using technology, students can develop coding skills by creating algorithms using pencil and paper. Learners can use cut-out command language cards in order to help a toy or figurine go to a certain location or complete a task.

Coding Resources

5 Ways to Get Your Students Coding across the Curriculum
https://kidsdiscover.com/teacherresources/5-ways-to-get-your-students-coding-across-the-curriculum/.
Computer Science in a Box: Unplug Your Curriculum
www.ncwit.org/resources/computer-science-box-unplug-your-curriculum-2018-update
5 Hands-On Activities That Teach Coding without a Computer
www.extendednotes.com/after-school-activities/5-hands-on-activities-that-teach-coding-without-a-computer

17. Makey Makey

Makey Makey (https://makeymakey.com/) is an invention kit designed by two MIT students that allows learners to use different options as a touchpad. Learners can use the alligator clips and wires in the kit to connect to conductive everyday objects. Through the invention kit, these objects then become touchpads that can interact with a computer program. Makey Makey promotes invention literacy and provides an extra level of interactivity to coding projects.

Makey Makey kits are often used to enhance learners' ability to interact with coding programs. The kits have natural science connections to explore conductive materials, circuits, and sensors. However, Makey Makey can be utilized in literacy activities to develop interactive poetry or interactive digital stories. In social studies, learners can create interactive maps or virtual city tours. Makey Makey's website provides lessons that can be explored through chapters such as "Hacking Literacy with Makey Makey" and "Intro to Everyday Inventing." The website also provides a database of a wide variety of cross-curricular, teacher-created projects, including how to develop a talking measuring cup, models of body systems, interactive tectonic plates, and many more.

Incorporating Makey Makey into the classroom does require technology and access to their invention kits, which can be ordered through their website. You can utilize a wide variety of everyday conductive objects such as fruits and vegetables, water, graphite pencils, and aluminum foil to create interactive projects. Many online coding programs such as Scratch are able to interact with the Makey Makey kits.

Makey Makey Resources

Academic Ways to use Makey Makey in the Classroom
www.thetechieteacher.net/2017/06/academic-ways-to-use-makey-makey-in.html
Makerspace for Education
www.makerspaceforeducation.com/makey-makey.html
A Surefire Way to Make Art History Less Boring
https://theartofeducation.edu/2017/01/05/surefire-way-make-art-history-less-boring/

18. Collage

Collages are created by gluing a variety of images or words together onto a larger surface, which creates one cohesive project. The artistic format of a collage can be creatively adapted to connect to a variety of learning goals or themes. Developing collages of topics requires learners to conceptually grasp the main ideas of the subject matter through a visual platform.

Collages can be adapted to all content areas. In social studies, a class can develop collages using words and letters from historical documents, use pictures of geographical features based on natural resources, or build one based on a specific time period. In science, learners can create collages that define scientific terms or demonstrate complex processes such as the water cycle using images. In literacy, learners can create collages based on texts or themes explored in literature. In writing, learners can use images and text from magazines to develop creative writing collages that can be published for an authentic audience.

The mediums used to create a collage can vary depending on available resources. Learners can develop projects using good old-fashioned scissors, paper, and glue. Students can use images, words, or letters from magazines, catalogs, newspapers, printed articles, text from fictional writing, or advertisements in their projects. Learners can also create digital collages, using online programs such as Adobe Spark (https://spark.adobe.com/make/photo-collage-maker/), Kapwing (www.kapwing.com/collage), Pic Collage (https://piccollage.com/), or BeFunky (www.befunky.com/features/collage-maker/). No matter the structure or format of the collage, students will be required to think both critically and creatively.

Collage Resources

Show Evidence of Learning with Collages
www.scholastic.com/teachers/blog-posts/kriscia-cabral/17-18/Collage-Creations-to-Show-Evidence-of-Learning/

A Creative Collage Lesson for All Students
https://theartofeducation.edu/2018/02/20/collage-canvasa-creative-lesson-students/
Unit Collage
www.scholastic.com/teachers/articles/teaching-content/unit-collage/

19. Comedy

Are dad jokes cool or lame? No matter what your answer is, people love experiencing comedy. Our world can be so serious nowadays that kids are seldomly given the opportunity to laugh and create funny content. If you have ever spoken to kids for an extended period of time, then you realize they are exceptionally funny. As educators, we must remember this generation of learners were raised on Pixar movies, Captain Underpants books, and an endless stream of 24/7 content of some of the best humor-based programming ever created. It is safe to infer that learners will want to try their hand at writing and delivering a comedic performance.

Most subjects and units in the classroom can be infused with comedy as a student product. Reading and language arts are subjects that can easily be connected to a comedic performance. As an educator, contemplate having learners use a book, text, or another literary theme as their inspiration for a two-minute performance. Both the comedian and the audience will enjoy the spectacle. For social studies, a comedic performance based on an event in history could change the everyday tone of the traditional lesson. Although science and math aren't the first subjects that come to mind for a comedy, we are sure there are plenty of long-division or periodic table routines for future comedians in the classroom.

Educators can assess both the script and performance for the content and research that went into the performance. To add more of an authentic appeal, teachers can feel free to create a classroom stage and record their performances. Finally, a connected educator can share a classroom set of comedic treasures by uploading each student's performance to YouTube or Google Drive to show to parents.

Comedy Resources

Robert McNeely's Using Humor in the Classroom
www.nea.org/tools/52165.htm
Kid Snippets: "Math Class" (Imagined by Kids)
www.youtube.com/watch?v=KdxEAt91D7k
Laughter and Learning: Humor Boosts Retention
www.edutopia.org/blog/laughter-learning-humor-boosts-retention-sarah-henderson

20. Comic Strip

Comic strips are an amazing medium for learners to share visual information with accompanying text. Made popular by their long history in newspapers, comic strips have been entertaining generations for decades. As an alternative to writing out long-drawn-out narratives, a comic strip rations text into small captions, dialogue callouts, and thought bubbles and lets the images communicate understanding.

The graphic outline of comics allows learners to integrate art and creativity into their storytelling endeavors while communicating any topic. Comic strips are very versatile and cater to pretty much every grade and every content area. Some integration ideas include creating biographies or autobiographies, reinforcing social skills among students, introducing creative writing, and highlighting new vocabulary words with visual cues. In science, learners can create comic strips to demonstrate understanding of any content area. For example, how could one volcano explain to another volcano how to erupt? In social studies, learners can use comic strips as a way to create dialogue between various historical figures or recreate historical events with alternative endings.

FIGURE 6.5 Image of a student-generated comic strip about volcanoes
Credit: Mayara Rudolph, Forsyth Country Day School

There are numerous online comic strip generators such as the Read Write Think's Comic Creator (www.readwritethink.org/files/resources/interactives/comic/), Storyboard That (www.storyboardthat.com/storyboard-creator), and Toondoo (www.toondoo.com/). Learners are also able to use more traditional materials, such as pencils, pens, colored pencils, markers, and paper, to fashion their own comics.

Comic Strip Resources

5 Minute Film Festival: Comics in the Classroom
www.edutopia.org/blog/five-minute-film-festival-comics-classroom
How to Use Comic Strip Making Websites to Enhance Your Teaching

https://elearningindustry.com/use-comic-strip-making-websites-enhance-teaching

MakeBeliefsComix.com

http://MakeBeliefsComix.com

21. Commercial

Although they can be annoying when watching television or online videos, commercials do have the ability to capture attention, sell a product, or persuade viewers in a very short time span. Their format is flexible, and they use a combination of visuals, music, imagery, actors, and dialogue to convince viewers to do something. Educators can use them as examples for exploring persuasive speaking and writing, consumerism, marketing, and media literacy. When learners write scripts and produce their own commercials, they are applying their content knowledge and creative skills in a real-world scenario. Commercials can inform, persuade, or invite their audiences to buy a product, make a decision, or select a position in a societal debate.

Producing commercials can benefit any age level learner in any content area. Writing commercials has a natural connection to literacy through the development of persuasive writing skills. Learners can also write commercials to advertise their favorite books or authors. In social studies, learners can watch older commercials as a method of exploring historical context. They can then use their inferences to develop their own commercials advertising game-changing historical inventions or even tickets to attend historical events. The content of the commercial can demonstrate mastery of academic content while learners are writing to an authentic audience.

Commercials can be performed live for classmates or using technology. Learners can film and edit their commercials using any editing software such as WeVideo or Animoto for Education. Learners can also create cartoon commercials using digital presentation tools such as Powtoon.

Commercial Resources

Teach Media Literacy with Super Bowl Ads
www.middleweb.com/20198/teach-media-literacy-super-bowl-ads/
Digital Communication: Student-Designed Commercials
www.scholastic.com/teachers/blog-posts/brent-vasicek/digital-communication-student-designed-commercials/
Animoto (Education)
https://animoto.com/business/education

22. Costume Design

Costume designers for theater and movies must create garments that correspond to the settings, themes, and other design elements of the final product. The costumes often communicate deeper elements of text, unveiling symbolism and layers of meaning and character. Costume design can include consideration of time period, fabric choice, colors, and cohesive design of the production. Designing costumes requires an understanding of historical context related to the time period of the setting, as well as higher-level reflections on themes and ideas of the text. To develop a memorable and effective costume, designers need to delve deep into an understanding of all factors that impact what a character would wear. Therefore, designing costumes for a character requires high-level critical-thinking skills through inferential interpretation of primary sources.

Costume design can be seamlessly integrated into history and language arts. Learners can develop costume designs based on historical content. Learners can research the typical fabric, dyes, patterns, buttons or fasteners, and decorations garment makers utilized in specific time periods. This research provides a gateway for a conversation on social hierarchy, geography, and the availability of natural resources. In literature, learners can develop costume designs of literary characters based on text evidence provided by the author. Learners can use quotes from novels to

FIGURE 6.6 Image of student-generated costume design poster for the book *Tuck Everlasting*

Credit: Elizabeth Smith

defend the reasoning behind their costume designs. They can also create costumes based on scientific vocabulary, using facts to defend their thinking. For example, a sedimentary rock costume would include stripes based on the layers of the rock.

Learners can create costume designs by sketching two-dimensional paper mannequins. Also, providing students with a pile of fabric is a great way to bring their costume designs to life. Inspiration boards using a variety of images can depict the colors, textures, and feelings of their design.

Costume Design Resources

Quarantine Costume Design Lesson Plan
www.stemread.com/wp-content/uploads/2017/05/Costume_Design_Lesson_Plan.pdf
Here's a Lesson You'd Never Expect: Costume Design
https://dramamommaspeaks.com/2018/11/23/heres-a-lesson-youd-never-expect/

23. Crossword

Arthur Wynne, a newspaperman who wrote for the now-defunct *New York World*, is credited for inventing the crossword puzzle more than a century ago. Crossword puzzles have a series of squares and grids that are then completed using clues that describe the words. Crossword puzzles mix the excitement of learning new vocabulary with learning their meaning through strategy.

For years, schools have used these puzzles as learning center worksheets or homework assignments – busy work that can be easily checked and tossed into the circular filing cabinet. The true power of the crossword puzzle for students is in learning new discipline-specific vocabulary. Crossword puzzles based on a book, unit, theme, topic, or subject can provide valuable vocabulary instruction to learners. Crossword puzzles are also ideal for reviewing previously learned words and their definitions.

Educators can also provide learners with the opportunity to assume ownership of the activity and ask them to create their own crosswords to share with their peers. Learners can develop crossword puzzles using graph paper or by using a multitude of free online programs such as Crossword Labs.

Crossword Puzzle Resources

Many educators have already had the smart idea of creating subject-specific crossword puzzles. If you are an educator looking for a crossword for your book, unit, theme, topic, or subject, complete a simple Google search to find one. "Solar system crossword," "Bridge to Terabithia crossword," and "countries crossword" are just a small sample of the crosswords available online.

> Instant Online Puzzle-Maker
> www.puzzle-maker.com/crossword_Entry.cgi
> Crossword Labs
> https://crosswordlabs.com/

24. Dance

Although effective teaching was once thought to require students to stay in their seats, dance is a format that allows students to express themselves and learn content kinesthetically. Dance arts integration allows students to develop skills needed for future-focused learning, including collaboration, critical thinking, and creativity. Dance is one facet of an arts-integration curriculum that encourages a high-level understanding of the curriculum.

Dance can be used to experience and explore the curriculum or demonstrate an understanding of content. Students often encompass their learning through written and spoken word, but dance allows students to absorb their learning into their bodies. Through dance, learners can become water droplets in the water cycle, transform quadrilaterals with their bodies, and experience historical events through creative movement. Learners can create movements that personify science vocabulary, represent a period of history, or express the theme or main idea of the text.

Utilizing dance in the learning process requires a large space where learners can move around freely. Although dance is typically performed live, dancers can be recorded digitally to allow students to reflect on their own creations.

Dance Resources

Let's Talk about Arts-Integration: Defining What You Do
www.danceadvantage.net/arts-integration/
How Dance Can Teach Literature
https://artsedge.kennedy-center.org/educators/how-to/
encouraging-arts/how-dance-can-teach-literature

25. Debate

Using debates as an instructional approach allows learners to work in a collaborative and cooperative group setting. As learners discuss and organize their perspectives, they are able to discover new information, contemplate their positions on a topic, and put their knowledge into action. It also encourages learners to examine an event or particular topic from perspectives that they might never have held before. These kinds of activities can help with the development of empathy and social-emotional learning.

Debates provide learners with the chance to research and become experts on real-world topics and authentic issues in all academic disciplines. Therefore, debates can be implemented in the classroom in any subject in which there are topics with a variety of views and opinions. Educators should select a complex and controversial topic that allows various stances to exist. Conducting classroom debates also allows the younger generations to see that differing points of view should be appreciated and respected.

Instructional debates can take on numerous forms. Student teams can consolidate their collaborative spirit, conduct research, and create convincing arguments about their shared topics. Educators can break their classes up into partners and provide them with a perspective of the issue to research and argue. The structure of the debate can be as follows:

- ♦ Students create their teams.
- ♦ Team 1 provides a presentation of positives or arguments for the topic.

- Team 2 provides a presentation of cons or arguments against the topic.
- Both teams meet to prepare their responses or rebuttals.
- Team 1 presents responses or rebuttals of positives or arguments for the topic.
- Team 2 provides responses or rebuttals of cons or arguments against the topic.

Debate Resources

120 Debate Topics for High and Middle School Students
www.theedadvocate.org/120-debate-topics-for-high-school-students/

Education World: Debates in the Classroom
www.educationworld.com/a_curr/strategy/strategy012.shtml

Debate Lesson: Refutation and Rebuttal
www.youtube.com/watch?v=l6_6i-OJ_e4

26. Demonstration

Parents first demonstrate how to ride a bike, how to turn on the TV, or how to buckle a seatbelt to teach their children these skills. Demonstrations that involve showing someone how something works have long been a tool used by teachers to instruct students. However, wouldn't it be far more effective and powerful to allow learners to do the demonstrating?

Incorporating student demonstrations in the classroom is as simple as giving a learner the dry erase marker to show classmates how to edit a sentence, complete a math problem, or balance a chemical equation. The demonstration could also be utilized to allow learners to encourage their own peers to think outside the box. Take the previous example of utilizing dance in the classroom. A student who has put together a particularly thoughtful dance piece about the water cycle can demonstrate to another student how the mechanisms of evaporation, condensation, and precipitation could all be represented by physical movements. In this way, other students might discover interpretations they have considered before. An added benefit might be the ability to communicate the notion that it is okay to think outside the box, be creative, or do something beyond their comfort zone.

Although demonstrations can be completed without any technology, students can also create videos that teach others how to complete a specific task. Learners can use screen-recording technology such as Loom, Screenflow, Camtasia, or any number of digital tools to record and provide voice over for a digital demonstration on any topic.

Demonstration Resources

>Preparing Effective Demonstrations for the Classroom and Laboratory
>www.nactateachers.org/Images/Jun11_1_Preparing_Effective_Demonstrations_for_the_Classroom_and_Laboratory.pdf
>From YouTube to Your School
>https://news.harvard.edu/gazette/story/2020/02/online-demos-can-be-as-effective-as-classroom-teaching/
>The Art of Effective Demonstrations
>www.ualberta.ca/centre-for-teaching-and-learning/media-library/catalysts/design-multidomain-demonstrations/effective-demonstrations.pdf

27. Design Thinking

Design thinking is an iterative process that challenges students to blems. It requires students to understand the needs of the people whose problem you are solving, develop solutions, design prototypes, and then gather feedback and assess the quality of solutions. By experiencing this process, learners can use these steps to solve any problem-based challenge.

Design thinking can be applied across many different curriculums. Because most subject matter involves problems, there are solutions that can be developed through design thinking. In science, learners might develop a plan to save an endangered species or create ways to use renewable power sources. In math, learners can develop a pricing system that will help a store be more profitable or determine what sizes of boxes a company should package their products in to be the most cost-effective. In social studies, learners can develop new laws that help solve a problem in a current event or design inventions that would have changed the face of history.

The power of design thinking lies in authenticity. By providing opportunities to experience learning through design thinking processes, learners gain a deeper understanding of content while also demonstrating the ability to apply these specific thinking processes to real-world scenarios. Although design thinking does not require the use of technology, it can be used to enhance experiences. Learners can create presentations on their solutions using digital applications such as Tinkercad or use 3-D printers to create a physical prototype. Low-tech prototypes can also be created with popsicle sticks, cardboard, glue, and tape.

Design Thinking Resources

What Is Design Thinking? A Handy Guide for Classroom Teachers
www.makersempire.com/what-is-design-thinking-a-handy-guide-for-classroom-teachers/
Design Thinking in the History Classroom
www.middle.com/31977/design-thinking-in-the-history-classroom/
The Beginner's Guide to Design Thinking
http://ajjuliani.com/the-beginners-guide-to-design-thinking-in-the-classroom/

28. Digital Games

Kids often stay up late playing video games fighting mythical creatures, creating their own imaginative world, or adventuring through storylines where they are actually growing in strategic thinking. Classrooms can capitalize on kids' natural obsession with gaming by going beyond the typical slew of educational games found online today and actually encouraging students to create their own digital games. Digital games include those that are played using an electronic device, including game consoles, computers, or smartphones. The development of digital games requires a high level of research, synthesis, and authentic application of problem-solving skills.

In order for learners to develop digital games that transport players to other time periods or even other worlds, students need to become experts in the content. The medium of video games propels the understanding of computer science but can be used cross-curricular. Students can create simplistic digital games that involve getting questions correct to progress in the game or more complex games involving coding. Digital game creation has a natural connection to literacy through the development of characters and storylines. In math, a simple Google search will help to locate tons of math computation digital games. Students can develop games that take place in specific time periods where characters face challenges related to historical events. In science, learners can create games that take place inside cells, the human body, or a specific biome.

There are a wide variety of online options for creating digital games. WISC-Online hosts a game builder (www.wisc-online.com/gamebuilder) that allows learners to develop games that help reinforce skills through quizzing. There are also many online programs that challenge students through coding skills to develop more complex games, such as Game Star Mechanic (http://gamestarmechanic.com/).

Digital Gaming Resources

Game On: Using Digital Games to Transform Teaching, Learning, and Assessment
www.amazon.com/Game-Transform-Assessment-practical-educators/dp/1936763974

14 Tools to Turn Game Obsessed Kids into Genuine Game Designers
www.commonsensemedia.org/blog/14-tools-to-turn-game-obsessed-kids-into-genuine-game-designers

What Students Learn When They Give Up Shoebox Dioramas for Video Games
www.edsurge.com/news/2013-08-19-video-games-the-shoebox-diorama-of-the-future

29. Digital Story

A digital story provides students with the experience to bring their writing to life through technology tools. Digital storytelling involves adding images, animation, and voice to help learners' writing jump off of the page and into the audience's imagination. The use of multimedia in stories creates a new level of engagement in the creators and viewers.

Although there is an obvious connection between digital storytelling and literacy, any element of the curriculum that involves telling a story can be enhanced through digital storytelling. In social studies, students can create historical fiction stories or diary entries of historical figures. Learners can write diary entries from the perspective of Harriet Tubman, Nelson Mandela, or Alexander the Great. The ability to add multimedia to their stories creates a transfluent experience. In math, students can create authentic real-world situations supported by imagery, sound, and other media and pose questions that their peers can solve. Using images and animations can help develop a greater context for math word problems. Students can create digital bar models, graphs, or tables that can serve as visual representations of the word problems.

There are a wide variety of platforms that allow students to develop digital stories. Story Board That (www.storyboardthat.com/) provides tools to create digital storyboards with cartoon characters to illustrate their writing. Animoto (https://animoto.com) allows for the addition of visuals into a video format. Storybird (www.storybird.com/) provides graphics that can inspire text. Exposure (https://exposure.co/) is another tool that provides the opportunity for users to embed photos, text, and other media into digital stories.

Digital Story Resources

6 Reasons You Should Be Doing Digital Storytelling with Your Students
www.gettingsmart.com/2016/01/6-reasons-you-should-be-doing-digital-storytelling-with-your-students/
30 Sites and Apps for Digital Storytelling
www.techlearning.com/tl-advisor-blog/30-sites-and-apps-for-digital-storytelling\
The Art of Digital Storytelling
https://creativeeducator.tech4learning.com/v04/articles/The_Art_of_Digital_Storytelling

30. Diorama

A diorama is a minute model that often includes 3-D objects with a painted background. Although they can be created using a wide variety of materials, shoebox dioramas are probably the most practical and popular today. Although dioramas may be considered an old-fashioned and outdated classroom project, as long as higher-order thinking skills are integrated into the design of dioramas, students can demonstrate a rich understanding of concepts.

For a diorama project to be effective, learners need to move beyond simply duplicating a picture in a textbook or representing a scene from a book. They need to purposefully create scenes based on their research and understanding of concepts. Learners should be thoroughly familiar with the styles, patterns,

FIGURE 6.7 Image of a student-generated wetland diorama
Credit: Mayara Rudolph, Forsyth Country Day School

architecture, and visual motifs of the literary pieces for their dioramas. In science, students might create a new animal that has adaptations that allow it to live in a different habitat. Students can design a scientifically accurate scenario based on the chosen habitat and then create this animal and its adaptations.

Diorama Resources

> Dioramas in the Classroom – Fun and Effective Project Based Learning
> http://judydodgecummings.com/dioramas-effective-project-learning/
> Not Your Dad's Diorama: Using Tech Tools to Enhance a Traditional Assignment

www.edutopia.org/article/not-your-dads-diorama-using-tech-tools-enhance-traditional-assignment
How to Make a Shoebox Diorama
https://feltmagnet.com/crafts/shoebox-diorama

31. Discussion

Discussions have always been a foolproof way to gauge student understanding in the learning environment. However, advancements in technology have resulted in additional platforms and venues to have these conversations. A discussion can simply be defined as an exchange of ideas. It could be a conversation between the teacher and a student or between a student and their peer or peers. Although traditional face-to-face discussions are impactful, digital conversations, both written and oral, enhance the benefits of this format through the ability to document academic growth over time.

Discussions can be implemented in all subject areas, as their power lies in the ability for ideas to build upon one another leading to more insightful reflections. Effective discussions are inquiry-based with a variety of question types based on the levels of Bloom's taxonomy. Through dialogue, learners grow in communication and active listening skills. Having discussions provides students with practice in developing appropriate etiquette when sharing ideas. Through conversation, learners develop speaking and listening skills, learning how to clearly express their thinking. Speaking and listening skills will be utilized in learners' futures no matter what profession they pursue. Thoughtful question stems can jumpstart conversations.

As conversations are being held more often through emails and texts, the ability to have a discussion has expanded to digital platforms. Written dialogue can be held digitally through blogs, Google Classroom Questions, or backchannel platforms such as Yo Teach! (https://yoteachapp.com/). Many digital tools allow for video and audio discussions. Voicethread (https://voicethread.com/) is a presentation platform that provides users with the ability to add video, audio, and text comments for learners and their peers to experience. Flipgrid (https://info.flipgrid.com/) is a similar online video and discussion app available on most digital platforms. Teachers can also upload documents to host conversations digitally through NowComment (https://nowcomment.com/).

Discussion Resources

Leading Effective Class Discussions
https://learninginnovation.duke.edu/faculty-opportunities/art-and-science-of-teaching/leading-effective-class-discussions/
Kialo
www.kialo-edu.com/
7 Free Online Discussion Tools
https://lindsayannlearning.com/7-free-online-discussion-tools/

32. Drawing

It is said that a picture is worth 1,000 words. In education, drawings also have amazing value. Sketches, doodles, drawings, and pictures allow learners to demonstrate their understanding in a creative and artistic format. According to John Medina, images can be interpreted by the human brain up to 60,000 times faster than text, meaning humans are all inherently visual learners. Therefore, integrating drawings and illustrations into learning activities can benefit today's generations of learners.

Many traditional classrooms rely on only words for learners to express their thinking. However, through visual representations like an image, learners are able to cultivate visual learning skills, which may lead to deeper understanding. Sketches can be used by educators as a quick way for learners to take notes or show their mastery of a subject in the form of formative assessment. Learners can draw pictures of vocabulary words or concepts, illustrate what they internally visualize after reading fiction or nonfiction, or create their own artwork inspired by others.

Drawings can be completed using no tech (crayons, colored pencils, etc.) or low tech. Online digital tools, such as Google Drawings, Autodraw (www.autodraw.com/), Kleki (https://kleki.com/), and Wixie (www.wixie.com/), allow learners to develop drawings on a digital canvas individually or collaboratively. Wixie also provides learners with the option to add voice recordings to correspond with their drawings.

Drawing Resources

10 Engaging Google Drawings Activities for Classroom
https://ditchthattextbook.com/10-engaging-google-drawings-activities-for-classes/

During Reading Response: Visual Response or Drawing through the Text
www.amle.org/BrowsebyTopic/WhatsNew/WNDet/TabId/270/ArtMID/888/ArticleID/960/During-Reading-Response-Visual-Response-or-Drawing-through-the-Text.aspx

10 Digital Art Projects That Will Spark Student Creativity
https://theartofeducation.edu/2017/12/11/10-digital-art-projects-that-will-spark-student-creativity/

33. Escape Room

Escape rooms have taken the world by storm. Paying money to get locked in a room until you figure out the answers to clues to escape has become a favorite activity for family and friends. An escape room, sometimes referred to as a breakout room, involves a narrative storyline that provides players with a series of puzzles and clues to solve within a time limit. Escape rooms add the elements of suspense and excitement while encouraging the development of problem-solving skills and collaboration.

Many teachers are using this format to bring excitement and creativity to the learning experience. However, learners can develop their own escape rooms using the content that they are experiencing. This gives learners the power to implement the curriculum in a way that is both challenging and authentic. Learners can create an escape room based on any learning goal in math, science, social studies, or language arts. In science, learners may need to figure out how to escape being trapped in a human body system. After reading the novel *Hatchet*, students may need to figure out how to use the symbols from the novel to escape the island they are stranded on. To further develop geography skills, learners may need to determine ways to get from one location to another so that they can trade for needed resources.

In order for learners to create their own escape rooms, they must develop a compelling storyline to immerse the other players in. As learners transition to escape room developers, they must design different puzzles based on the skills and concepts they are exploring. Kesler Science (www.keslerscience.com/escape-room-puzzle-ideas-for-the-science-classroom/) has an incredibly helpful list of suggestions for puzzles that can be adapted to any content area. Once they have the puzzles developed, all that's needed to add is a timer that counts down. By having learners design and self-assess their escape rooms, educators have a front-row seat to the development of their problem-solving, collaboration, and creativity skills, in synthesis with content knowledge.

Escape Room Resources

Escape Rooms Created by Kids
www.youtube.com/watch?v=anShY2bdojw
How to Create a Digital Breakout for the Classroom
https://engagingandeffective.com/how-to-create-a-digital-breakout-for-the-classroom/
Top 11 Puzzle Ideas for Escape Rooms

https://escapehour.ca/blog/27-top-11-puzzle-ideas-for-escape-rooms/

34. Event Planning

When it comes to planning a special occasion, every detail needs to be considered. Event planning involves making a guest list, gathering addresses, sending invitations, creating a budget, designing the menu, planning the order of activities, and creating a seating chart while following all of the proper rules of etiquette. Extensive research is required to complete these tasks in terms of guest relationships, etiquette, and protocol, as well as the context of the celebration. This provides learners with fun and authentic ways to engage with the content.

With some creativity, event planning can be incorporated into all subject areas. Math students can develop budgets and calculate the costs of various choices for an event. In literacy, learners can create invitations, guest lists, and seating charts based on a character or event that takes place in the novel. In social studies, students can plan out what a celebration for independence might have looked like. What would the seating chart look like for the founding fathers as they sat next to other historical figures? In science, learners might plan a birthday party for an apex predator and carefully design a seating chart that ensures that the predators and prey aren't seated next to one another.

Although no technology is needed, depending on the structure and specific goal of the planning event project, it can be incorporated as a way for learners to communicate their ideas. Students can use presentation software to explain their design process or use design tools such as Canva to create invitations and seating charts.

Event Resources

Plan an Event
https://creativeeducator.tech4learning.com/2014/lessons/plan-an-event

Event Planning Project
www.familyconsumersciences.com/2010/02/event-planning-project/

35. Experiment

Although experiments are typically used in science class and determined by the teacher or textbook, learners can develop experiments that result in self-constructed knowledge. An experiment is any construct in which you strive to test a hypothesis or demonstrate a fact. In a situation where learners can develop their own hypothesis to test, they can design an experiment. Even when the experiment ends without the predicted result, placing learners in charge of the experiment promotes authentic conversations based on unexpected outcomes.

Experiments can occur in any subject area where the power of the purpose lies in learners' questions to test the hypothesis. Math can be connected to experimentation through the collection of data and the development of tables and graphs. Students can design research that tests the laws of probability and design experiments to determine whether the order of operations affects the outcome. To bring health and science concepts to life, learners can use experimental design to determine which forms of exercise most effectively increase heart rate. Through experiments, learners participate in active learning that is meaningful and based on problem-solving.

Authentic experiments are effective experiments. When learners conduct investigations based on learner interests, the engagement level is naturally higher. Teachers can help develop experiments with learners based on a student questionnaire or provide resources for learners to create their own research from scratch. In order for learners to have successful experiences, teachers must provide a framework for understanding experimental design.

Experiment Resources

How to Teach Your Students to Design an Experiment
www.amybrownscience.com/2013/08/how-to-teach-your-students-to-design.html

An Experiment Design Project That Is Not a Cookbook Lab
https://sunrisescience.blog/experimental-design-project/

36. Fake Text Conversations

Today's students tend to communicate with their peers using text far more than they do face-to-face. Although many teachers beg students to put away their cell phones, creating fake text conversations can capitalize on this technology trend. Learners can develop fake texts that explore relationships between historical and contemporary figures.

Learners can use text conversations as a means of demonstrating understanding in a variety of subject areas or topics. After reading a piece of fiction, they can summarize the storyline through text conversations between characters. In social studies, learners can recreate historical events through group texts. Learners can also practice the use of vocabulary words and grammar rules in the space of the text bubbles.

Learners do not need to use their smartphones to demonstrate understanding. Instead, they can write down text conversations using Post-it notes or a template. They can also use digital tools such as ifaketext or Texting Story Chat Story Maker that provide the opportunity to create imagined text conversations.

Fake Text Conversation Resources

ifaketext
http://ifaketext.com/
Make Your Lessons Memorable with the Texting Story App

www.thetechieteacher.net/2017/04/make-your-lessons-memorable-with.html

Texting Story Chat Story Maker

https://apps.apple.com/us/app/textingstory-write-chat-stories-save-as-video/id1083676922

37. Fashion Show

Students often compare their clothes to those of others to figure out the latest fashion trends. Their outfits are a form of self-expression where everyone is able to communicate without words. Since students are already fixated on the latest fashion trends, turning the classroom into a fashion show is an easy way to create a virtual catwalk for students to express themselves. Learner-led fashion shows can be informal with learners wearing their outfits for the day or as sophisticated as transforming the learning environment into a runway from fashion week.

A fashion show can be adapted to work with a wide variety of learning goals. Learners can research clothing styles from specific historical periods and strut down the runway in outfits inspired by that era. Putting together an outfit based on history allows learners to research the period deeply and requires learners to apply their findings to their ensemble. Learners can also dress as various scientific vocabulary terms and put together outfits that depict "low pressure" or "igneous rocks."

Furthermore, fashion shows can be integrated into literacy studies. Learners can write about their fashion for others to read as they walk down the runway. The description of the outfit can focus on expressive language goals. The flexibility of the fashion show connects period clothing to various learning goals. This strategy is a fun and exciting way for learners to express their understanding and extend their learning experience.

Fashion Show Resources

How One School Fashions Geometry Lessons from Recyclables
www.scpr.org/news/2015/06/10/52314/arts-opening-door-to-common-core-learning-in-socal/
Kim Bearden's Fashion Extravaganza
www.facebook.com/watch/?v=10156249572508599
End of Year Fashion Show
https://modelsofexcellence.eleducation.org/projects/end-year-fashion-show

38. Flowcharts

A flowchart can be simultaneously dynamic and simple when used to demonstrate complex connections in the form of graphic representations. Learners can use flowcharts to explain the relationships between concepts, vocabulary, or events, allowing them to comprehend ideas at a much deeper level. Learners can develop flowcharts identifying the stages of a project or as a means of organizing ideas or research to scaffold into larger writing projects.

The flexibility of flowcharts allows for the development of a wide variety of formats. Flowcharts are most useful when utilized to express understanding related to cause and effect, sequence of events, or the relationship between events. Flowcharts can be used to connect historical events or describe the relationship between scientific phenomena or the relationships of characters in a novel. The format allows for self-differentiation, as students can use pictures, words, sentences, or paragraphs as content for their flowcharts.

Learners can easily develop flowcharts using a piece of paper, sticky notes, or a poster utilizing string or arrows to symbolize connections. They can also design digital flowcharts using Google Docs, Google Slides, or other online tools such as

Edraw or LucidChart. Flowcharts allow learners to be creative in how their thoughts are represented using visual-rich media.

Flowchart Resources

Edraw
www.edrawsoft.com/flowchart-examples-for-students.html
20 Flowchart Templates, Design Tips, and Examples
https://venngage.com/blog/flow-chart-template/
Teaching Kids to Code with Lucidchart
www.lucidchart.com/blog/coding-for-kids-in-lucidchart

39. Foldables

Foldables are three-dimensional interactive graphic organizers that use folds and cuts to create visual representations of content using paper-based materials. Foldables are a means for practicing and reviewing different ideas using a hands-on, brains-on learning approach.

Foldables can be easily integrated into any subject area. Although traditionally created by teachers and given to learners to complete in a predetermined way, learners can develop foldables to demonstrate their own understanding. In math, students can create foldables that organize estimations, solutions, and representations of word problems. In social studies, learners can create foldables that demonstrate the cause and effect of historical events. In science, students can use foldables to understand the chemical equation of photosynthesis or definitions of other concepts and key vocabulary words. In language arts, learners can craft foldables to study word definitions or even to generate a list of synonyms to utilize when writing.

Foldables can be created using any materials that you can cut and glue or using a blank piece of paper with folds and cuts serving as tabs. Sticky notes also make the perfect flap to add an additional dimension to the foldable. Foldables can also be designed using online publishing programs. Lines and dashed lines can show students where to cut and fold. Foldables can also be created using manilla envelopes or file folders.

Foldable Resources

5 Other Ways to Use Foldables in Your Math Classroom
https://ideagalaxyteacher.com/5-ways-to-use-foldables-in-math-classroom/
Alternative Assessments: Othello Foldables
http://ellmatters.blogspot.com/2015/05/alternative-assessments-othello.html
How to Create Your Own Digital Foldables
https://howweteach.com/how-to-create-your-own-digital-foldables/

40. Genius Hour

Adults typically mandate what subjects and content areas learners should become experts in. However, Genius Hour gives learners some of the power back. Genius Hour is a movement that provides students time to explore a topic that they are passionate about. Genius Hour is inspired by the company Google. Google allows its engineers to spend 20% of their time working on projects that they are interested in, hence the name Genius Hour. The format revolves around learners conducting independent research on their topic and then developing a product of their choice to share with the class.

Although Genius Hour projects are purposefully based on learner interests, passion-based projects can be based on specific curriculum topics. Learners can complete a Genius Hour project on a chosen historical time period, a self-selected famous mathematician, or an interesting scientific theory. As long as learners get to choose the topic and select the format of the project, they will benefit from the power of independence of a Genius Hour project.

The level of technology required for each learner's project depends on their selected topic and project format. Mini-lessons on how to effectively research using online search engines and databases will help students find pertinent information.

Genius Hour Resources

What Is Genius Hour?
www.teachthought.com/learning/what-is-genius-hour/
You Get to Have Your Own Genius Hour
www.youtube.com/watch?v=COF-bqZuE-I
Your Top 10 Genius Hour Questions Answered
www.cultofpedagogy.com/genius-hour-questions/

41. Google Earth Tour

All teachers strive to transport learners to different areas of the world through history, geography, and literature. Although once an expensive feat, Google Earth (www.google.com/earth/) makes it possible for learners to travel to every inch of the globe. Google Earth is an application accessed through a web browser that allows learners to explore the earth through satellite imagery. Through Google Earth tours, learners can design their own virtual sightseeing tours by embedding location-based information and images.

Google Earth tours can enhance any lesson that can be brought to life through digital geographic tours. Using Google Earth's creation tools, world explorers can pinpoint locations and add photographs, information, shapes, and lines to the satellite images. In language arts, learners can further immerse themselves into a novel by visiting the historical settings or use locations to develop a timeline based on a biography. Using the ruler feature, mathematicians can determine the perimeter around a space to identify the correct length of fencing or the area of sod needed to cover an area. In science, learners can examine geographic features such as volcanoes and fault lines to develop evacuation plans for residents. In social studies, students can develop guided tours through historical landmarks such as the Colosseum or the Taj Mahal.

Creating Google Earth tours does require a computer or tablet and access to the internet. However, no matter your level of technical expertise, videos on YouTube help demonstrate how to utilize Google Earth's creative tools to manipulate satellite images.

Google Earth Tour Resources

> Creating with Google Earth: 10 Activities to Try
> https://ditchthattextbook.com/google-earth-creation-tools/
> Teaching with Google Earth
> www.nationalgeographic.org/education/google-earth/
> Tips for Google Earth in the Classroom
> https://tommullaney.com/2018/10/24/7-tips-for-google-earth-in-the-classroom/

42. Graffiti Art

Although over the years, graffiti has developed a bad reputation, when created without permission, graffiti murals and walls provide learners with a different way to express their thinking. Graffiti is an expressive art form that includes both words and images. Through graffiti art, learners can collaborate creatively, leading to a deep understanding of content. The art form also gives students a chance to develop deeper comprehension and create connections with the content while also promoting student voice. The collaborative aspect of graffiti art allows students to display their collective experience through their connections to the content.

Graffiti walls can be incorporated across the curriculum. Teachers can use any prompt to kick off the creation of one based on a historical timeline or a vocabulary word. Learners can respond to a quote, image, or open-ended question. In math, teachers can start graffiti walls by writing "the answer is 13" and asking students to write expressions or word problems that will lead to the answer of 13.

It is crucial for educators to remember that art does not have to be permanent. Although graffiti is authentically created with spray paint, students can create graffiti walls on a whiteboard, or they can use crayons and markers on large butcher paper. Incorporating graffiti into learning does not require technology. However, digital graffiti walls can be created through Padlet or Google Jamboard.

Graffiti Art Resources

> 20 Engaging Ways to Teach with Graffiti Walls
> www.weareteachers.com/graffiti-walls/
> Tag It – Graffiti in the Classroom
> www.amle.org/BrowsebyTopic/WhatsNew/WNDet/TabId/270/ArtMID/888/ArticleID/683/Tag-It%E2%80%94Graffiti-in-the-Classroom.aspx
> Graffiti Walls: Discussing and Responding to Literature Using Graphics
> www.readwritethink.org/classroom-resources/lesson-plans/graffiti-wall-discussing-responding-208.html

43. Graphic Design

Kids recognize stores, signs, and boxes of their favorite snacks because of the logos. This happens before they even learn to read. Graphic designers apply research and creativity to develop memorable designs using font color and image choices using road signs, billboards, advertisements, and logos. Through the connection of graphic design and media literacy, students can interpret messages and use their analysis to develop their own designs.

Any product that includes visual elements and communicates messages relates to the theories of graphic design. Products are developed and used as a means for learners to expand their ideas for a creation. In literacy, learners can develop billboards

FIGURE 6.8 Image of a student-generated graphic on innovation
Credit: Annabelle Bailor and Mayara Rudolph, Forsyth Country Day School

to advertise novels or logos that represent a character's specific traits. In math, students can develop signs that clearly explain the steps of math algorithms, rules that are applied to certain mathematical situations, or explanations of mathematical theories. In social studies, learners can develop logos for life-changing historical inventions or billboards recruiting others to join the fight for a cause. In science, students can develop billboards that demonstrate cellular respiration or logos that represent the organelles of a cell.

Students can develop graphic design projects with no technology at all, using art supplies and paper. However, there are many ways that students can develop digital versions of these graphic design projects. Google Drawings is a free digital drawing app that allows students to create anything from logos to billboards to advertisements. Online programs such as Media Modifier and Canva also allow learners to quickly create and export graphic designs.

Graphic Design Resources

Math in Graphic Design
https://prezi.com/ucrd2ffrgdf7/math-in-graphic-design/
Pictures and Slogans Persuade an Audience
www.scholastic.com/teachers/lesson-plans/teaching-content/pictures-and-slogans-persuade-audience/.
3 Graphic Design Opportunities Perfect for Students
https://theartofeducation.edu/2020/11/30/3-graphic-design-opportunities-perfect-for-students/

44. Graphic Organizer

Our brains are not designed to organize information into paragraphs and pages. Rather, our brains systematize information and facts in classified structures that show relationships between pieces of information. Graphic organizers provide a structure for learners to organize thought processes or content. They are paper or digital templates that include structural elements and images, such as arrows and connecting webs. Graphic organizers are used as a starting point to organize information while developing connections and relationships between ideas because they provide a means to demonstrate ideas so that the brain can categorize facts and information to promote retention.

Graphic organizers provide the flexibility for learners to organize topics and subjects. Inserting text into a graphic organizer requires students to analyze and evaluate information. Learners can gather materials such as videos, articles, trade books, novels, presentations, websites, word problems, class discussions, or primary sources. Graphic organizers can be quickly developed to help provide structure when solving a difficult word problem or used to organize quotes that support various themes of novels.

Provide learners with the opportunity to choose the design of their graphic organizer to access and utilize new information. Learners can also exchange their own graphic organizers to compare their ideas with peers.

The design of a graphic organizer is dependent on the thinking applied when analyzing the sources. Common graphic organizers include cause and effect, main idea with supporting details, Venn diagrams, webs, and timelines. Tables on Google Docs or Microsoft Word provide a simple platform to develop personalized graphic organizers. Several digital graphic organizer resources exist, including Mindmeister (www.mindmeister.com/), which provides an element of online collaboration.

Graphic Organizer Resources

Mindmeister
www.mindmeister.com/
General Graphic Organizers
www.teach-nology.com/worksheets/graphic/
10 Sites for Creating Graphic Organizers
www.techlearning.com/tl-advisor-blog/9736

45. Hexagonal Thinking

Hexagonal thinking is a framework that involves making connections between various ideas, words, or phrases that are written on hexagons referred to as thinking decks. Using this strategy, learners develop connections using the six-sided shape. When coupled hexagons are connected, they demonstrate relationships between words, phrases, and ideas. This strategy results in deep discussions and productive debate about the organization and relationship of the words or phrases, as it is unlikely that two learners will develop identical connections.

Hexagonal thinking is a process of deep connection and can be applied to all content areas. In social studies, learners can make connections between historical events, influential figures, or important dates. In math, learners can develop relationships between geometric shapes, mathematical conjectures, or any math vocabulary words. To further literary analysis, learners can develop connections between characters in novels, topics of nonfiction writing, or literacy themes and symbols.

Hexagonal thinking can be incorporated by simply writing vocabulary words on hexagonal shapes. This process can easily be adapted to a digital format using Google Slides, allowing learners to virtually manipulate their shapes. Learners can share analysis of their connections through a wide variety of platforms and mediums, such as audio and video recordings of their choice.

Hexagonal Thinking Resources

Hexagonal Thinking: A Colorful Tool for Discussion
www.cultofpedagogy.com/hexagonal-thinking/
What Is Hexagonal Thinking? Plus 13 Examples to Inspire You
www.weareteachers.com/hexagonal-thinking/
Hexagonal Thinking in ELA: The Ultimate Guide
www.nowsparkcreativity.com/2020/03/hexagonal-thinking-in-ela-ultimate-guide.html

46. Hyperdoc

A hyperdoc is a digital document, such as a Google Doc, that provides the steps for learning through various links and resources. Hyperdocs are similar to webquests or playlists where teachers provide helpful resources and learning activities that will guide learners through a learning progression. Student choice can be embedded in a teacher-created hyperdoc through resources to gain knowledge and the ability for learners to determine their own pace. Learners can choose between reading an article, watching a video, or playing a digital game on the same topic or subject. Furthermore, effective hyperdocs provide opportunities for learners to develop ownership over their work by creating a product within the digital lesson.

Learners can also develop their own hyperdocs with activities for a peer to complete, placing the power of learning in their own hands. A learner-designed hyperdoc can contain an article, a video, an online simulation, or an image related to the topic. Through explaining the process by which they selected the resources, learners practice assessing the credibility and relevance of resources furthering media literacy skills. Designing hyperdocs provides the opportunity for learners to further their communication, information, and digital literacy skills.

Hyperdocs rely on technology tools' ability to insert hyperlinks to different resources. Hyperdocs can be created using Google Docs or Google Slides or website builders, such as Weebly, that allow for hyperlinks to connect to other webpages or digital resources.

Hyperdoc Resources

    HyperDocs Academy
    https://hyperdocs.co/
    How Hyperdocs Can Transform Your Teaching
    www.cultofpedagogy.com/hyperdocs/
    Using Hyperdocs in Class
    www.kidsdiscover.com/teacherresources/
       using-hyperdocs-in-class/

47. Infographics

Infographics combine words and pictures to depict connections between ideas. Developing infographics allows learners to express a deep understanding of concepts by relating literacy to pictorial images. Infographics rely on common symbols and well-thought-out placement of words to represent information. Developing an effective infographic involves using critical thinking skills and creativity to determine the relationships of ideas to be presented in the infographic.

Infographics can be used to express understanding of a wide variety of content. They are a creative format in which understanding of scientific processes, cause and effect of historical events, or illustration of a theme in novels can be depicted. Infographics can also be used for learners to brainstorm and demonstrate conceptual ideas, such as classroom expectations or the characteristics of leadership. Infographics also serve as a format for public service announcements to save an endangered species, a how-to guide on writing effective paragraphs, or a way to demonstrate the relationship between groups of people involved in historical conflicts.

Infographics can be developed using markers and poster boards. However, digital tools such as Canva and Piktochart can be used to develop digital infographics. The templates and images offered in the programs increase the level of design quality.

Infographic Resources

Piktochart
https://piktochart.com/
Infographics as a Creative Assessment
www.schrockguide.net/infographics-as-an-assessment.html
How to Make Infographics with Students
www.easel.ly/blog/how-to-make-infographics-with-students/

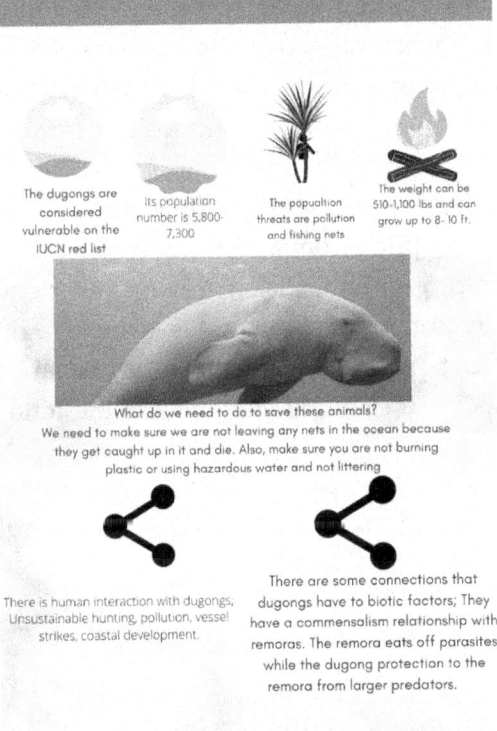

FIGURE 6.9 Image of a student-generated infographic about dugongs
Credit: Colin Nicolay, Forsyth Country Day School

48. Infomercial

Everyone has been forced to watch a cheesy infomercial late at night in between TV reruns. An infomercial is a longer television commercial that promotes a product, often through demonstrations and entertaining customer reviews. When developing infomercials, learners summarize information and apply facts to express understanding in a fun and quirky format.

Infomercials can be incorporated across the curriculum. In social studies, learners can develop infomercials based on historical inventions or as a pitch from a historical figure. In science, learners can develop an infomercial that solves a scientific problem. In math, students can create infomercials encouraging viewers to follow specific steps of a mathematical procedure or advertise a specific number. An example may include the following:

> Why would you purchase a fraction when you can buy a mixed number that includes a free whole number with your fraction?

Students can further develop their writing skills by creating informational text to explain how the product works, producing creative writing through customer reviews, and practicing persuasive writing to convince viewers to purchase this product.

Infomercials can be produced using either audio or video. Depending on access to technology, infomercials can be performed live or recorded and edited. There are a wide variety of student-friendly video-editing software programs that can be downloaded or used via the internet, such as WeVideo.

Infomercial Resources

What Is an Infomercial? Creating the Storyboard
www.cteonline.org/lesson_plans/adebj0/what-is-an-infomercial-creating-the-storyboard

Fun Video Project! Produce a TV Commercial for an Invention

https://teacherrebootcamp.com/2018/07/inventionTVad/
Teacher Reboot Camp
https://teacherrebootcamp.com/2018/07/inventionTVad/

49. Interactive Word Wall

Lists of vocabulary, high-frequency, or tricky spelling words are often displayed in learning environments. Interactive word walls take classroom displays to the next level by making learners the creators. Because all content areas require vocabulary acquisition, interactive word walls can be implemented across the curriculum. Learners can repeatedly add words on the wall and adjust its overall structure. The words can be organized in a T-chart, Venn diagram, or idea web, depending on the focus of the unit. As vocabulary words come up during lessons, students can add words to the display. Words can then be moved based on new observations that demonstrate visible thinking.

Interactive word walls can be created using sticky notes and a large open space on a wall, the floor, or even a table. Painter's or washi tape serves as a great way to create the template for the word wall. However, there are also digital tools that can be used to create virtual interactive word walls, such as Padlet (https://padlet.com/dashboard) or Google Jamboard (https://jamboard.google.com/).

Interactive Word Wall Resources

Building a Better Word Wall
www.edutopia.org/article/building-better-word-wall
Interactive Word Walls Enliven Vocabulary Learning
www.middleweb.com/37209/interactive-word-walls-enliven-vocab-learning/
Word Wall Ideas – Ready for an Interactive Word Wall Makeover?
https://learningfocused.com/word-wall-ideas-interactive-classroom-word-wall-makeover/

50. Interview

An interview involves one person asking another a series of questions to gain understanding from the interviewee's expertise or perspective. Interviews can consist of a list of interview questions, a script that includes the possible responses from the interviewee, audio or video recorded interview, or a live talk show performance. Within the format of an interview, learners have a choice in what details of the task are included.

Interviews can deepen understanding of a wide variety of topics. Learners can write interviews of famous scientists, inventors, mathematicians, historical figures, or characters in a novel. Learners can also write interviews in which they creatively write responses for inanimate objects. How might a triangle respond to questions in an interview versus a square? What questions would an exponent ask a base number? What questions does the nucleus have for the mitochondria? In social studies, learners can conduct imaginary interviews with distinguished individuals, political figures, or living witnesses to historical events.

Depending on the format of the interview, technology is not always needed. However, learners can record interviews as an audio or video clip using software tools such as iMovie or WeVideo. Learners can also add sound clips and music to enhance the presentation.

Interview Resources

Learning to Interview Builds a Range of Communication Skills
www.edutopia.org/article/learning-interview-builds-range-communication-skills

Lights, Camera, Action: Interviewing a Book Character
www.readwritethink.org/classroom-resources/lesson-plans/lights-camera-action-interviewing-140.html

Incorporating an Oral History Interview PBL in Your Social Studies Class
https://letscultivategreatness.com/incorporating-an-oral-history-interview-pbl-into-your-social-studies-class/

51. Jackdaw Project

A jackdaw is a crow-like bird that scavenges to gather items to create its nest. A jackdaw project is a learning experience in which learners, like the jackdaw bird, gather important objects based on a textual theme. Artifacts can be based on the topics and themes of novels or nonfiction texts. These objects can be literal or figurative. Along with the artifact, students can include a quote from the text or description that explains their choices of the artifact based on the relevance to the text.

Jackdaw projects can also include learner-written artifacts based on events of a novel or historical event. In literacy, some examples of jackdaw artifacts include a letter written from a character, a menu from a character's favorite restaurant, or a wanted poster based on a novel's antagonist. In social studies, some examples of written artifacts include advertisements from a historical speech, a postcard from someone who attended the event, or a news report describing the event. Physical artifacts may include symbols from text or meaningful objects.

The jackdaw project can be a poster, a shoebox, a container, or a Google Slides deck that organizes all of the artifacts. Instead of weaving a nest like a jackdaw, students weave together their understanding of a novel or historical text through artifacts, symbols, themes, quotations, character relationships, and connections with the text. Learners select the advertisements, develop writing artifacts, and design the presentation format. Learners can gather physical materials, create models of the artifacts, or print out images of the objects. The inherent elements of choice and creativity in a jackdaw project result in a high level of student ownership.

Jackdaw Project Resources

Touchcast Martin Luther King Jr. Lesson Example
https://bbc-vip.touchcast.com/lesson/Social_Studies_8_Grade_Dr_Martin_Luther_King_Jr

Salem Literature Circle Projects
www.msstringfellow.com/home/category/literature-circles

52. Journal

Modern learners should not just be able to recite facts and recall information. Rather learners need opportunities to develop their metacognitive skills by reflecting on their learning and developing thoughtful questions. Journaling is a reflective writing format that can further these goals through the focus on curiosity and the development of deep connections.

Journals can be centered on self-guided reflection choice, or they can be guided through sentence starters or graphic organizers based on academic goals. Journals that focus on reflection of thinking and personal investigation allow learners to develop skills that promote lifelong learning. Journals also provide a simple assessment tool and a way for teachers to connect with students through individual communication and feedback.

Journals are a simple way for learners to communicate their ideas in all content areas. In science, students may have a year-long KWL journal that encourages curiosity and documents learning. In literacy, students can journal about the class read-alouds or personal choice books. In social studies, learners can write a journal from the perspective of a historical figure. No matter which approach is used, journaling is an effective way for students to share their thinking in an individualized manner.

Journals can be written in spiral notebooks, copybooks, or digital formats. For historical journals, learners may want to make their books look old by using coffee grounds to brown the paper. Learners can alternatively create digital diaries using website creators, such as Weebly, or using Google Docs or Google Slides.

Journal Resources

20 Types of Learning Journals That Help Students Think
www.teachthought.com/literacy/20-types-of-learning-journals-that-help-students-think/

Journaling
www.teachervision.com/journaling
The Importance of Student Journals and How to Respond Efficiently
www.edutopia.org/blog/student-journals-efficient-teacher-responses

53. Learning Logs

Learners should explore content in a variety of ways to develop their own conclusions. However, this form of interactive and student-centered learning can be difficult to assess. Learning logs make it possible for learners to document their own attitudes and reasoning. A learning log is a digital or physical document that keeps track of newfound ideas or changes in thinking to engage with in the learning process. Learning logs also often include self-reflections on the relevance of knowledge and application to future learning.

Using any of these formats, learners think about their learning, furthering metacognitive skills. Learning logs can list facts or information gained or provide reflections of thinking through guiding questions. Learning logs can serve as a form of note-taking or as a way for learners to document higher-level connections or developed conjectures. Learning logs also serve as documentation of student learning while students play content-based digital games. In social studies, learners can reflect on new strategies or acquired content knowledge while playing digital games, such as the Oregon Trail or games hosted on iCivics. In math, learners can solve equal sharing problems or any similar type of word problem format and then log discoveries with examples to prove their thinking.

A learning log could be structured as an organized table hosted on Google Docs, which also allows for real-time peer collaboration. A learning log can also be organized in a spiral notebook or binder. A quick Google search unearths digital learning log templates that can be adapted for a wide variety of learning activities

Learning Log Resources

Learning Logs in the Science Classroom
www.nsta.org/publications/news/story.aspx?id=51883
Collaborative Strategic Reading Learning Logs
www.adlit.org/strategies/22355/
WordPress
https://wordpress.com/

54. Literature Circle

In literature circles, learners meet in small groups to discuss their reading. Literature circles' formats can vary and look different depending on goals. The common ingredients are the reading of the same text and learner-guided discussion. In literature circles, learners guide the conversation. In other situations, learners are given roles in which they prepare the discussions for the various elements of the piece of literature. Literature circles have inherent elements of choice as students can choose the books they read, the element of the novel or text they focus on, and even their group members.

Literature circles were initially created as a format to deeply discuss novels. However, that does not mean that literature circles cannot be implemented in science or social studies to discuss nonfiction text, historical fiction, or informational picture books. When conducting science or social studies literature circles, each learner can be responsible for focusing on vocabulary, important figures, steps or processes, or connections beyond the book. Educators have also utilized literature circles in math classrooms, in which learners focus on deciphering math tasks rather than novels.

Literature circles usually entail learner reflections and the development of discussion questions using graphic organizers prior to meetings and then discussing face-to-face. With the availability of digital discussion tools, students can lead literature circle conversations via online chats or through online video conferencing programs, such as Zoom or Google Meet.

Literature Circle Resources

The Power of Literature Circles in the Classroom
www.edutopia.org/blog/literature-circles-how-to-and-reasons-why-elena-aguilar

Literature Circles for Science
https://stultzjn.files.wordpress.com/2013/01/literature-circles_straits-and-nichols-2006.pdf

Math Circles . . . Discussion Groups . . . Collaboration. . .
http://flippedclassroom.blogspot.com/2013/04/math-circlesdiscussion.html

55. Magazine

You may just skim the covers of interest-based periodicals while waiting to check out at the grocery store or while sitting in a doctor's office's waiting room. No matter what level of a magazine reader you are, you recognize that the wide variety of colorful and multifaceted content scattered throughout magazines provides engaging entertainment. A magazine is a publication typically centered around a specific theme or topic that includes miscellaneous writing pieces and illustrations. Because magazines have a wide variety of publications within them – articles, advertisements, fictional narratives, games, puzzles, comics – the creation of magazines in classrooms provides learners with the opportunity to creatively design their own printed media format.

Magazines are an expressive format that can be developed to meet a wide range of learning goals. Magazines are literacy-rich and therefore have a clear connection to developing language arts learning goals. Learners can write articles that include narratives, essays, poetry, eyewitness accounts, interviews and so much more. To deepen social studies understanding, learners can develop magazines based on conceptual themes. A magazine on the topic of conflict might include articles about famous conflicts throughout history and current events that depict current conflicts. In science, learner-created periodicals can center on any science concept that includes articles on how to become a molecule or how to tell the difference between chemical and physical changes. To further math understanding, students can write articles that include data, graphs, and elements of probability to reinforce their articles.

Although magazines are typically published and printed on paper, there are digital tools that allow learners to add a variety of interactive media to their creations. Lucid Press (www.lucid-press.com/pages/examples/free-digital-magazine-software) provides easy-to-use digital magazine templates for learners to adapt. Flipsnack (www.flipsnack.com/) is a digital program that provides learners the ability to embed voiceover, video, and audio throughout their magazines. Free Google Slide magazine templates are also available to utilize, providing learners with a quick way to edit and adapt the format to make it their own.

Magazine Resources

> Making a Middle School Magazine
> www.amle.org/making-a-middle-school-magazine/
> Reading and Writing in Math Class
> www.edutopia.org/article/reading-and-writing-math-class
> I've Got It Covered! Creating Magazine Covers to Summarize Text
> www.readwritethink.org/classroom-resources/lesson-plans/covered-creating-magazine-covers-1092.html?tab=4

56. Maps

Before GPS existed, road trips relied on passengers interpreting large colorful folded maps anxiously taken out of glove compartments. Although GPS has turned road maps into artifacts, maps continue to be informative representations of themes or geographical attributes. Maps are two-dimensional representations of specific areas that can include landforms, roads, data such as population, or locations of specific landmarks. Transforming learners into cartographers provides learners with the experience of developing relationships between physical landscape, location, and facts.

Learners can design and publish maps to illustrate concepts across the curriculum. In language arts, learners can develop maps of a character's home or town based on text evidence. Learners can also add quotes and key plot points onto maps to demonstrate the entire plot of the story throughout a map. In social studies, students can create maps that demonstrate the relationship between locations where important historical events occurred or depict the areas where world explorers landed. In science, learners can create maps based on the locations of active volcanoes or current habitats of endangered species. Learners can also design maps of the inside of a cell or a map of the digestive system. To build authentic connections to math understanding, students can develop thematic maps based on data from current event articles or research or use geometric shapes to create maps of their bedrooms or homes.

Maps can be created using a wide variety of media, including paper or poster board, or designed digitally for increased interactivity. Learners can add color and dimension with markers, paint, clay, or even discarded materials found around the house, such as egg cartons and bottle caps. Google Earth and MapQuest can serve as inspiration. Learners can also develop online maps from scratch using digital drawing tools such as Wixie, Pixie, or Google Drawings. Online tools such as Google My Maps offer features such as embedding videos, pictures, information, or links to pins dropped on locations.

Maps Resources

Map It
https://creativeeducator.tech4learning.com/v01/lessons/Map_It_with_Pixie
How to Create Media-Rich, Interactive Maps for Deeper Learning

https://ditchthattextbook.com/how-to-create-media-rich-interactive-maps-for-deeper-learning/

10 Ways to use Google Maps in the Classroom

http://blog.whooosreading.org/10-ways-to-use-google-maps-in-the-classroom/

57. Memes

Everyone loves searching through social media, chuckling at a particularly witty meme, and sharing it with others you think might enjoy it. A meme is an entertaining and humorous expression through words and images. Memes are a current element of pop culture as many are virally copied, slightly adjusted, and reshared through social media. Memes inspire ingenuity through their ability to apply curriculum into humorous combinations of pictures and words.

FIGURE 6.10 Image of a student-generated meme

Credit: Ramzi Badreddine, Forsyth Country Day School

Learners can create memes in all subject areas. A quick Google search will provide you with hundreds of memes based on assorted subject materials to use as examples. In math, memes can be used to demonstrate an understanding of vocabulary or concepts. Learners can create memes based on common errors that occur in the current mathematical theme being learned or about the importance of estimation to determine the reasonableness of solutions. In social studies, learners can use historical images and use their sense of humor to depict the thinking of one of the figures or think up a clever subtitle. To demonstrate understanding of literacy learning goals, learners can use plot, characters, or elements of literature, such as theme and irony, to create a witty statement that coincides with an image.

Learners can create memes using pencil and paper or digitally. There are many teacher-created meme templates for students. There are also many online meme creators, but these should be vetted prior to use for inappropriate content. Fortunately, there are school-safe meme templates that teachers have created for just this purpose.

Memes Resources

7 Creative and Smart Ways to Use Memes in the Classroom
www.weareteachers.com/memes-in-the-classroom/
Safe for School Meme Generator
https://meredithakers.com/2017/12/10/meme-generator/
Memes in the ELA Classroom
https://juliefaulknersblog.com/memes-in-ela-classroom/

58. Mind Map

Humans process knowledge through connections. Educators encourage students to make connections with their observations, their reading, and the world around them. Mind maps, also referred to as concept maps, are visual diagrams that depict connections between content using lines, similar to webs. They are often based on specific topics. From the topics, branches stem containing information about the main topic. Additional stems can then connect to the first level of branches, adding more details or connections. Learners can then add images and colors to help demonstrate the relationships between the content.

Mind mapping can enhance instruction for learners in all content areas. They are beneficial as ways to introduce concepts and assess prior knowledge, as a way to demonstrate thinking processes, and as a way to develop and evaluate understanding. In language arts, learners can complete a mind map based on the topic of their next novel study to develop background knowledge. In writing, learners can develop a mind map of the elements of the process of completing a persuasive essay or a literary essay. For deep scientific understanding, learners can develop mind maps to depict the steps of metamorphosis or mitosis using lines and arrows with additional facts about the processes. To demonstrate understanding of complex ideas in social studies, students can use mind maps to depict relationships between related historical events or historical figures.

Mind maps can be created on large pieces of butcher paper using markers or on any dry erase surface. When developing mind maps collaboratively, try having each student use different colored markers, so you can evaluate the participation of students and assess understanding. They can also be created digitally using any publishing program or online programs such as Mindmeister and Padlet.

Mind Map Resources

10 Mind Mapping Strategies for Teachers
www.teachthought.com/pedagogy/10-mind-mapping-strategies-for-teachers/

10 Ways Mind Mapping Improves Learning in the Classroom
http://blog.whooosreading.org/mind-mapping-improve-learning/

15 Creative Mind Map Examples for Students
www.mindmeister.com/blog/students-guide-to-mind-mapping/

59. Model

Many learners, when given the opportunity to choose how to demonstrate their understanding, select building and creating. Learners who enjoy learning kinesthetically benefit from interacting with models because they are able to learn by feeling and experimenting. Learners can develop models that demonstrate understanding and lead to deeper learning for a wide variety of topics.

Models can integrate multiple subject curriculum standards while simultaneously promoting collaboration, problem-solving, and creativity skills. Learners can develop models of important symbols from literature or physical representations that demonstrate math theories and proofs. They can develop scientific models or models of buildings, tools, or structures from throughout history. Students can create models of important state monuments and government buildings. Learners can then integrate their science understanding of circuits by developing an alarm system that sounds when the circuit is closed. This integrated activity allows students to experience the interconnectedness of subjects and innovation.

Learners can develop models using a wide variety of mediums. Learners can use Legos, cardboard, pipe cleaners, paper, or any other classroom supply. The sky's the limit! They can also develop models using technology with the development of 3-D printers or online using digital programs such as Tinkercad.

Model Resources

Physical Models in the Classroom
www.robomatter.com/blog-physical-models-classroom/
Making Models

www.nsta.org/science-and-children/science-and-children-march-2020/learning-models
Tinkercad
www.tinkercad.com/

60. Monologue

"But soft, what light through yonder window breaks?" Shakespeare's famous words in impactful monologues have entertained audiences for centuries. These solo reflections sometimes become the most memorable moments in plays and movies. Monologues involve actors speaking to themselves, often sharing their intimate thoughts and feelings with the audience. In order to write monologues, learners need to make inferences based on an artifact that inspires their writing and also practice essential speaking and listening skills when presenting.

Monologues have a natural connection to literacy, but they can also easily be incorporated into any subject area. Younger learners can create monologues based on the images in picture books. In social studies, students can create them based on historical portraits, paintings, or photographs. In science, students can write in this genre to express the challenges of plants growing through photosynthesis or a bison's frustration with ecological changes in their environment, or they can write from the perspective of a famous scientist on the cusp of making an earth-changing discovery. Monologues can combine literacy and creativity with any subject area in which words bring forth a subject's innermost thoughts and feelings.

Monologues can be written on paper or typed digitally. They allow students to perform their writing live or to capture their performance on video so they can be presented at a later time. Learners can utilize any online video platform such as Flipgrid to quickly capture their performance or practice editing skills using software such as iMovie.

Monologue Resources

Monologues
https://betterlesson.com/lesson/607537/monologues
Dramatic Monologues and the C3 Framework: An Oscar-Winning Pair
https://thekeep.eiu.edu/cgi/viewcontent.cgi?article=1132&context=the_councilor

61. Movie/Book Review

Roger Ebert, one of the most famous and influential American movie critics, once said that "the point is not to avoid all stupid movies, but to avoid being a stupid movie-goer." Before deciding to spend money on a movie ticket or before downloading your favorite author's latest book on your Kindle, you often turn to reviews to determine whether the movie or book is worth your time. Reviews often impact the success of movies and books. By learners writing their own movie and book reviews, they are challenged with critically evaluating the media, developing a strong and clear opinion, and then communicating that opinion with evidence to support their thinking.

Composing movie and book reviews encourages learners to think critically about many content areas. Naturally, when writing book or movie reviews, learners develop writing skills, advancing their ability to persuade readers. Writers need to use specific words and descriptive phrases so readers can gain an accurate picture of the reviewed media. To immerse learners in a historical time period, they can write reviews on media from different time periods based on primary and secondary sources. Learners can also write reviews as various historical figures, inspiring them to step into the shoes of another, deeply analyzing their individual perspectives on a piece of media. Students can also use historical fiction as a way to review the historical accuracy of a novel. In science, students can write reviews based on science trade books or based on an informational documentary. Learners can analyze the clarity and accuracy of the scientific information or reflect on the format and stylistic elements of science nonfiction books.

Although learners can compose reviews using pencil and paper, they can also be published digitally, attracting an authentic online audience. Book reviews can be published as blog posts or podcast episodes. Scholastic also allows students to submit their book reviews through Share What You're Reading (http://teacher.scholastic.com/activities/swyar/index.asp) so that other students can read recommendations.

Movie/Book Review Resources

> How to Write a Book Review
> www.literacyideas.com/how-to-write-a-great-book-review
> Two Thumbs Up! Get Students Writing and Publishing Book Reviews
> www.readwritethink.org/classroom-resources/lesson-plans/thumbs-students-writing-publishing#ResourceTabs1
> Writing Movie Reviews: Lights, Camera, Publish
> www.scholastic.com/teachers/lesson-plans/teaching-content/writing-movie-reviews-lights-camera-publish/

62. Multi-Genre Project

Through writing, learners have the opportunity to express themselves in a creative manner through the medium of language. Multi-genre projects are student-driven through the variety of choices in the genres in which learners can creatively express their ideas or knowledge. The element of student choice leads to student buy-in and ultimately student engagement. In multi-genre projects, learners can select from a wide variety of nonfiction and fiction writing styles. Products may include menus, postcards, invitations, theatrical scripts, text conversations, wanted posters, and so on. Students research the topic and then

The List ◆ 175

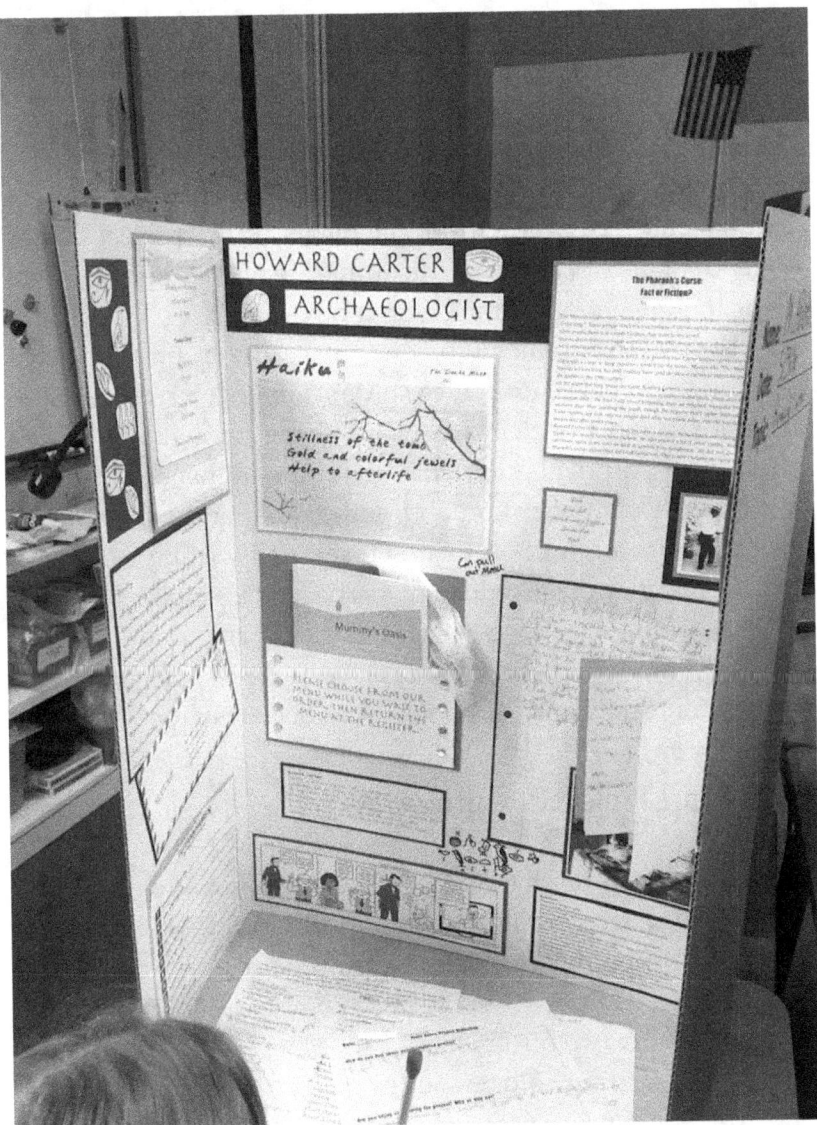

FIGURE 6.11 Image of a student-generated multi-genre project
Credit: Maggie Runyon

can select the writing genres that most excite them and align them to their strengths to synthesize information.

Multi-genre projects can focus on a wide range of topics. A teacher can structure a multi-genre project around a time period, a novel, a historical event, or a scientific process. Multi-genre projects that are centered on big ideas, such as conflict or perspective, allow a teacher to include a variety of standards that require deep critical thinking by students. For example, a multi-genre project can be based on the construct of influence. Learners can focus the writing elements of the project on the influence of historical events, the influence of scientific discoveries, or the impact of characters in a novel.

If the project is centered on one subject, for example, history, the conceptual lens encourages students to develop connections and understand the elements of influence throughout various time periods. Students can write about the influence of the historical figures, immigration and emigration, and battles in the outcome wars all through their self-selected writing genres.

Consolidation of the writing pieces penned for multi-genre projects can be displayed together on a poster board, foam board, or trifold. Digital multi-genre projects can be unified on a Google Slides presentation, an interactive Google Docs document, or a website.

Multi-Genre Project Resources

11 Reasons to Teach the Multi-genre Research Project
www.readingandwritinghaven.com/11-reasons-your-students-need-to-be-rocking-out-the-multigenre-research-project-n-o-w/

Multi-genre: An Introduction
https://writing.colostate.edu/gallery/multigenre/introduction.htm

Multi-genre Mapper
www.readwritethink.org/classroom-resources/student-interactives/multigenre-mapper-30047.html?tab=4

63. Murals

Murals are large pieces of artwork painted directly on walls or ceilings, often displayed in public locations. They can be designed as a means to beautify a public space's location, as a way to express an opinion or to promote specific ideals or values. In order to design and paint expansive murals, learners must develop collaborative skills to organize the timely completion of a project.

Designing and painting murals can allow students to delve deeper into a content area through arts integration while also creating a provocative piece of art for your school community to enjoy. In order to integrate mural design into the social studies classroom, students can research historical perspectives and symbols applicable to a specific time period. They can create a mural with the goal of expressing cultural opinions, depicting current events, or demonstrating multiple perspectives through historical symbolism. In science, learners can create murals that demonstrate scientific processes such as metamorphosis, seed germination, or the interrelationship between human body systems. To deepen understanding and connections with novels, students can design a mural based on their readings using symbolism and quotes from the text. The student-designed mural will become an educational resource for all learners who view a piece of art.

To create an authentic mural, students need a blank canvas in the form of a large wall or ceiling, pencils to sketch out the design, and paints to bring their vision to life. Learners can work collaboratively to design the full mural or be given individual sections to be responsible for eventually creating a large mural using the individual pieces.

Mural Resources

How to Create a Successful Mural with Younger Students
https://theartofeducation.edu/2018/10/24/how-to-create-a-successful-mural-with-younger-students/
Murals
www.pbs.org/americanfamily/teacher2.html
Activate Activism: Planning Our Mural
www.pbs.org/americanfamily/teacher2.html

64. Music Composition and Lyrics

Everyone has experienced the nuisance of getting the latest catchy song on the radio stuck in their head. Educators can capitalize on this phenomenon. Any earworm or catchy tune can encourage learners to create their own music and lyrics. By transforming into music producers, learners can transfer academic content into long-term memory by repeated exposure to the lyrics as they craft their songs.

Learners can compose music and lyrics to demonstrate their understanding and connection to all content areas. By creating lyrics, learners deepen their writing ability using short, succinct phrases to communicate their ideas. They can also develop lyrics that rhyme, use literary devices such as simile and metaphors, and incorporate humor to help listeners connect to the music. To deepen historical understanding, students can explore the musical trends popular during a specific time period and use those trends in music compositions and subjects to write their own hit song. Musicians can also be challenged to develop theme music for a historical figure or specific cultural event. In math and science, learners can create lyrics to help remember measurement conversions or steps of the scientific method.

Music lyrics can be written using tunes from already composed popular songs. There are also online programs, including Chrome Music Lab, that allow students to create their own music compositions. Using online composition programs interweaves technology skills into musical creativity.

Music Composition and Lyrics Resources

> 7 Great Tools for Kids to Make Music Online
> www.fractuslearning.com/kids-make-music-online/
> 12 Tips and Tricks for Using Music in the Social Studies Classroom

https://historytech.wordpress.com/2017/03/14/12-tips-and-tricks-for-using-music-in-the-social-studies-classroom/

Singing in Science: Writing and Recording Student Lyrics to Express Learning

https://files.eric.ed.gov/fulltext/EJ1094959.pdf

65. News Report

Extra, extra – read all about it! We interrupt this regularly scheduled programming to bring you an important message. As advances were made in technology, the delivery method for broadcasting important news changed. From letters to newspapers, radios, TVs, and now the internet and social media, the content of news reports has enthralled people for centuries. A news report is an account of a current event organized to be informative and often includes quotes and interviews from those who witnessed the event. News reports can be written as in the case of a newspaper or recorded such as on television or radio. News reports allow for students to synthesize and apply understanding in a creative and authentic format. When creating news reports, students get to transform into journalists.

In the process of researching, interviewing, and publishing, students develop critical thinking, media literacy, and communication skills through reflection. In science, learners can create meteorology reports based on scientific understanding of weather or develop reports on issues related to sustainability or interdependence of ecosystems. In social studies, learners can report on eyewitness accounts based on historical events or develop their own reports of an impactful global issue or current event. In math, learners can use Olympic world record statistics to develop their own report of the action and use authentic data to inform the public.

News reports can be created as newspaper articles on paper. However, learners can also create digital versions using Fodey (www.fodey.com/generators/newspaper/snippet.asp), which is a newspaper clip generator. Learners can also film and edit radio or television news reports.

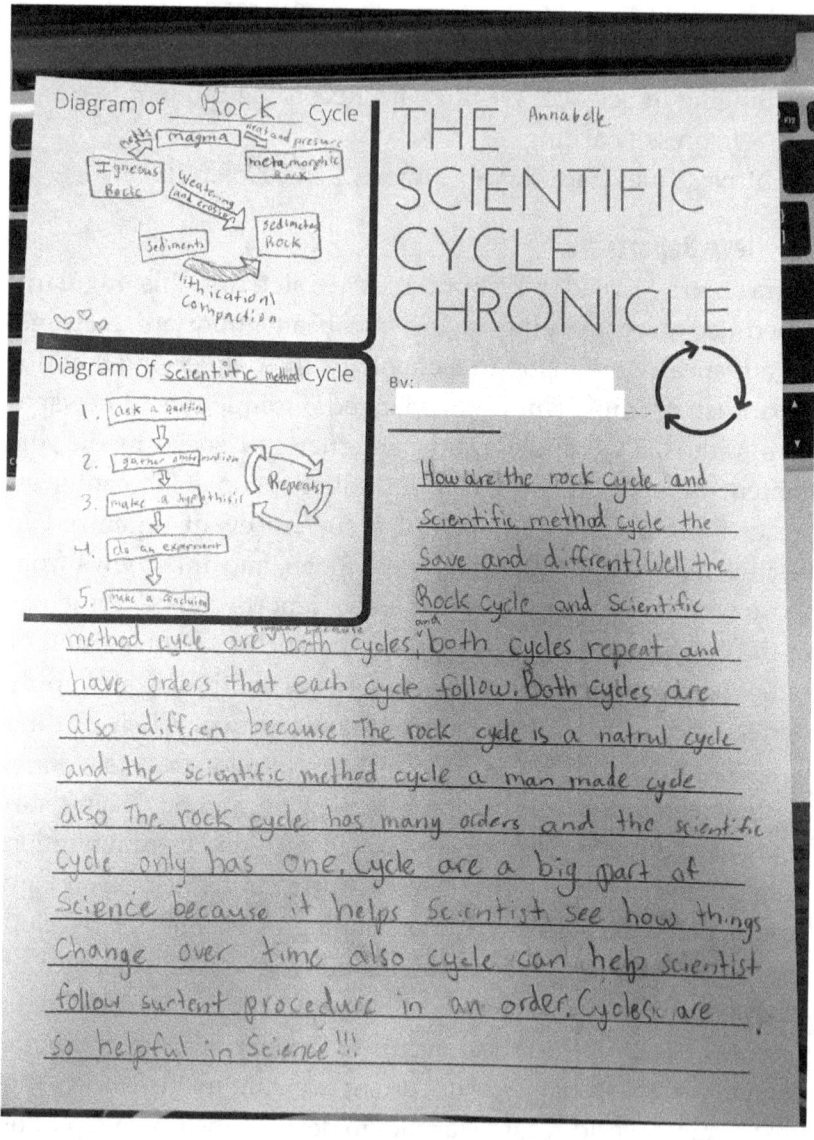

FIGURE 6.12 Image of a student-generated newspaper
Credit: Annabelle Bailor, Forsyth Country Day School

News Report Resources

Student Reporting Labs
https://studentreportinglabs.org/lesson-plans/
Roving Reporters
https://edex.adobe.com/resource/v69afee91
Newsela
https://newsela.com/

66. One-Pager

One-pagers are a strategy for students to summarize the main ideas of any content using words and images on a single piece of paper. They include a combination of visuals and written ideas to convey important information. One-pagers can include images, quotations, connections, thoughts, names, dates, and so on – anything that demonstrates understanding and analysis of the subject matter can be incorporated.

One-pagers have a very flexible format. Guidelines can be adjusted based on learning objectives. They allow learners to express their own interpretations of a novel by incorporating important quotes, symbols, or personal connections. In science and social studies, learners can develop this product based on themes such as ecosystems, human body systems, the civil rights movement, or World War II. Learners can incorporate facts, quotations from historians or scientists, timelines, or diagrams. In math, learners can create one-pagers that depict the relationship between rational and irrational numbers, fraction operations, or even geometry utilized in architecture. One-pagers' direct structure and extensive range of guidelines allow learners to creatively communicate their knowledge.

One-pagers can be designed simply using a blank piece of printer paper. Teachers can help students who are intimidated by the creative aspect of the project by developing templates using shapes to help form the one-pager. Learners can also develop digital one-pagers using Google Docs, Canva, or Padlet – all of which provide the opportunity to include digital media.

One-Pager Resources

> A Simple Trick for Success with One-Pagers
> www.cultofpedagogy.com/one-pagers/
> Digital One Pagers: How to Harness the Power of Technology
> www.readingandwritinghaven.com/digital-one-pagers-how-to-harness-the-power-of-technology/
> Using Art in Assessments
> www.edutopia.org/article/using-art-assessments

67. Photography

Photography is an art form that relies on light to interpret form and record images of objects in space. Once a much more demanding and time-consuming process, the advancement of digital tools has allowed digital photography to be an easily accessible art form for all. Using photography as a way for students to develop inferences and make connections is an effective approach in the classroom; however, putting students behind the lens gives them a voice through the camera. When taking a photograph, learners get to make choices in camera placement, shutter speed, and exposure level, just to name a few.

Learners photograph people, objects, or scenes to depict thinking visually. For literacy, learners can take photographs around the school or at home that inspire a creative writing piece. Students can also illustrate their nonfiction or fiction writing by adding photographs. A how-to book can be taken to the next level by learners photographing the different steps of the creative process. In science, students can take photographs of experiments to depict and prove scientific conclusions. Learners can also take pictures to be edited into scientific diagrams. In social studies, learners can create photographs of what historical events would be like if cameras had existed during that time period. In math, students can take photos that demonstrate geometry understanding or that can serve as inspiration for learner-developed word problems.

Photographs do require some technology, but with most tablets and phones having cameras on them, separate devices do not need to be purchased. The level of photo editing students are expected to do for the projects will impact the level of technology experience required. There are several free and paid applications and websites that are available that allow students to add elements of creativity to their photographs, such as Adobe Photoshop Express and BeFunky.

Photography Resources

Best Photography and Photo Editing Apps for Students
www.commonsense.org/education/top-picks/best-photography-and-photo-editing-apps-for-students
Picture This: Using Photography to Teach Science, Math, and Writing
www.edutopia.org/photography-how-to-project-learning

68. Podcast

Named after the combination of the popular Apple *iPod* and the term broad*cast*, a podcast is an audio file transmitted through the web. Most podcasts are free for users to download and listen to. With the ability to stream directly from the internet or be stored on a mobile device for listening to later, podcasts provide an auditory method for learning.

Learners can create podcasts on a wide range of topics, allowing for strong cross-curricular connections. Podcasts require development in literacy skills. From researching, planning, organization, the writing of scripts, and interviewing others, learners will develop skills that are applicable to many career paths.

When working with learners, teachers can use podcasts as a phenomenal method for producing and sharing authentic student voices. To demonstrate scientific knowledge, learners can write and produce podcasts that answer common why and how questions; for example, why is the sky blue or how do we get our drinking water? In social studies, learners can compare and contrast historical events to current global events or even interview witnesses of world-changing historical events. To further math understanding, learners can use podcasts as a platform to demonstrate the steps to solve problems, share their reasoning behind an estimation, or even interview peers on varied strategies used to solve an authentic math problem.

As for learner consumption, there are numerous sources for listening and learning with podcasts. Podcast outlets such as *The Walking Classroom* (www.thewalkingclassroom.org/walking-classroom-works/), *Story Time* (https://bedtime.fm/storytime), and *But Why: A Podcast for Curious Kids* (http://digital.vpr.net/programs/why-podcast-curious-kids#stream/0) offer hungry, young minds exciting and informative audio content. More importantly, learners can record their own podcasts with relative ease, sharing their perspective or newly acquired knowledge. Podcasters would require a digital device that can record audio and upload to a service, such as Buzzsprout (www.buzzsprout.com/index_new), SoundCloud (https://soundcloud.com/), Stitcher (www.stitcher.com/), and PodOmatic (www.podomatic.com/).

Podcast Resources

Bam! Radio
www.bamradionetwork.com/
Voices.com
www.voices.com/resources/articles/podcasting/plan-your-podcast
Read Write Think: Teaching with Podcasts
www.readwritethink.org/professional-development/strategy-guides/teaching-with-podcasts-30109.html

69. Poetry

Roses are red. Violets are blue. Poetry is an effective way to demonstrate learning too!

In order for students to create poetry, they need to have a high level of understanding of content vocabulary. Learners can utilize the content vocabulary to develop poetry using rhyme, rhythm, form, or any combination of these. Although poetry has strong literacy connections, the wide variety of poetry formats opens a wide door of possibilities for the use of poetry in all subject areas. Integrating literacy through poetry in other subjects allows students to comprehend the connections between content areas. The typically short format of poetry provides an effective structure combining creative writing and a full understanding of vocabulary.

Poem templates provide direction and guidance to allow students to take more risks as they experiment with the wide variety of poem types. There is no right or wrong way to write poetry, which benefits learners becoming poets.

Some poem templates include diamante, haiku, sonnet, and acrostic. Poetry Machine (www.poetrygames.org/poetry-machine/), an online poem creator, has 48 poem templates to choose from. Poetry's short and concise format provides a wide variety of connections to content areas. To demonstrate historical understanding, learners can write a haiku that summarizes a historical event or use a sonnet structure to differentiate between the 13 colonies or famous world explorers. Budding scientists can write diamante poems to describe the relationship between rocks and minerals. The diamante poem may start with minerals, use adjectives and verbs to describe minerals, then transition into adjectives and verbs about rocks. Learners can also write an acrostic poem using any science vocabulary words. For example, an acrostic poem written about photosynthesis can include the stages and facts about the process.

Free verse poetry is less guided but just as substantial of a format to demonstrate understanding. Students can develop free-verse poems by using magnetic vocabulary words of any content to create the poem. Students can also create blackout poems, which involves learners taking a written piece of text from a book, newspaper, or magazine and redacting words in order to come up with their very own poetry using the most important vocabulary words in a fictional or informational text.

Poetry Resources

> Poetry Machine
> www.poetrygames.org/poetry-machine/
> Interactive Poetry Resources Your Students Will Love
> www.readitwriteitlearnit.com/blog/2017/03/28/high-interest-poetry-activities
> Integrating Daily Poetry in the Classroom: 5 Tools to Support Your Efforts
> www.edutopia.org/blog/integrating-daily-poetry-5-tools-brett-vogelsinger

70. Portfolio

Throughout a learner's educational journey, stacks of worksheets, notes, projects, and assignments pile up underneath a layer of dust. However, portfolios provide an opportunity for learners to assess their work and share their learning with others in an authentic manner. Furthermore, portfolios provide a way for learners to see their growth in understanding and documenting their varied learning experiences.

Portfolios can be utilized to demonstrate understanding of a topic or as a way to show growth of learning in any discipline. In fact, portfolios may be used to demonstrate cross-curricular understanding through the integration of subjects. Literacy portfolios may include a wide range of writing samples, analyses of novels, or general reflections on skills gained throughout a unit or course. Portfolios centered on social studies may have a work sample for each studied historical time period. Or the portfolio could showcase assignments using a variety of thinking structures, such as cause and effect, problem and solution, and compare and contrast. Scientific or mathematical portfolios can include performance-based tasks and learner reflections on their experiences throughout the year.

One benefit of portfolios is the power of choice within an assignment. Learners can select the format of the portfolio that most excites them. Portfolios can be created by using folders to display work, attaching assignments to pages in a book similar to a scrapbook format, or organizing work samples on a poster. Portfolios can also be created digitally using Google Slides or a free website developer, such as Weebly. There are also many digital programs such as Evernote, LiveBinders, and OneNote that are well-designed for digital portfolio creation.

Portfolio Resources

    4 Tips for Meaningful Student Portfolios
    www.commonsense.org/education/articles/4-tips-for-meaningful-student-portfolios
    Getting Started with Student Portfolio Projects in Virtual and Hybrid Courses
    https://spencerauthor.com/student-portfolio-projects/
    10 Tools to Create Online Student Portfolios
    www.gettingsmart.com/2016/01/10-tools-to-create-online-student-portfolios/

71. Public Service Announcement

Public service announcements (PSAs) provide a format for students to demonstrate understanding through an authentic platform based on persuasion. The goal of PSAs is to educate the consumer and convince them that they should reconsider their opinion related to a situation or to perform an action that aligns with the perspective of a PSA.

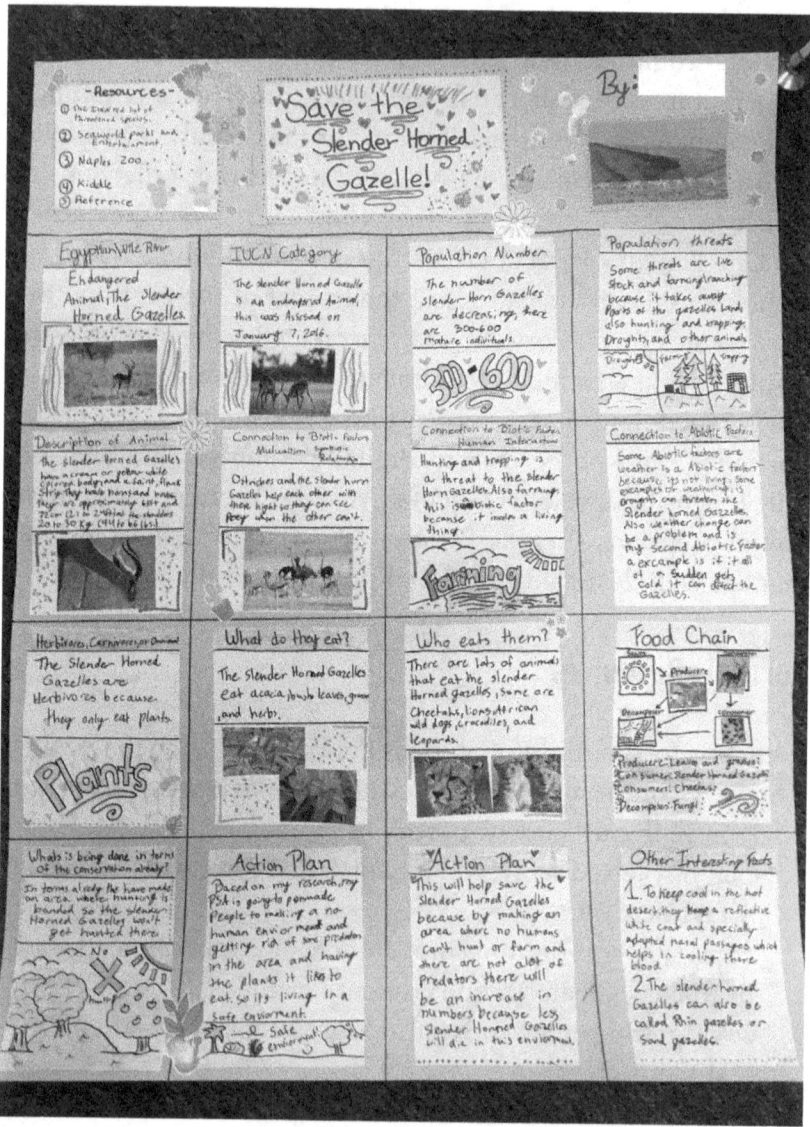

FIGURE 6.13 Image of a student-generated public service announcement about gazelles

Credit: Annabelle Bailor, Forsyth Country Day School

In an era where information is everywhere, students can develop their own media in the form of a PSA to reflect on how media impacts them. Students analyze PSAs as a means of developing media literacy skills which can then be utilized to develop their own PSAs.

PSAs can be developed for any content area in which a perspective is developed. In science, students can write PSAs to save an endangered species, explain the danger of driving without a seatbelt using physics, or discuss the importance of not doing drugs. In social studies, students can encourage viewers to get involved in a current event, convince loyalists that they should gain independence from the king, or explain the dangers of prejudice or bias based on historical figures. In literacy, students can develop PSAs to convince others that they should read a specific book. Furthermore, learners can create PSAs that bring to light an issue explained in informational text. PSAs allow for students to analyze and select the information that would most likely convince a listener or observer.

PSAs can be designed as posters or brochures. This form of media can also be created as a radio advertisement or video PSA.

Public Service Announcement Resources

Public Service Announcements: A How-To Guide
www.teachwriting.org/blog/2018/4/11/public-service-announcements-a-how-to-guide-for-teachers
My Tube: Changing the World with Video Public Service Announcements
www.readwritethink.org/classroom-resources/lesson-plans/mytube-changing-world-with-1069.html
Storyboard That
www.storyboardthat.com/articles/e/public-service-announcements

72. Puppet Show

From *The Muppets* to *Sesame Street*, puppets have proven to be entertaining and humorous while also often being educational. A puppet show is a theatrical performance that stars inanimate objects. These puppets can be easily created out of socks, paper bags, or as intricately designed as a marionette. The creation of puppet shows requires literacy skills, creativity, and often collaboration.

Through the design and implementation of creating the puppets, as well as writing and performing the story, learners develop a wide variety of skills. By writing the script and accompanying stage directions, learners grow in literacy skills. The development of puppet shows can also incorporate cross-curricular connections while also encouraging the development of speaking skills. Younger learners may even feel more comfortable presenting in front of the class through a puppet. Puppet shows can be performed based on student-authored short stories or as a way to adapt a novel into a performance piece. Puppet shows can also be used to creatively demonstrate scientific processes or reenact historical events.

Puppets can be created from a wide variety of materials. Characters can be simply designed using paper bags or oven mitts to create sock puppets. Puppets can also be designed using rods to easily allow for the movement of the characters. Puppet shows can be performed live or filmed and posted on a video streaming platform, such as YouTube, to provide an authentic audience. Online applications such as PuppetMaster allow learners to create digital puppet shows using characters from a self-created drawing or photo.

Puppet Show Resources

6 Reasons Why Puppets Will Change Your Classroom Forever www.edutopia.org/blog/puppets-will-change-your-classroom-sam-patterson-cheryl-morris

PuppetMaster

www.shmonster.com/puppetmaster/

The Science of Shadow Puppets
www.kennedy-center.org/education/resources-for-educators/classroom-resources/lessons-and-activities/lessons/6-8/the-science-of-shadow-puppets/

73. Rap

In the 1970s, when MCs introduced DJs, many began to provide introductions through rhyme over the beats of the music. Thus, began rap music. Rap is a musical art form that uses words and phrases spoken rhythmically that often include a beat or music in the background. Many videos of students using rapping to passionately and creatively share their learning through rhyme and catchy beats have gone viral. Introducing rap music as a way for students to express their understanding brings rhythm and energy into the classroom.

There is a natural connection between rap and literacy development. When creating raps, learners develop connections between content in creative and rhythmic ways. As students create their own raps, they are writing poetry relevant to current pop culture while at the same time increasing vocabulary and experimenting with figurative language. With Lin-Manuel Miranda's creation of the musical *Hamilton* in 2015, the relevance of telling historical stories through rap became evident. History learners can create debates on democratic policy inspired by *Hamilton*'s Cabinet Battles #1 and #2. In science, students can write raps that synthesize any scientific information. Science-based raps may help students to memorize the order of the periodic table or how to remember the difference between physical and chemical changes. In math, learners can create raps to remember the order of operations or the steps to estimate the product of two decimal numbers.

Student-created rap songs do not require the use of technology, but online digital libraries and digital tools can enhance learner-created rap songs. Flocabulary (www.flocabulary.com/)

is a low-cost online hip hop resource library that hosts videos across content areas to serve as inspiration for student-created rap songs. Rhyme Zone (www.rhymezone.com/) and Thesaurus.com (www.thesaurus.com/) are online websites that provide resources for students to find rhyming words and synonyms to include in their rap. Tony-b Machine (www.tony-b.org/) is a free online program in which students can create their own beats to back up their rhymes.

Rap Resources

Writing Academic Raps II: The Remix
https://mrmikekaufman.com/2018/04/25/writing-academic-raps-ii-the-remix/
Teaching with Rap: Rapping Their Minds
www.educationworld.com/a_curr/profdev/profdev161_b.shtml
Flocabulary: Write Your Own Rhymes
www.flocabulary.com/warp/intro/

74. Recipe Card (Inspired by Katie Powell's Book *Boredom Busters*)

Although paper recipe cards have become somewhat archaic with the birth of the internet, home chefs continue to rely on recipe cards to cook their favorite dishes. Recipe cards include information needed to replicate a culinary treat. The content often includes ingredients needed, preparation time, cooking time, and directions.

Recipe cards can be used to demonstrate understanding creatively across curriculum areas. A recipe card might share the makeup of a character using adjectives and descriptions of the plot through cooking actions. The ingredients (or qualities) that make up the character might include one ounce of sweetness, a pinch of pride, and two cups of perseverance. Directions may tell you to first remove him or her from his or her hometown and then stir in a group of new friends from a new school.

Learners can use quotes from the text to support their character recipe. In math, students can create recipe cards with variations of doubling the batch to practice multiplying with whole numbers of fractions. In science, learners can develop recipe cards that express the contents of a body system or the parts of an animal cell. In social studies, learners can name the ingredients and steps that led to a historical conflict or event.

Recipe cards can be easily created using pencil and paper. Cardstock paper or index cards can be used to better duplicate the feel of recipe cards. Recipe cards can be placed in a classroom recipe box for learners to peruse peers' work. They can also be created digitally using any publishing program using templates. Virtual recipe boxes can serve as a place to publish all recipe cards in a central location, allowing learners to make observations and connections between the cards.

Recipe Card Resources

> Teach Beyond the Desk: Recipe Card
> www.teachbeyondthedesk.com/recipe-card.
> Character Recipe Cards
> https://learn.k20center.ou.edu/lesson/434

75. Resume

Before applying for most jobs, people are usually asked to share a resume that documents past experience. A resume is a document used to apply for jobs that provide general information about a person, such as a name, address, and contact information. A resume also explains the person's education, past accomplishments, past employment, description of the employment, and references. Not only is the development of resumes a skill needed for future employment, but resumes can also be used as a creative way for learners to demonstrate understanding.

In order for learners to write resumes, they need to have a deep understanding of the person or character and research skills. Students can develop resumes for historical characters, using informational text and inferences from primary sources to gather information. They can develop resumes based on characters or people from picture books, novels, or biographies. Before designing creative writing pieces, learners can flesh out resumes of their developed characters. Developing a resume of a character helps to build a deeper understanding of a character's wants, needs, and dreams. In science, learners can create resumes of organs, organelles, or cells as a way to demonstrate the functions of various biological systems.

Written resumes can be created using lined paper or fancy resume paper. Resumes can also be created digitally using Google Docs or any publishing software. A quick Google search for resume examples will give you plenty of template options.

Resume Resources

Digital templates can also be created using Google Docs or Google Slides. www.google.com/docs/about/

You're Hired: An Introduction to Resumes, Job Applications, and Job Interviews

www.scholastic.com/teachers/unit-plans/teaching-content/resume-writing/

76. Scavenger Hunt

A scavenger hunt is a game in which participants are required to gather specific lists of items or take pictures at various locations based on clues. Although teachers can design scavenger hunts for the class, students can also use their understanding to create their own scavenger hunts for peers to complete. Scavenger hunts can be created to complete at school, or students can research museums or historical locations before visiting to develop a field trip scavenger hunt.

Scavenger hunts are an easily adaptable format for learners to explore a wide variety of content areas. Students can create scavenger hunts with clues that take classmates to different geographical locations or through various historical time periods. For literacy, students may need to find specific items that relate to symbols or themes in a novel or find items that a character from a novel would collect. A scientific scavenger hunt might involve students taking pictures of examples of physical or chemical reactions or biological relationships they observe. For math, learners can find objects of various 2-D or 3-D geometric shapes.

Students can create scavenger hunts without the use of technology or by incorporating QR codes (www.qr-code-generator.com/) as a way to share clues through the scavenger hunts. Scavenger hunts can also be developed as webquests where participants hunt throughout specific websites to find facts to help solve clues.

Scavenger Hunt Resources

20 Zoom Scavenger Hunt Ideas for Teachers
https://vestals21stcenturyclassroom.com/zoom-scavenger-hunt-ideas-for-teachers/
Using Scavenger Hunts to Get Students Moving in Virtual Learning
https://spencerauthor.com/scavenger-hunts/
Activities for Engagement: The Scavenger Hunt
www.maneuveringthemiddle.com/activities-for-engagement-the-scavenger-hunt/

77. Scrapbook

After any vacation or a once-in-a-lifetime experience, people longingly look through photos reminiscing and reflecting. Scrapbooks provide blank pages to add photos, newspaper clippings, and other mementos to preserve memories. Scrapbooks allow creators to creatively design, label, and illustrate the mementos while telling a story throughout their scrapbook pages.

Scrapbooks provide a unique way for learners to express themselves and their knowledge acquisition across the curriculum.

Scrapbooks can serve as a way to document student understanding throughout a unit or course, much like a portfolio. A scrapbook format provides opportunities for learners to attach work samples and their own comments and reflections. In literacy, learners can document the lives of characters in a novel by designing scrapbooks for them. In social studies, learners can create historical scrapbooks, designing memory books including created mementos and pictures a person would want to document from a specific time period or living through an impactful historical event. Learners can recreate brochures, news articles, photographs, and so on to incorporate into the historical scrapbooks. In science, learners can create nature scrapbooks that incorporate learners' observations, questions, reflections, and learned information from interacting with nature. In math, learners can scrapbook attempts of thinking tasks throughout the year, providing snapshots of understanding and a roadmap of a learner's deepening understanding throughout the year.

Basic scrapbooks can be created using stapled pieces of paper, notebooks, or any sort of bound book. Learners can cut out elements of artifacts, photographs, and news articles to paste into the scrapbook. Learners can then reflect on the media with reflective captions. However, digital scrapbooks can be developed using Google Slides, Canva, or Wixie. Digital scrapbooks allow creators the opportunity to incorporate videos, sound clips, and music in their scrapbooks.

Scrapbook Resources

Academic Scrapbooking: Snapshots of Learning
www.edutopia.org/academic-scrapbooking-photographs-journals

Character Scrapbook Lesson
https://creativeeducator.tech4learning.com/v09/lessons/Character_Scrapbook

Making Memories: An End of Year Digital Scrapbook

www.readwritethink.org/classroom-resources/
lesson-plans/making-memories-year-digital

78. Sculpture

Sculpture is an art form that results in a three-dimensional model of a figure or object. Sculpture is a fun, hands-on way for students to express themselves while also demonstrating understanding. Learners have the opportunity to design sculptures that directly model another object, person, or place or to design an abstract sculpture that can be representative of an idea or theme.

Sculpture is a learning activity that can be applied to any subject area. In mathematics, students can develop sculptures of 3-D shapes, explore volume, or develop their own math manipulatives to understand word problems. In science, students can create sculptures to illustrate understanding of scientific phenomena, express understanding of scientific vocabulary, or demonstrate thinking regarding scientific processes. Students can also explore the science behind sculpture or the physics behind kinetic sculptures. In social studies, students can develop sculptures based on historical figures, create designs based on a specific time period, or design representations of a historical piece of technology. In literacy, students can create sculptures of characters from their reading, a representation of a symbol from literature, or a model of a novel's setting.

Sculptures can be created using any materials you can get your hands on. Learners can use clay, Model Magic, paper clips, buttons, string, paper – the list goes on and on! With the increased sophistication of creative technology, students can develop sculptures using online programs and 3-D printing.

Sculpture Resources

Adjective Monsters
www.kennedy-center.org/education/resources-for-educators/classroom-resources/lessons-and-activities/lessons/k-2/adjective-monster/

FIGURE 6.14 Image of a student-generated pyramid sculpture
Credit: Sally Dunnagan, Maggie Wiley, Maryann Teuschler, Forsyth Country Day School

Geometry and Tony Smith Sculpture
www.nga.gov/education/teachers/lessons-activities/new-angles/tony-smith.html
How to Use Art to Teach History
www.edutopia.org/article/how-use-art-teach-history

79. Service Learning Project

Service-learning projects involve students applying classroom learning to activities that center on community service. Simply put, service-learning projects have the potential to bring positive change to communities based on community needs. Discussion with community members and reading local bulletins can provide inspiration for service-learning projects.

Service-learning projects can connect to a wide variety of curriculum areas, as long as their final service project relates to classroom learning. In all service-learning projects, students will grow in literacy skills through conducting research, planning the community service element, communicating with members of the community, and promoting the summative project or event. In science, students can develop projects around sustainability, building community gardens, or working to protect and save wildlife. Service-learning connects to math when the project requires budgeting or determining the prices for materials or products.

Service-learning projects do not require the use of digital devices. However, technology can be incorporated by creating digital advertisements or brochures and using social media to gather interest or promote an event. Communication technologies also make it possible for service learning projects to extend beyond the school, or even the city, developing projects that benefit those in a different state or across the world. Projects such as this develop global citizens.

Service Learning Project Resources

> What the Heck Is Service Learning?
> www.edutopia.org/blog/what-heck-service-learning-heather-wolpert-gawron
> More Service Learning
> www.plt.org/news-stories/teacher-stories/more-service-learning/
> Service Learning Projects to Engage Math Students

https://miraclemathcoaching.com/service-learning-projects-to-engage-math-students/

80. Set Design

When attending a musical or play, the first thing that you probably notice is the set. You are able to determine the setting and maybe infer some themes of the show just based on your observations. You might even be able to make some predictions regarding the plot. Determining the design of a set is one of the first things that happens before a director is able to start blocking the actors. Although set design is an essentially creative aspect of theater, teachers rarely utilize it as a way for students to express themselves through the arts.

Set design directly correlates to multiple learning goals in mathematical studies. For example, students can develop set designs that include practice in measurement, geometry, or ratios. From

FIGURE 6.15 Image of a student-created set design

Credit: Darian Pisapia

exploring set designs, students can recognize and name various geometric shapes and patterns while also estimating linear measurement. Students can be challenged to create a set design that includes a list of 2-D or 3-D shapes. The list of elements required in a set design might include a square with an area of four square inches, a rectangle that is also a square, and a trapezoid with only one set of parallel lines. Students in upper grades could develop sketches with accurate measurements using ratios and proportions.

Furthermore, set design can be used for students to deeply connect with literature. In order to develop a set for a novel-based musical adaptation, students could develop a high-level understanding of the setting and its relationship to the plot and theme. Students can develop a 2-D or 3-D model of a set design that would be utilized if a piece of literature was to be adapted into a stage production. Students can gather quotes and text support related to their set design to use as text evidence. Furthermore, set design is an authentic way for learners to explore scale, deepening mathematical understanding. Set design is a unique way for students to interact with the curriculum in a creative way.

Learners can create their designs using pencil and paper. Developing set designs on gridded graph paper will allow students to incorporate scale into their design. Set designs can also be created using online programs such as Wixie, which allows students to provide voice-over descriptions of their creative layout.

Set Design Resources

> "How I Learned Not to Be Afraid of Theatre:" 8 Ways to Bring the Theatre Arts into the 3–5 Classroom www.weareteachers.com/how-i-learned-not-to-be-afraid-of-theater-8-ways-to-bring-the-theater-arts-into-the-3-5-classroom/
>
> Theatre Educator Pro
> https://learn.schooltheatre.org/creating-a-set-design
>
> Tinkercad
> www.tinkercad.com/

81. Simulation

Simulations allow students to play roles in scenarios that imitate real-world situations. Observation, analysis, and reflection during and after participation in simulations provide students with an opportunity to develop their own understanding. Although the simulated reality is most often defined by the teacher, learner-designed simulations provide the opportunity for students to test out theories through trial and error while practicing critical thinking and problem-solving skills.

Simulations provide learners with an environment to explore complex situations in an interactive way. In math, simulations can provide learners with an authentic context in which they will apply their math skills. Learners can develop and initiate business plans or participate in a stock market simulation in which they set the parameters to evaluate the impact on a classroom economy. In science, learners can develop simulations that depict natural phenomena, such as earthquakes, wildfires, or hurricanes. Learners will need to figure out what supplies to use and how to create an accurate simulation. Simulations involve making decisions in order to survive on the Oregon Trail or win a mock election to deepen connections between historical events and events today. These simulations can be designed much like the game of Life, where learners need to draw events randomly that impact their simulation and may alter future decisions.

Simulations can be designed to take place right in the classroom. However, there are online programs such as StarLogo that provide learners with a tool to develop digital simulations.

Simulation Resources

Extended Role Play Exercises in the History Classrooms
www.edutopia.org/discussion/extended-roleplay-exercises-history-classroom
Simulation and Computing Tools

https://education.mit.edu/project-type/coding-tools/
Interactive Simulations for Science and Math
https://phet.colorado.edu/

82. Sketchnote

As a student, how many times did you have to listen to a monotone lecture while staring at slides mindlessly as you simultaneously copied down notes verbatim? It is very likely that you did not retain the information you frantically jotted down. Sketchnoting is a way for learners to deepen learning by combining words, illustrations, symbols, and shapes in a way that makes the learning more memorable.

Any subject that involves retaining information can be enhanced by sketchnoting. Learners can sketchnote vocabulary words, use symbols to demonstrate relationships between concepts, or summarize the content. Learners can create sketchnotes before a new unit, while actively listening to a class discussion, and after a lesson as an assessment.

Sketchnoting can easily be implemented using paper and pencil. Dotted paper can provide an outline for sketching. Posters with suggestions for symbols and icons can be shared to create inspiration. Or they can be created digitally. Hand-Drawn Goods (http://handdrawngoods.com/freebies/) provides many free icons licensed under Creative Commons that can be used for digital sketchnotes. There are also online websites and apps that provide a platform for virtual sketchnoting, including Paper (https://paper.bywetransfer.com/), Tayasui Sketches (https://tayasui.com/sketches/), and Notability (https://apps.apple.com/us/app/notability/id736189492?mt=12).

Sketchnote Resources

Skills and Strategies: Doodling, Sketching, and Mind Mapping as Learning Tools https://learning.blogs.nytimes.com/2015/09/24/skills-and-strategies-doodling-sketching-and-mind-mapping-as-learning-tools/

Sketchnoting in the Classroom: 12 Ways to Get Started

https://ditchthattextbook.com/sketchnoting-in-the-classroom-12-ways-to-get-started/

How – and Why – to Introduce Visual Note-Taking to Your Students

www.edutopia.org/article/how-and-why-introduce-visual-note-taking-your-students

83. Slideshow

Slideshows are a true and tested way for learners to synthesize information and share what they have learned. Slideshows involve a digital visual presentation of slides that includes text, images, and sometimes video. The slides are ordered in a way that persuades audience members, tells a story, or shares facts about a topic. Although slideshows can be one-dimensional, the advance of technology has increased the number of features that are available when creating presentations, including video, sound, and animation. Slideshows also allow students to be at the front of the classroom, developing their speaking and listening skills.

Slideshows provide a digital format for writers to develop their literacy skills. They start as a blank canvas for students to customize by adding text, images, video, sound, transitions, animations, and hyperlinks that help tell the story. Learners can create slideshows to complement a persuasive writing piece, informational presentation, or a biography of a historical figure.

Using internal hyperlinks in Google Slides provides opportunities for learners to create their own "choose your own adventure" stories. This can be applied to science understanding by developing a story that follows food as it goes through the digestion process. Hyperlinks provide readers with the opportunity to predict which organ the food would travel to next and provide information explaining the accuracy of their prediction.

There are a wide variety of online programs developed to create slideshows with features and abilities to make them interactive. Google Slides allows learners to remotely and simultaneously access the same presentations, allowing for peer collaboration. Prezi provides an interactive slide format that zooms in and out from the presentation, helping the consumer "travel" throughout the content.

Slideshow Resources

A Beginner's Guide to Google Slides in the Classroom
www.theedublogger.com/google-slides/
The Ultimate Google Slides Teacher Resource
https://ditchthattextbook.com/google-slides/
5 Clever Google Slides Projects for Kids
https://fluxingwell.com/google-slides-projects/

84. Social Media Content

Today's learners do not remember a time when they were unable to Google an answer to a question, stream the latest TV shows, or see what their best friend posted on Facebook. Social media includes applications in which users create and share content to create a digital community – this includes applications, such as Facebook, Twitter, Instagram, TikTok, and Yelp. Educators can capitalize on students' interest in social media by designing opportunities for them to express their learning through their favorite digital platforms.

Social media pages can be incorporated into any content area. Writing has a natural connection with the creation of social media content. In literacy, learners can develop social media profiles using Facebook or Instagram based on characters in a novel to delve deeper into a character. Furthermore, learners can contribute to a collaborative classroom Twitter account, highlighting the current events taking place in the classroom. To demonstrate historical understanding, learners can create a social media post from the perspective of any historical figure. What would George Washington's latest TikTok say? How would Martin Luther King Jr. utilize Instagram to share his message to the world? To demonstrate math concepts, learners can create TikTok videos that show how to convert fractions to percentages. Learners can also develop their own social media page to help younger students solve tricky math problems, much like an online tutoring program.

Social Media Content Resources

12 Social Media-Inspired Google Slides Templates
https://ditchthattextbook.com/social-media-templates/
22 Ways to Use Social Media in the Classroom
www.theedadvocate.org/22-ways-use-social-media-classroom/
Social Networks for Students and Teachers
www.commonsense.org/education/top-picks/social-networks-for-students-and-teachers

85. Socratic Seminars

Although many classrooms rely on discussions to engage students, assess current thinking, and synthesize ideas and information, most of these discussions are led by the teacher. However, Socratic seminars put students in the driver's seat of the classroom discussion. Socratic seminars are based on Greek philosopher Socrates's theory that it is essential that students develop deep connections through examining opinions and open dialogue. The incorporation of Socratic seminars requires students to prepare for discussions by analyzing rich text and arriving at the discussion with thought-provoking questions.

Since Socratic seminars are based on student inquiry questions, they can be incorporated into all curricular areas. Learners may engage in a Socratic seminar after reading primary sources, poems, news articles, blogs, or any other text that examines values or debatable subjects. To deepen scientific understanding, learners could engage in a Socratic seminar after reviewing an authentic article that brings to light scientific ethics issues. In social studies, learners can discuss a current event article that might possess similarities to historical events or a controversial textual artifact.

Socratic seminars are typically implemented in the classroom with seats arranged in a circle. However, the Socratic seminar structure can still be incorporated into a digital discussion via Zoom or Google Meet. In the same way, learners can engage in similar conversations through online social media applications or Google Classroom.

Socratic Seminar Resources

Socratic Seminars: Building a Culture of Student-Led Discussion
www.edutopia.org/blog/socratic-seminars-culture-student-led-discussion-mary-davenport

AVID Socratic Seminar
http://pms.pasco.k12.fl.us/wp-content/uploads/pms/2014/08/Socratic-Seminar.pdf

Facing History and Ourselves
www.facinghistory.org/resource-library/teaching-strategies/socratic-seminar

86. Speech

Some of the most powerful phrases have come from impactful speeches that have changed the face of history. A speech is an expression of ideas and thoughts presented before an audience. Some speeches may be written to persuade the audience to complete a task or support a specific ideal. Some speeches are designed to share information that helps the audience to understand a topic. Some speeches are given with the mere purpose to entertain and provide enjoyment allowing the audience to connect with the speaker through personal anecdotes and oftentimes humor.

This form of public speaking can have a wide variety of goals designed to help learners develop and deliver speeches in a variety of content areas. The process of writing a speech for a specific audience with a clear purpose provides learners with an authentic opportunity to practice expressive writing. In social studies, learners can develop speeches inspired by famous historical figures that have changed the course of history. In science, learners can formulate speeches persuading the audience of the most important part of a cell, element from the periodic table, or law from Newton's three laws of motion.

Although speeches can be composed using paper and pencil, slide presentations can add digital components to amplify speeches. Further, speeches can be filmed in order to be shared with authentic audiences. Flipgrid is an online application that allows students to film short videos in which speeches can be documented and shared with classmates for peer feedback and questions.

Speech Resources

Original Speech Writing
www.fords.org/for-teachers/teaching-oratory/original-speech-writing/

Speeches from History: A Cross-Curricular Unit
www.theatrefolk.com/blog/speeches-history-cross-curricular-unit/

Public Speaking Activities for Secondary Students
https://languageartsclassroom.com/2015/04/public-speaking-activities.html

87. Tableau

Kids often have difficulty staying in their seats because they naturally want to learn actively. Having learners create tableaus in the classroom is one way for them to be physically active in their learning. A tableau, originally implemented in theater classrooms, asks learners to create a picture that has various levels, facial expressions, and poses that represent a vocabulary word or concept. Although tableaus are silent pictures, students can unfreeze to share the thinking behind their pose, facial expression, or energy.

Tableaus can be utilized to assess understanding in all subjects. In literacy, tableaus are a great way for students to explain the content of a chapter of a novel or a new vocabulary word. In social studies, students can create tableaus of historical events or their reactions to a famous quote. In science, learners can create a tableau of scientific processes or vocabulary words. In math, students can create tableaus of geometric vocabulary.

Incorporating tableaus in the classroom does not require any technology. However, tableaus can be documented by taking pictures with a camera or smartphone. Students can also publish them digitally and add text to explain their thinking.

Tableau Resources

>Assessments through Tableau
>www.artfulteaching.org/artstories/assessments-through-tableau
>Tableau
>www.theteachertoolkit.com/index.php/tool/tableau
>The Magical Tool of Tableau
>https://elearningindustry.com/how-to-use-wiki-in-the-classroom

88. TED Talk

TED Talks first originated in 1984 as a way for powerful speakers to share their ideas in a short public speaking presentation. Although TED Talk conferences were not always successful, as video platforms emerged, they were shared via the internet and created a movement in sharing ideas. TED Talks are a format for learners to develop public speaking skills by expressing their ideas in a short speech (often 18 minutes or less).

TED Talks have an obvious connection to literacy skills through writing a well-thought-out speech that engages listeners.

They have a clear theme that learners can use to share their own ideas. TED Talks can be geared to focus on creative writing, persuasive writing, literary essays, or informational writing. Through informational TED Talks, learners can create speeches about scientific phenomena or historical events. Learners can create TED Talks to prove their own mathematical conjectures or explain their ideas for helping an endangered animal survive.

TED Talks can be performed live without the need for technology or can be filmed and posted on video streaming services such as YouTube or Vimeo. Filming and sharing the TED Talks provides students with an authentic audience.

TED Talk Resources

How My Students Create Their Own TED Talks
www.teachthought.com/pedagogy/students-create-ted-talks/
33 Must-Watch TED Talks for Students
www.weareteachers.com/ted-talks-students/
History of TED
www.ted.com/about/our-organization/history-of-ted

89. Theatrical Play

A theatrical play tells a story through the relationship of characters and the dialogue between them – their conversations tell the story in the script. A play provides students with the opportunity to creatively write a story that focuses on conversations between the characters. Often, these conversations center around conflict, and the dialogue explains the events of the problem and the solutions. Students can independently or collaboratively create their own script as the final product, or they can perform the play.

Although theatrical plays have a natural connection to literacy growth, they are also a format students can creatively express themselves and demonstrate knowledge of content. In science, scripts can be used to express an understanding of the connections between living things. For example, students can create a script based on an energy chain. What would the characters of sun, apex predator, herbivore, primary consumer, producer, and decomposer say to one another? In math, students can create scripts in which one character explains the steps of a math problem to another character. In social studies, playwriting can easily be integrated into the classroom by giving students choices of topics that relate to various historical events or time periods.

Creating theatrical play scripts does not require any technology. Students can write their plays using paper and pencil. However, there are also digital tools such as Writer Duet (www.writerduet.com/) that use templates to format scripts so that they look like professional submissions.

Theatrical Play Resources

Teaching Playwriting in Schools
www.learningtogive.org/sites/default/files/06play
   wrightshandbook.pdf
Writing Aloud: Staging Plays for Learning
www.edutopia.org/student-playwrights-project-playwriting

90. Thought Bubbles

Thought bubbles are simple graphics often used in comic strips or cartoons to communicate the thoughts of different characters. Speech bubbles can be easily used in the classroom as a way for students to demonstrate their own thinking or to use both their learning and imagination to show what characters in photographs or artwork are thinking. Using thought bubbles provides opportunities for students to reflect on their own understanding and metacognition as well as develop their ability to make inferences using images or text.

Using speech bubbles' simple format makes it easy for them to be used across the curriculum. In the math classroom, students can create thought bubbles for characters in word problems or for annotating their thinking of the steps needed to complete a word problem. In social studies, students can add thought bubbles to historical art, photographs, or political cartoons. In science, students can demonstrate their understanding of concepts or add thought bubbles to pictures of scientific vocabulary words.

Thought bubbles can be quickly drawn on paper by students, teachers can print out templates for students to cut out and glue on top of the images, or sticky notes can be used.

Thought Bubble Resources

A Dozen Ways to Use Speech and Thought Bubbles in the Classroom
www.scholastic.com/teachers/blog-posts/shari-edwards/dozen-ways-use-speech-and-thought-bubbles-your-classroom/#:~:text=Encourage%20students%20to%20think%20more,they%20have%20about%20the%20lesson.

How a Simple Thought Bubble Can Send Students Deep into Literature
www.thethinkerbuilder.com/2017/03/how-simple-thought-bubble-can-send.html

Thought Bubbles
www.redesignu.org/design-lab/learning-activities/thought-bubbles

91. Timeline

Although there are a variety of ways to communicate sequential events, none of them are as straightforward as a classic timeline. A timeline is a way to chronologically order events using a line to illustrate the passage of time. They can be used to demonstrate understanding of the time period of events or the relationship between events based on time.

Timelines' depiction of chronological events easily connects to a number of content areas. In literacy, learners can use timelines to organize the structure of a writing piece or to comprehend fiction and nonfiction texts. In science, learners can create timelines that demonstrate the relationship between scientific events. For example, a timeline can be used to illustrate the sequence of events leading up to the first man walking on the moon, focusing on the scientific understanding needed prior to this historical event occurring. In history, learners can develop timelines that outline the chronology of events of an important historical event. Learners can even create multiple timelines for the same event – each taken from the perspective of different individuals or groups – thus allowing learners to better appreciate how timelines influence frames of reference for historical events.

Timelines can easily be created with no technology using sentence strips, index cards, Post-it notes, or a large piece of paper. There are also multiple digital tools such as Tiki-Toki (www.tiki-toki.com/) and Preceden (www.preceden.com/) that can be used to develop webpage based timelines.

Timeline Resources

> Deeper Thinking with Timelines
> https://ditchthattextbook.com/deeper-thinking-with-timeline-projects/
> Timeline Creators and Templates
> www.commonsense.org/education/top-picks/best-timeline-creators-and-templates
> 10 Engaging Ways to Create Timeline
> https://theowlteacher.com/10-different-timelines/

92. Trading Cards

Throughout time, kids have loved trading coveted items – things like baseball cards, slap bracelets, and Pokemon cards, just to name a few. This desire to trade and interact with others can be utilized to encourage learners to create their own trading cards. Trading cards are typically about 2.5 by 3.5 inches and typically

Name of Science Tool: Graduated Cylinder 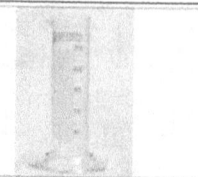	Name of Science Tool: Light Microscope 
Description: Tall cylinder with measurements on the side.	Description: A light microscope works like a refracting telescope except that the object is very close to the objective lens.
Function in Science Lab: To measure the volume of liquid and certain amounts of liquid.	Function in Science Lab: It is used to magnify an image so it appears closer and larger.
Name of Science Tool: Beaker 	Name of Science Tool: Test Tubes 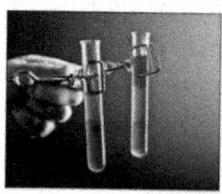
Description: A beaker is small and wide with measurements on the side, kind of like a graduated cylinder, except smaller and wider.	Description: Test Tubes are small individual tubes that are about 4 inches tall and 1 inch wide.
Function in Science Lab: A beaker's function in a Science Lab is to hold volume and amounts of liquids.	Function in Science Lab: Test Tubes are tubes that are used to hold liquids so that you can compare the liquids in an experiment.

FIGURE 6.16 Image of student-created trading cards of science tools
Credit: Cara Freeman, Forsyth Country Day School

contain an image and information that is a part of a set based on a single theme or topic.

Designing and creating a set of trading cards is extremely engaging for learners, and trading cards are a format that can be applied to any content area. In literacy, learners can design trading cards based on book characters, different authors, or vocabulary. In science, students can create trading cards based on famous scientists, scientific terms, or scientific processes. In social studies, learners can develop cards based on historical characters, events, or time periods. Trading cards based on math content might include geometric shapes or proofs, math vocabulary, or math properties. One of the best things about creating trading cards is that they provide a flexible format that is adaptable to any content area.

Trading cards can be created using paper and colored pencils or any other classroom supplies. Teachers can create a template listing the required information for each trading card, or they can give students complete freedom in the design. Trading cards can also be created online using digital tools such as Read Write Think's Trading Card Creator (www.readwritethink.org/classroom resources/student-interactives/trading-card-creator-30056.html) or on a computer using any word processing or presentation software.

Trading Card Resources

Trading Card Creator
www.readwritethink.org/classroom-resources/student-interactives/trading-card-creator-30056.html
Vocabulary Trading Cards
https://creativeeducator.tech4learning.com/2019/lessons/vocabulary-trading-cards

93. TV Show

From the early black-and-white TV sitcoms to today's reality shows where people compete for money or even love, TV shows continue to entertain all. With the availability of favorite TV shows, 24/7 through digital streaming, the variety of viewing options has never been greater. Teachers can take advantage of today's binge-watching society by having learners develop their own TV shows.

As there are a wide variety of TV shows, this media format can be used for learners to demonstrate a wide assortment of learning skills. The predictable format and script of today's shows means that literacy skills can easily and naturally be embedded. Learners can practice creative writing by developing sitcom scripts. In social studies, scripts can be created based on historical events. The young TV producers can even develop documentaries that recreate interviews and eyewitness accounts of events. In science, students can create cooking shows that explain the science behind baking their favorite dishes, or they can develop reality TV shows that depict natural selection in an ecosystem.

Although student TV shows can be performed live in front of an audience, technology can also be incorporated to enrich the task. Learners can film and edit their programming, developing a new set of skills in the process. The online application Flipgrid can be used as a quick and simple means for students to film and upload TV shows that are up to ten minutes long.

TV Show Resources

Beyond the Stigma: 9 Ways to Use Television in the Classroom
www.opencolleges.edu.au/informed/features/beyond-stigma-9-ways-use-television-classroom/

5 Steps to Creating Student Documentaries in Middle School
www.weareteachers.com/student-documentaries-middle-school/

60 of the Best Educational Shows on Netflix
www.weareteachers.com/educational-netflix-shows/

94. Twitter Tweet

Twitter is a social media platform and application that allows users to send 140-character tweets or posts. The 140-character limit provides a way to challenge students to analyze, summarize, and consolidate information into a few short phrases. A signature of tweets is the use of the hashtag symbol #. The hashtag symbol is a way to use words or phrases that connect tweets of related themes. The hashtag provides a means for students to make connections with classroom material by creating hashtags that link their tweets to big cross-curricular ideas.

Tweets provide learners with the opportunity to share their thinking with both individuals and groups. In literacy, students can create tweets from the perspective of a character from a novel they are reading or as a response to a character's comments. In social studies, students can create tweets from the perspective of historical characters or as fictional characters experiencing a historical event. In math, students can create word problem tweets to which other students hashtag their responses, or they tweet from the perspective of a math vocabulary word, such as a rhombus or a factor.

Tweets can be created using paper and pencil. There are also online programs such as Simitator that allow you to create fake digital tweets. Twitter threads can also be "recreated" by using Google Sheets, Google Forms, or any application that allows for real-time collaboration.

Twitter Tweet Resources

> Mock Twitter Chat with Students
> https://alicekeeler.com/2016/12/27/mock-twitter-chat-students/
> Fake Tweet Generators
> https://tweetfull.com/blog/fake-tweet-generator/
> Students Tweet as Historical Figures
> https://alicekeeler.com/2018/02/05/students-tweet-historical-figures-mrsashleybfort/

95. Video

Through the availability of social media applications such as Snapchat and TikTok and with the creation of websites such as YouTube, where users can quickly upload videos, students have become inundated by videos – a format that allows learners to use their voices in a variety of ways. Having students create videos provides an easily accessible and versatile format in which to express their creativity.

Videos can be created to demonstrate understanding in all content areas. They are also an easy means to use as formative assessment by having learners share their current thinking. Video can also be used for multidisciplinary projects in which students demonstrate a rich understanding of content areas. These videos can be music videos, soap operas, stop motion films, commercials, documentaries, news reports – the sky's the limit. As a result of the wide variety of video types, videos can be used in any subject area.

Although creating videos does require the use of technology, cameras are a common feature on most digital devices these days, including tablets, phones, or laptops. There are many editing apps and websites for students to create their own videos. Flipgrid (https://info.flipgrid.com/) is an app that allows students to quickly and simply create and upload videos. Edpuzzle (https://edpuzzle.com/) is a digital tool that allows students to embed questions into their self-created videos. Touchcast (https://touchcast.com/learningk12) is another digital resource that allows students to add multimedia to further engage viewers.

Video Resources

Student-Created Videos in the Classroom
www.edutopia.org/article/student-created-videos-classroom
The Best Video Creation Tools for Teachers and Students
www.kathleenamorris.com/2020/06/01/video-tools-teachers/
PlayPosit
https://go.playposit.com/

96. Visible Thinking

At one time or another, every educator has wished to be able to get inside a student's head to better comprehend his or her understanding of a concept. Visible thinking is a research-based framework that relies on making students' thinking visible. The goal of using flexible thinking routines is to develop connections between content and apply the thinking routines to other situations. Visible thinking helps show learners how to think in a variety of ways, thus allowing them to take ownership of their own learning.

Because visible thinking relies on "thinking moves" such as asking questions, making connections, considering viewpoints, and uncovering complexity, visible thinking can be used as a way for students to share their thinking in all subject areas. Visible thinking moves provide structure and tools for learners through routines that can be applied to all content areas. For example, learners can use the thinking routine of "claim, support, and question" as they analyze a lab report, a primary historical source, a student's solution to a word problem, or a short story. By creating thinking routines, learners develop strategies to deeply explore content, conduct analysis, and concisely share their thinking with others.

Visible thinking routines do not require technology to implement. They can be implemented using sticky notes, large posters, or graphic organizers. Online tools such as Padlet (https://padlet.com/) and Google Jamboard (https://jamboard.google.com/) allow students to practice visible thinking strategies in a digital format.

Visible Thinking Resources

What Is Visible Thinking Really?
https://seanhamptoncole.wordpress.com/2017/09/02/what-is-visible-thinking-really/
Project Zero's Thinking Routine Toolbox

https://pz.harvard.edu/thinking-routines
A Teacher's Guide to Visible Thinking Activities
www.inquisitive.com/blog/2019/03/27/visible-thinking/

97. Vocational Role Play

From an early age, kids love to play pretend. Toddlers play house, pretend to prepare meals in a toy kitchen, or rule an imaginary kingdom. Although preschool and kindergarten capitalize on kids' love for imaginary play, as learners continue on in higher grades, the use of pretend play is an often forgotten strategy that can be used to encourage student voice. Vocational role play involves developing situations in which learners take on a vocational role to make authentic decisions, experience a day in the life of a job, and practice higher-order thinking skills.

Vocational role play allows students to explore curriculum and content in authentic ways. Learners are able to develop their ability to write and read fluidly by designing menus, writing children's books, or designing advertisements. Young scientists can step into the shoes of a doctor by diagnosing "patients." Mathematicians can double recipes applying fraction knowledge or transform into accountants giving advice on houses a family can afford. In history, learners can become lawyers by creating opening statements for famous historical trials or by creating their own legislation as a member of Congress.

The level of technology use required depends on the format and structure of the vocational role play experience. Learners may use digital tools to enhance any product they are designing. Role play experiences can also be digitized by building websites using Weebly or Google Sites.

Vocational Role Play Resources

Role Playing
www.niu.edu/citl/resources/guides/instructional-guide/role-playing.shtml

5th Grade Residency
http://5thgraderesidency.weebly.com/
Young Chefs: From Cooking to Science
https://youngchefsprogram.org/educators/plans/

98. Webpage

The creation of the internet has transformed the ways that learners can access and obtain information. While at one point in the past, learners needed to physically go through card catalogs to find a book related to their topic of study, they can now quickly type in a word in a search engine and find an overwhelming assortment of resources related to that topic. Webpages are online hypertext documents that can not only embed a variety of multimedia but also provide a dynamic platform for learners to express their thoughts and understanding.

Learners can create web pages that relate to any content area, can be used for a single project to demonstrate mastery of content, or can be utilized as a portfolio for learning. Websites have flexibility in their organization through the creation of subpages. They also allow for creativity and interactivity through the use of multimedia to enhance a website. Many website creators allow learners to embed quizzes and forms into the web pages. In science, learners can create a webpage that provides information on an endangered species or how to decrease pollution. In social studies, learners can create websites about a specific country or advertise tours of historical sites.

Creating websites used to require being fluent in HTML coding. However, there are now a wide variety of website creators such as Weebly and Google Sites that automate the coding process for learners.

Webpage Resources

12 Best Free "Website Creator" Software
www.hostingadvice.com/how-to/website-creator/

20 Google Sites Tips and Tricks
https://ditchthattextbook.com/20-google-sites-tips-and-tricks/

Give Kids Choices with a Google Slides Project
https://teachingwithoutaquill.wordpress.com/2015/12/03/give-kids-choices-with-a-google-sites-project/

99. Wiki

Almost everyone has used Wikipedia as a means for looking up a quick fact. However, many people do not know that Wikipedia can be edited by anyone. A wiki is a collaborative website that allows users to edit and modify pages without requiring an understanding of coding and instantaneous publishing.

Wikis can be incorporated in any content area, and learners can use the platform to become authors of any type of written project. They can post book reviews, publish research, or share digital projects as a portfolio. The collaborative nature of wikis also allows digital discussions, debates, and project collaboration. Learners can cooperate digitally to solve a math thinking task or to share or present ideas in order to solve social issues. Wikis can truly be jacks of all trades.

There are multiple online learning management programs that allow you to develop wikis, including EditMe (www.editme.com/), PBWorks (www.editme.com/), and WikiDot (www.wikidot.com/), which allow you to upload text, images, and tables into the online wiki.

Wiki Resources

How to Use Wiki in the Classroom
https://elearningindustry.com/how-to-use-wiki-in-the-classroom

Wikis in Education: How Wikis Are Being Used in the Classroom
https://educationaltechnology.net/wikis-in-education/

100. Word Cloud

It is said that a picture is worth a thousand words, but a word cloud increases the worth of words. Word clouds take words and use them to create a picture. A word cloud, also referred to as a tag cloud, is simply a visual representation of words. Word clouds help to demonstrate how many times a specific word is included based on font size or color.

Word clouds can be used as an effective means to assess student understanding after reading fiction or nonfiction text. By creating lists of important vocabulary words after reading texts, word clouds can then be created that depict the vocabulary words that most students deemed to be important. They are effective in helping students to summarize then discuss their readings. Furthermore, word clouds can be created as a way to demonstrate an understanding of science vocabulary by creating word clouds in the shape of the definition.

Although there are several digital tools that allow you to build word clouds, they can also be created using paper and markers to depict the frequency of words using color or font size. Some digital word cloud websites include TagCrowd (https://tagcrowd.com/) and WordItOut (https://worditout.com/word-cloud/create). Other word cloud digital resources, such as word-art.com and wordclouds.com, add an extra element of creativity by creating the word arts in a chosen shape. Mentimeter's Word Cloud Creator (www.mentimeter.com/features/word-cloud) allows word clouds to be created in real-time as students enter their text to answer questions.

Word Cloud Resources

10 Education Word Cloud Activities That Get Students Talking
https://blog.polleverywhere.com/10-word-cloud-activities-classroom/
200 Ways to Use Word Clouds in the Classroom

TABLE 6.1 Planning Table for the List

Strategy	Subject	Grade Level	Preparation (Prep Time)	Instructional Time	High, low, no tech	Solution Fluency	Collaboration Fluency	Creativity Fluency	Information Fluency	Communication Fluency
Advertisement	ELA, Social Studies, Science, Health	2–12	Medium	Low	Low, no		x	x	x	x
Annotation	ELA, Social Studies, Science, Health	3–12	Low	Medium	Low, no		x			x
Audio Recording	ELA, Social Studies, Science, Health	K–12	Low	Low	Low, no			x	x	x
Avatar	ELA, Social Studies, Health	3–12	Medium	Medium	High			x		x
Blocking of a Scene	ELA, Social Studies, Science, Health	4–12	Medium	Medium	No	x	x	x	x	x

Blog	ELA, Social Studies, Science, Health	4–12	Medium	Medium	Low, high	x	x	x	x
Board Game	ELA, Social Studies, Math, Science, Health	4–12	Low	Low	Low, —	x	x		
Book Bento Box	ELA, Social Studies, Science, Health	K–12	Low	Low	Low, —	x	x		
Book Jacket/Cover	ELA, Social Studies, Science, Health	K–12	Low	Low	Low, —	x	x		x
Brochure	ELA, Social Studies, Science Math, Health	2–12	Low	Low	Low, —	x	x	x	x

TABLE 6.1 (*Continued*)

TABLE 6.1 (*Continued*)

Strategy	Subject	Grade Level	Preparation (Prep Time)	Instructional Time	High, low, no tech	Solution Fluency	Collaboration Fluency	Creativity Fluency	Information Fluency	Communication Fluency
Bulletin Board	ELA, Social Studies, Math, Health	2–12	Low	Low	No		x	x		
Cartoon	ELA, Social Studies, Science, Math, Health	K–12	Low	Low	Low, no			x		x
Cereal box	ELA, Math, Social Studies, Science, Health	2–12	Medium	Low	Low, no		x	x	x	x
Choice Board	ELA, Social Studies, Science, Math, Health	K–12	Medium	Low	Low		x	x		x

Class Books	ELA, Social Studies, Science, Math, Health	3–8	Medium	Medium	No, low	x	x	x	x
Coding	ELA, Social Studies Science, Math, Health	3–12	Medium	Medium	High	x	x		
Collage	ELA, Social Studies Science Math, Health	K–12	Low	Medium	No, low		x	x	
Comedy	ELA, Social Studies, Science, Math, Health	3–12	Medium	Medium	No		x	x	

TABLE 6.1 (*Continued*)

TABLE 6.1 (*Continued*)

Strategy	Subject	Grade Level	Preparation (Prep Time)	Instructional Time	High, low, no tech	Solution Fluency	Collaboration Fluency	Creativity Fluency	Information Fluency	Communication Fluency
Comic Strip	ELA, Social Studies, Science, Math, Health	K–12	Low	Low	No, low			x		
Commercial	ELA, Social Studies, Science, Health	K–12	Low	Medium	No, low		x	x	x	x
Costume Design	ELA, Social Studies	3–12	Medium	Medium	No, low	x		x	x	
Crossword	ELA, Social Studies, Math, Science, Health	3–12	Low	Low	No, low	x				
Dance	Science, Math, Social Studies	K–12	Medium	Medium	No	x	x	x		

Strategy	Subjects	Grades	Col A	Col B	Col C				
Debate	ELA, Social Studies, Math, Science, Health	3–12	Medium	Medium	No	x	x		x	x
Demonstration	ELA, Social Studies, Math, Science, Health	K–12	Low	Low	No	x	x			x
Design Thinking	ELA, Social Studies, Math, Science, Health	3–12	High	High	Low, high	x	x	x	x	x
Digital Game	ELA, Social Studies, Math, Science, Health	3–12	Medium	Medium	Low, high	x	x	x	x	x
Digital Story	ELA, Social Studies, Math, Science, Health	K–12	Medium	Medium	Low high	x	x	x	x	x

TABLE 6.1 (*Continued*)

TABLE 6.1 (Continued)

Strategy	Subject	Grade Level	Preparation (Prep Time)	Instructional Time	High, low, no tech	Solution Fluency	Collaboration Fluency	Creativity Fluency	Information Fluency	Communication Fluency
Diorama	ELA, Social Studies, Math, Science, Health	K–12	Low	Low	No			x		
Discussion	ELA, Social Studies, Math, Science, Health	K–12	Low	Low	No, low		x		x	x
Drawing	ELA, Social Studies, Math, Science, Health	K–12	Low	Low	No, low			x		
Escape Room	ELA, Social Studies, Math, Science, Health	6–12	Medium	Medium	Low, high	x	x	x		

Activity	Subject	Grade								
Event Planning	ELA, Social Studies, Math	6–12	Medium	Medium	No, low			x		x
Experiment	Math, Science	3–12	Medium	Medium	No	x				x
Fake Text Conversations	ELA, Social Studies, Math, Science, Health	K–12	Low	Low	No, low			x		x
Fashion Show	ELA, Social Studies, Math, Science, Health	K–12	Low	Low	No			x		
Flowchart	ELA, Social Studies, Math, Science, Health	K–12	Low	Low	No				x	
Foldable	ELA, Social Studies, Math, Science, Health	K–12	Low	Low	Low					x

TABLE 6.1 (*Continued*)

TABLE 6.1 (*Continued*)

Strategy	Subject	Grade Level	Preparation (Prep Time)	Instructional Time	High, low, no tech	Solution Fluency	Collaboration Fluency	Creativity Fluency	Information Fluency	Communication Fluency
Genius Hour	ELA, Social Studies, Math, Science, Health	K–12	High	High	Low	x	x	x	x	x
Google Earth Tour	Social Studies, Science,	6–12	Medium	Medium	High				x	x
Graffiti Art	ELA, Social Studies, Math, Science, Health	3–12	Low	Low	No		x	x		
Graphic Design	ELA, Social Studies, Math, Science, Health	3–12	Low	Low	No, low			x		
Graphic Organizer	ELA, Social Studies, Math, Science, Health	K–12	Low	Low	Low, no		x	x	x	x

Hexagonal Thinking	ELA, Social Studies, Science, Math, Health	5–12	Low	Medium	Low, no		x	x	x
Hyperdoc	ELA, Social Studies, Math, Science, Health	3–12	Medium	Medium	Low		x	x	x
Infographic	ELA, Social Studies, Math, Science, Health	3–12	Medium	Medium	Low	x	x	x	x
Infomercial	ELA, Social Studies, Math, Science, Health	3–12	Medium	Medium	No, low		x	x	x
Interactive Word Wall	ELA, Social Studies, Math, Science, Health	K–12	Low	Low	No	x	x		

TABLE 6.1 (*Continued*)

TABLE 6.1 (Continued)

Strategy	Subject	Grade Level	Preparation (Prep Time)	Instructional Time	High, low, no tech	Solution Fluency	Collaboration Fluency	Creativity Fluency	Information Fluency	Communication Fluency
Interview	ELA, Social Studies, Math, Science, Health	3–12	Medium	Medium	No				x	x
Jackdaw Project	ELA, Social Studies, Health	K–12	Medium	Medium	No, low			x		x
Journal	ELA, Social Studies, Math, Science, Health	K–12	Medium	Medium	No, low					x
Learning Log	ELA, Social Studies, Math, Science, Health	3–12	Medium	Medium	No, low					x
Literature Circle	ELA, Social Studies	K–12	Medium	Medium	No		x			x

Magazine	ELA, Social Studies, Math, Science, Health	2–12	Medium	High	High, low, no	x	x	x	x
Makey Makey	Science, Math	3–12	Medium		High	x			
Map	ELA, Social Studies, Math, Science, Health	K–12	Low	Medium	High, low, no	x	x	x	x
Meme	ELA, Social Studies, Math, Science, Health	3–12	Low	Low	Low, no		x	x	x
Mind Map	ELA, Social Studies, Math, Science, Health	K–12	Low	Low	High, low, no	x	x	x	x

TABLE 6.1 (*Continued*)

TABLE 6.1 (*Continued*)

Strategy	Subject	Grade Level	Preparation (Prep Time)	Instructional Time	High, low, no tech	Solution Fluency	Collaboration Fluency	Creativity Fluency	Information Fluency	Communication Fluency
Model	ELA, Social Studies, Math, Science, Health	K–12	Low, medium, or high depending on medium and complexity	Medium, high	High, low, no	x	x	x	x	x
Monologue	ELA. Social Studies, Science, Health	4–12	Low	Medium	Low, no	x	x	x	x	x
Movie/Book Review	ELA, Social Studies, Science, Health	3–12	Medium	Medium	High, low, no	x	x	x	x	x
Multi-Genre Project	ELA, Social Studies, Health	4–12	Medium	High	High, low, no	x	x	x	x	x
Mural	ELA, Social Studies, Science, Math, Health	3–12	Low	High	Low, no		x	x		x

Activity	Subjects	Grade							
Music Composition or Lyrics	ELA, Social Studies, Science	3–12	Medium	Medium	High, low, no	x		x	x
News Report	ELA, Social Studies, Science, Health	3–12	Medium	Medium	High, low, no	x	x	x	x
One Pager	ELA, Social Studies, Science, Health, Math	3–12	Low	Medium	High, low, no		x	x	
Photography	ELA, Social Studies, Science, Health	K–12	Low	Medium	High, low	x	x		x
Podcast	ELA, Social Studies, Science, Math, Health	3–12	Medium	High	High low	x	x	x	x

TABLE 6.1 (*Continued*)

TABLE 6.1 (Continued)

Strategy	Subject	Grade Level	Preparation (Prep Time)	Instructional Time	High, low, no tech	Solution Fluency	Collaboration Fluency	Creativity Fluency	Information Fluency	Communication Fluency
Poetry	ELA, Social Studies, Science, Math, Health	3–12	Medium	Medium	Low, no		x	x	x	x
Portfolio	ELA, Social Studies, Science, Math, Health	K–12	Low	Medium or high	High, low, no	x	x	x	x	x
Public Service Announcement	ELA, Social Studies, Science, Health	3–12	Medium	Medium	High, low, no	x		x	x	x
Puppet Show	ELA, Social Studies, Science, Health	K–4	High	Medium	Low, no	x		x	x	x
Rap	ELA, Social Studies, Science, Math, Health	2–12	Medium	Medium	Low, no	x		x	x	x

Product	Subjects	Grade								
Recipe Card	ELA, Social Studies, Science, Health, Math	3–12	Medium	Medium	Low, no	x		x	x	x
Resume	ELA, Science, Social Studies	4–12	Medium	Medium	Low, no	x		x	x	x
Scavenger Hunt	ELA, Social Studies, Science, Math, Health	K–12	Medium	Low	Low, no	x				x
Scrapbook	ELA, Social Studies, Science, Health	3–12	Medium	Medium	Low, no	x		x	x	x
Sculpture	ELA, Social Studies, Science, Math, Health	3–12	Low	Medium	No	x	x	x	x	x

TABLE 6.1 (*Continued*)

TABLE 6.1 (Continued)

Strategy	Subject	Grade Level	Preparation (Prep Time)	Instructional Time	High, low, no tech	Solution Fluency	Collaboration Fluency	Creativity Fluency	Information Fluency	Communication Fluency
Service Learning Project	ELA, Social Studies, Science, Math, Health	K–12	High	High	High, low, no	x	x	x	x	x
Set Design	ELA, Social Studies, Math	4–12	Medium	High	High, low, no		x	x		
Simulation	ELA, Social Studies, Science, Math, Health	K–12	Medium	Low	No, low, high	x	x	x	x	x
Sketch Notes	ELA, Social Studies, Science, Math, Health	3–12	Low	Low	No, low			x	x	x
Slideshow	ELA, Social Studies, Science, Math, Health	3–12	Low	Medium	High, low		x	x	x	x

Social Media Page	ELA, Social Studies, Science, Health	5–12	Low	Medium	No, low, high	x	x	x
Socratic Seminar	ELA, Social Studies, Science, Health	5–12	Medium	Medium	No, low	x		x
Speech	ELA, Social Studies, Science, Health	3–12	Medium	Medium	No, low	x	x	x
Tableau	ELA, Social Studies	2–12	Medium	Medium	No, low	x	x	x
TED Talk	ELA, Social Studies, Science	6–12	Medium	High	Low, high	x	x	x
Theatrical Play	ELA, Social Studies	4–12	High	High	No, low, high	x	x	x
Thought Bubble	ELA, Social Studies, Science, Math, Health	2–12	Low	Low	No	x		x

TABLE 6.1 (*Continued*)

TABLE 6.1 (*Continued*)

Strategy	Subject	Grade Level	Preparation (Prep Time)	Instructional Time	High, low, no tech	Solution Fluency	Collaboration Fluency	Creativity Fluency	Information Fluency	Communication Fluency
Timeline	ELA, Social Studies	3–12	Low	Low	No, low		x		x	x
Trading Cards	ELA, Social Studies, Science, Health	2–8	Low	Medium	No, low		x	x	x	x
TV Show	ELA, Social Studies, Science, Math, Health	3–12	Medium	High	No, low, high	x	x	x	x	x
Twitter Tweet	ELA, Social Studies, Science, Math, Health	3–12	Low	Low	No, low			x	x	
Video	ELA, Social Studies, Science, Math, Health	K–12	Medium	Medium	Low, high	x	x	x	x	x

Tool	Subjects	Grades							
Visible Thinking	ELA, Social Studies, Science, Math, Health	K–12	Medium	Medium	No, low	x	x		x
Vocational Role Play	ELA, Social Studies, Science, Math, Health	K–12	High	Medium, high	High, no	x	x	x	x
Webpage	ELA, Social Studies, Science, Math, Health	3–12	Medium	Medium	Low, high	x	x	x	x
Wiki	ELA, Social Studies, Science, Math, Health	5–12	High	High	Low high	x		x	x
Word Cloud	ELA, Social Studies, Science, Math, Health	K–12	Low	Low	No, low	x	x		x

www.k12blueprint.com/blog/michael-gorman/200-ways-use-word-clouds-classroom

Ten Active Learning Strategies Using Word Clouds
https://community.macmillanlearning.com/t5/bits-blog/ten-active-learning-strategies-using-word-clouds/ba-p/6010

At first glance, there are a lot of ideas here to take in. However, for educators, it might be easier if all of these strategies were listed and organized into some form of visual aid for instructional planning. The following table provides a comprehensive list of potential products and instructional strategies for educators to develop authentic learning experiences infused with modern fluencies. And as another benefit, most of these are easily adapted to meet the needs of learners who have exceptionalities, who are English language learners (ELLs), or who are in different grade levels, or they can be just as a way for educators to think outside the box. Instructional modifications or scaffolding strategies are welcomed to meet the needs of all learners. In the next chapter, we offer insights on how to assess the learner experiences organized in the List.

Reference

Spencer, J., & Juliani, A. J. (2017). *Empower: What happens when students own their learning.* Columbia, SC: IMPress.

7

Authentic Assessment for Authentic Learning

Dylan Wiliam, a professor and educational advocate, observed,

> When a teacher teaches, no matter how well he or she might design a lesson, what a child learns is unpredictable. Children do not always learn what we teach. That is why the most important assessment does not happen at the end of learning – it happens during the learning when there is still time to do something with the information.
> (as cited in Marshall, 2019, para. 16)

The rethinking of learning assessment can be best illustrated in George Bernard Shaw's popular quote: "Those who cannot change their minds cannot change anything." As educational stakeholders, we must come to terms that using antiquated teaching, learning, and assessment approaches will not be enough to resolve 21st-century problems. Trying to improve traditional pedagogy will not allow educators to cultivate next-generation learning skills such as problem-solving, innovation, critical thinking,

DOI: 10.4324/9781003102984-8

communication, collaboration, and creative thinking skills in their students. These skills are growing essential to operate in an ever-changing world. The present and future state of education depend on what we can do to ensure that our students are ready to conquer their challenges and thrive as they graduate.

This chapter articulates the differences between assessment types, explains authentic assessment, and provides suggestions for creating practical tools to assess authentic learning experiences. It also highlights the importance of student self-reflection and articulates how educators can provide constructive feedback and feedforward to promote a growth mindset in all learners. Most importantly, this chapter shows educators how to add their students' voices to the assessment cycle to create an instructional copartnership. After all, if learners see they are an essential part of this process, they will see the value of buying in and flourish as a result.

Traditional education systems place too much emphasis on standardized testing – testing that only focuses on one type of intelligence. In the triarchic theory of intelligence, psychologist Robert Sternberg identifies three kinds of human intelligence: the analytic type reflected in IQ scores; practical intelligence, which is more commonly known as street smarts; and creative intelligence (Sternberg, 1985; Wallis, 2017).

Sternberg's Triarchic Theory of Intelligence

Analytical intelligence: this intelligence is associated with analyzing and evaluating ideas, solving problems, and making decisions.

Practical intelligence: this intelligence is associated with individuals applying their knowledge to real-world contexts.

Creative intelligence: this intelligence is associated with using existing knowledge and skills to deal with new problems or situations.

Many of the standardized tests used in schools today measure analytical intelligence only while completely ignoring both practical and creativity-based intelligence. The vision of modern education must be to prepare learners to survive and thrive in their futures. A prosperous future for our learners will require them to develop the other two intelligences just as purposefully. Authentic, real-world learning experiences can perpetuate the development of creativity and practical intelligence in learners. However, these experiences require a different approach to assessment and evaluation other than standardized tests. We must remember this – how can educators use standardized tests as the only means to measure non-standardized students?

Summative and Formative Assessments

Summative assessments (such as achievement or standardized tests) occur at the end of an instruction program. Although summative assessments have their uses as instruments to provide data about each learner and, in some ways, the classroom they learn in, this only represents one single data point. To use an analogy, it is like assuming that all of the apples in a tree are rotten because the first one you picked was bad. Educators require multiple means from multiple data points to conclude student performance. As educators, we cannot determine the success and potential of our learners during a single high-stakes test.

On the other hand, formative assessment is ongoing and can be used by both teachers and students to evaluate and make adjustments throughout the learning experience. Formative assessment is a crucial way for educators to check students' understanding and then use the information to guide future instruction. Unlike the linear design of summative assessment, where learners participate in a learning progression and finish with a test at the end, formative assessment is nonlinear. Educators continuously guide students to access their prior knowledge, engage them in learning activities to build on their knowledge base, help them to demonstrate their instructional gains (through a variety of assessment methods), and then reflect upon the process, product, and outcome of the learning cycle.

Authentic Assessment

Authentic assessment involves a more practical approach to student evaluation, requiring more hands-on involvement than traditional assessments. Martin-Kniep (2004) identified an assessment as authentic when it requires students to engage in real-world problems, issues, or tasks for a relevant audience who has a stake in what students learn. Authentic tasks require learners to apply what they have learned and establish connections between what they have learned in the classroom and the world in which they live.

According to Grant Wiggins (1989), "authentic assessment is 'a true test' of intellectual achievement or ability because it requires students to demonstrate their deep understanding, higher-order thinking, and complex problem-solving through the performance of exemplary tasks. Authentic tasks replicate real-world challenges and 'standards of performance' that experts or professionals (e.g., mathematicians, scientists, writers, doctors, teachers, or designers) typically face in the field" (p. 703).

Authentic assessment approaches evaluate both the process and products of learning and better measure Sternberg's three types of intelligence – practical, analytical, and creative. This type of evaluation also provides students, teachers, parents, and other stakeholders with performance data that informs decision-making and supports students' success both inside and outside of schools.

Rubrics

A rubric is a scoring tool that definitively communicates the required performance expectations for a learning task, assignment, or project (Brookhart, 2013). A rubric dissects the assigned work into different components called criteria. It must provide precise descriptions of the characteristics of the work associated with each criterion at varying levels of performance. In essence, rubrics attempt to take away the subjectivity sometimes practiced during the assessment process by providing a clear roadmap to success in an instructional activity. Popham (1997) also adds that rubrics should have a scoring strategy if they are used to evaluate students' work for a traditional grade or performance score.

A well-constructed rubric can be used to assess an array of authentic learning assignments: research papers, creative writing, role play, oral presentations, artistic performances, group projects, podcasts, videos, and models, to name a few. Figure 7.1 provides a visual to identify the components of a rubric created to assess the development, publication, and analysis of a podcast created by a team of fourth-grade learners. Once their podcasts have been published, each student is provided with another team's podcast to analyze its message. The teacher then assesses the podcast development (the process) as well as the finished podcast (the product).

For the rubric (Figure 7.1), you will observe that several Common Core State Standards (CCSS) have been selected that align with a persuasive podcast project for a fourth-grade student.

(a) Common Core State Standards ELA, Grade 4, Writing 1. Conduct short research projects that build knowledge through investigation of different aspects of a topic.
(b) Common Core State Standards ELA, Grade 4, Reading Informational Texts 9. Integrate information from two texts on the same topic to write or speak about the subject knowledgeably.
(c) Common Core State Standards ELA, Grade 4, Writing 1. Write opinion pieces on topics or texts, supporting a point of view with reasons and information. (1) Introduce a topic or text, state an opinion, and create an organizational structure in which related ideas are grouped

Podcast Rubric Example with Labels

Performance Levels (For this rubric, a four-point scale is used to differentiate student performance.)

Criteria (aligned to a CCSS; each is observable and measurable)	(4) Exemplary	(3) Proficient	(2) Developing	(1) Unacceptable
Research topic for a podcast (a)	All relevant information is obtained, and sources are valid.	Most Information is obtained from numerous sources.	Some information is obtained from different unverified sources.	Little or no information is found. Sources not provided.
Integrate information from multiple sources (b)	Information was obtained from more than three verified and authenticated sources for the podcast script.	Information was obtained from two verified sources for the podcast script.	Information was obtained from one verified source for the podcast script.	Information was obtained from no verified source for the podcast script.
Construct a podcast script (c)	The script included a compelling – opening introducing the topic and organizational structure for the podcast; – set of at least three complete details, reasons, or opinions supporting the topic; and – conclusion summarizing the topic and the podcast's content.	The script included a mostly compelling – opening introducing the topic and organizational structure for the podcast; – set of three complete details, reasons, or opinions supporting the topic; and – conclusion summarizing the topic and the podcast's content.	The script included a somewhat compelling – opening introducing the topic and organizational structure of the podcast; – set of at least three complete details, reasons, or opinions supporting the topic; and – conclusion summarizing the topic and the podcast's content.	The script included an uncompelling – opening introducing the topic and organizational structure of the podcast; – set of at least three complete details, reasons, or opinions supporting the topic; and – conclusion summarizing the topic and the podcast's content.

Collaborate with a team to produce and perform the podcast (d)	Each member of the team demonstrated a captivating performance by – assuming the role of a leader open to the team's input and ideas, – supporting the leader and team by performing required tasks, – completing all required podcast tasks, and – providing feedback and suggestions to aid their team members.	Each member of the team demonstrated a good level of a mostly captivating performance by – assuming the role of a leader open to the team's input and ideas, – supporting the leader and team by performing required tasks, – completing all required podcast tasks, and – providing feedback and suggestions to aid their team members.	Most members of the team demonstrated an acceptable level or a somewhat good performance by – assuming the role of a leader open to the team's input and ideas, – supporting the leader and team by performing required tasks, – completing all required podcast tasks, and – providing feedback and suggestions to aid their team members.	Most or all members of the team did not demonstrate an acceptable level of performance (tiresome, tedious, or boring) and failed to – assume the role of a leader open to the team's input and ideas, – support the leader and team by performing required tasks, – complete all required podcast tasks, and – provide feedback and suggestions to aid their team members.
Analysis of a podcast's message (e)	Learners accurately analyze the message of another team's podcast to determine its purpose.	Learners are mostly accurate in analyzing the message of another team's podcast to determine its purpose.	Learners are somewhat accurate in analyzing the message of another team's podcast to determine its purpose.	Learners are inaccurate in analyzing the message of another team's podcast to determine its purpose.

Descriptors for Performance Levels

FIGURE 7.1 Example of a rubric aligned to academic standards

Rubric by Ryan Schaaf based on *Literacy Is Still Not Enough*, 2021

to support the writer's purpose. (2) Provide reasons that are supported by facts and details. (3) Link opinions and reasons using words and phrases. Provide a concluding statement or section related to the opinion presented.
(d) Common Core State Standards ELA, Grade 4, Writing 7. Participate in shared research and writing projects (e.g., explore several how-to books on a given topic and use them to write a sequence of instructions).
(e) Common Core State Standards ELA, Grade 4, Speaking and Listening 3. Identify the reasons and evidence a speaker provides to support particular points.
(National Governors Association Center for Best Practices & Council of Chief State School Officers, 2010)

The academic language and instructional actions defined in each of the selected academic standards have been infused into the rubric's criteria and descriptors for each performance level. Each criterion and rubric descriptor must be observable and measurable. A flawed criterion will frequently try to measure something that cannot be measured, such as student thinking or their understanding of a topic. The secret to overcoming this malpractice is to assess ways learners demonstrate or reflect upon their thinking and understanding of content.

Coverage/Organization: What counts in a student's work?

1. Content. Does the rubric cover everything of importance? Does it leave out unimportant content?
   - Does the content of the rubric represent what it means to perform well on the skill or product being evaluated?
   - Does the content align directly with the academic standards or learning goals it is intended to assess?
   - Does the rubric measure what it is meant to measure? Is it what you look for when you evaluate the quality of a student product or the learning process?

2. Criteria Organization. Is the rubric divided into understandable criteria as needed?
   - Is the number of criteria appropriate for the complexity of the learning goals or product?
   - Are the descriptors for each criterion clear, understandable, observable, and measurable?
   - Does the relative emphasis among criteria represent their importance?
   - Is each criterion clear and unique with no overlap?
3. Appropriate Number of Performance Levels. Is the number of performance levels appropriate for the intended learning goal?
   - Can learners and users distinguish among each performance level?
   - Clarity: Does everyone understand what is meant?
4. Levels Defined Well. Is each level of the rubric clearly defined?
   - Do definitions include descriptive words and phrases rather than non-specific terms such as exemplary and detailed, or counting the number or frequency of something? (Both quantitative and qualitative descriptions)
   - Would two separate raters give the same rating to the same product or performance?
   - Are the descriptors non-evaluative?
5. Performance Level Parallel. Are the levels of the rubric parallel in content?
   - If an element is mentioned at one level, is it also mentioned at all other levels?

(Adapted from Arter & Chappius, 2006)

Types of Rubrics

There are many variations and design choices present in rubrics. For this book, we will examine three rubrics – holistic, analytic, and single-point. Educators should choose the type of rubric most appropriate for tracking or measuring student performance and the data they wish to collect and use to inform teaching and learning. Educators are encouraged to use single-point rubrics to provide students with feedback and feedforward throughout the learning process. Holistic and analytic rubrics should be used when assessing multiple performance areas across different levels.

A *holistic rubric* maps out the project, challenge, or task by listing all the criteria at the same time. The use of this rubric structure facilitates an overall judgment of the quality of student work as the assessor evaluates across several different performance levels. An *analytic rubric* splits the description into individual criteria and requires assessors to evaluate each separately.

A *single-point rubric* is constructed with only a single dimension for measuring the quality of student work by focusing on a single performance level (Fluckiger, 2010).

The single-point rubric contains two additional columns for extensive educator or peer feedback. The first column represents a place for educators to explain how student performance must grow and improve. This feedback and feedforward must be constructive, personalized, non-subjective, and actionable for students. The second column is a space articulating how student performance exceeded the expectations for the solution, challenge, or task and is a performance level above the proficient standard. (Consult Figures 7.1, 7.2, and 7.3 for rubric examples.)

Positive instructional practice is for educators to cocreate a rubric with learners before the task begins. By cocreating a rubric with a teacher, students feel a sense of ownership in their work because they helped to create the expectations for the assignment.

Creating Assessments and Rubrics

Creating rubrics is made more accessible and more potent if educators first brainstorm the expectations and criteria for the learning journey with their students. This action provides a clear understanding and transparency for the learner in what the expectations are for the problem, task, or challenge since they are codesigning the rubric with the educator. Here is an example of a science, mathematics, and geography unit plan called Full of Hot Air. What follows is a brief overview of a real-world scenario along with a holistic, analytic, and single-point rubric that an educator could use to assess student work.

An Overview of Full of Hot Air

A weather team is required to prepare a weather report based on the air pressure readings in specific parts of the country for the next five days. The readings will help the audience determine what the weather might be according to the air pressure reports. Using the collaborative team's knowledge of decimals, they must record the millibars or inches of mercury (exact and rounded to the nearest whole number) in various locations throughout the country and observe air pressure and weather changes for the next five days to report to the local (and global) audience.

An Example of a Holistic Rubric Based on Full of Hot Air

Exemplary (4) – Student groups thoroughly examined air pressure, its effects on weather, and weather safety procedures. The group recorded or calculated the estimated and air pressure measurements with 100% accuracy. They constructed accurate weather maps with labels, cities, and weather data. The team created a weather report script that included all of the following: an introduction to air pressure and how it's measured, the five days of barometric pressure readings on the map, weather predictions based on the data observations, and weather safety tips. Learners performed the weather report for the viewers at home or in the studio audience and delivered a segment on preparing for extreme weather in a compelling manner.

Proficient (3) – Student groups mostly examined air pressure, its effects on weather, and weather safety procedures. The group recorded or calculated the estimated and accurate air pressure

Criteria	(4) Exemplary	(3) Proficient	(2) Developing	(1) Emerging
Conducting Air Pressure Research	Student groups thoroughly examined air pressure and its effects on the weather.	Student groups mostly examined air pressure and its effects on the weather.	Student groups performed a limited examination on air pressure and its effects on the weather.	Students performed little or no examination on air pressure and its effects on the weather.
Calculating Air Pressure	The group recorded or calculated the estimated and accurate air pressure measurements with 100% accuracy.	The group recorded or calculated the estimated and accurate air pressure measurements with at least 80% accuracy.	The group recorded or calculated the estimated and accurate air pressure measurements with at least 60% accuracy.	The group recorded or calculated the estimated and accurate air pressure measurements with less than 60% accuracy.
Constructing Weather Maps	They constructed accurate weather maps with labels, cities, and weather data.	They constructed mostly accurate weather maps with labels, cities, and weather data.	They constructed somewhat accurate weather maps with labels, cities, and weather data.	They constructed inaccurate weather maps with labels, cities, and weather data.
Creating a Weather Report Script	The team created a weather report script that included all of the following: an introduction to air pressure and how it's measured, the five days of barometric pressure readings on the map, weather predictions based on the data observations, and weather safety tips.	The team created a weather report script that included most of the following: an introduction to air pressure and how it's measured, the five days of barometric pressure readings on the map, weather predictions based on the data observations, and weather safety tips.	The team created a weather report script that included some of the following: an introduction to air pressure and how it's measured, the five days of barometric pressure readings on the map, weather predictions based on the data observations, and weather safety tips.	The team created a weather report script that included few of the following: utilized an introduction to air pressure and how it's measured, the five days of barometric pressure readings on the map, weather predictions based on the data observations, and weather safety tips.

Performing a Weather Report	They performed the weather report for the viewers at home or in the studio audience and delivered a segment on preparing for extreme weather in a compelling manner.	They performed the weather report for the viewers at home or in the studio audience and delivered a segment on preparing for extreme weather in a mostly compelling manner.	They performed the weather report for the viewers at home or in the studio audience and delivered a segment on preparing for extreme weather in a somewhat compelling manner.	They performed the weather report for the viewers at home or in the studio audience and delivered a segment on preparing for extreme weather in an uncompelling and unfocused manner.

FIGURE 7.2 An example of an analytic rubric based on a podcast assignment

Rubric by Ryan Schaaf based on *Literacy Is Still Not Enough*, 2021

Areas to Further Develop	Proficient	Areas That Are Exemplary
	Conducting Air Pressure Research Student groups examined air pressure and its effects on the weather. **Calculating Air Pressure** The group recorded or calculated the estimated and accurate air pressure measurements with at least 80% accuracy. **Constructing Weather Maps** They constructed mostly accurate weather maps with labels, cities, and weather data. **Creating a Weather Report Script** The team created a weather report script that included most of the following: an introduction to air pressure and how it's measured, the five days of barometric pressure readings on the map, weather predictions based on the data observations, and weather safety tips. **Performing a Weather Report** Performed the weather report for the viewers at home or in the studio audience and delivered a segment on preparing for extreme weather in a mostly compelling manner.	

FIGURE 7.3 An example of a single-point rubric based on a podcast assignment Rubric by Ryan Schaaf based on *Literacy Is Still Not Enough*, 2021

measurements with at least 80% accuracy. They constructed mostly accurate weather maps with labels, cities, and weather data. The team created a weather report script that included most of the following: an introduction to air pressure and how it's measured, the five days of barometric pressure readings on the map, weather predictions based on the data observations, and weather safety tips. Learners performed the weather report for the viewers at home or in the studio audience and delivered a segment on preparing for extreme weather in a most compelling manner.

Developing (2) – Student groups performed a limited examination of air pressure, its effects on the weather, and weather safety procedures. The group recorded or calculated the estimated and accurate air pressure measurements with at least 60% accuracy. They constructed somewhat accurate weather maps with labels, cities, and weather data. The team created a weather report script that included some of the following: an introduction to air pressure and how it's measured, the five days of barometric pressure readings on the map, weather predictions based on the data observations, and weather safety tips. Learners performed the weather report for the viewers at home or in the studio audience and delivered a segment on preparing for extreme weather in a somewhat compelling manner.

Emerging (1) – Students performed little or no examination on air pressure, its effects on weather, and weather safety procedures. The group recorded or calculated the estimated and accurate air pressure measurements with less than 60% accuracy. They constructed inaccurate weather maps with labels, cities, and weather data. The team created a weather report script that included a few of the following: utilized an introduction to air pressure and how it's measured, the five days of barometric pressure readings on the map, weather predictions based on the data observations, and weather safety tips. Learners performed the weather report for the viewers at home or in the studio audience and delivered a segment on preparing for extreme weather in an uncompelling manner.

Peer and Self-Assessment

There is not enough focus placed upon peer and self-assessment in schools. In essence, both peer and self-assessments share many of the same advantages and provide a crucial opportunity for students to use their voices to help each other and themselves during the learning process. Peer assessment is a collaborative learning strategy in which learners evaluate their peers' work and, in turn, have their work evaluated using a set list of criteria. There are numerous advantages to using peer assessment in the classroom (adapted from the University of Exeter, 2019).

- Establishing shared criteria lessens confusion and subjectivity about the outcomes and expectations of the task.
- It encourages student involvement, participation, and responsibility.
- It encourages students to reflect on their thinking and roles as a contributor and evaluator of the task.
- It focuses on developing students' critical analysis skills.
- It involves students in the instructional and assessment processes so they can be empowered and have a voice in how they are evaluated.
- It provides an opportunity for multiple assessors – not just the teacher.

Self-assessment is a process of critical evaluation of one's performance, in which explicit criteria are being used to evaluate and scrutinize work against a set of agreed-upon criteria (Tillema, 2010). Tillema also goes on to unveil that learners engaged in self-assessment are found to be more engaged in their work and more able to interpret why and what they are doing. Self-assessment goes beyond learners, providing themselves with a grade. This practice involves more self-reflection and self-analysis of their product and process throughout their work.

Feedback, Feedforward

A study by John Hattie and Helen Timperley (2007) found that students engaged in strong feedback loops showed a remarkable 29-percentile gain in student achievement. Using a range of assessment strategies to create constructive feedback and feedforward loops promotes growth mindsets in learners. Educators spend a great deal of time providing students with feedback, suggestions, advice, guidance, gentle reminders, and coaching – it is built into their DNA! However, the feedback loop should not end with the teacher providing feedback to students without student action or time to respond. In this scenario, the feedback becomes a lost opportunity for student growth.

Authentic learning tasks suggested in the List chapter provide many opportunities for peer and self-assessment for learners. These learning tasks also offer numerous chances for educators to provide formal and informal feedback to their students. It is critical that the feedback provided by educators not rate or demean students' work. Feedforward is the practice of helping learners develop and grow for the future. Instead of rating and judging a person's performance in the past, feedforward represents actionable suggestions and guidance meant to perpetuate a growth mindset in learners. While positive feedback is good, it may only verify what the learner already knows. When educators provide feedforward instead of simple feedback, they are helping their learners to see what is possible. Educators must look for opportunities to provide both feedback and feedforward to their students each day.

Reflection

John Dewey, regarded as one of the most influential and prominent American scholars, stated, "We don't learn from experience. We learn from reflecting on experience" (1910, p. 3). When students develop reflective skills and practices, they empower their capacity to learn. Metacognition is thinking about one's thinking. When learners develop and utilize reflection, they can adapt their learning to new contexts and tasks, identify their strengths and weaknesses, make connections to prior experiences, plan the next steps, and assess their learning (Chick, n.d.).

Using reflection during the learning process is a crucial practice for learners and teachers alike. Zohar and David (2009) found that metacognition is most effective when it is adapted to reflect the distinct learning contexts of a specific topic, course, or discipline. This keen observation is why it is critical to provide students with guidance on how to perform self-reflection. Learners will gain agency and grow as individuals if they reflect upon their learning experiences. They will make fewer mistakes and also learn from the ones they make. When an educator asks a student to reflect upon their learning experiences, the students seldomly take more than a few seconds and move on with their lives. Reflective practices should go deeper than a superficial recall of the learning situation. Learners must connect what they have learned with what they already know. They should also think about how they performed (both the positive and negative aspects) during instruction.

By including learners in the assessment process, educators pull back the curtain on one of the most oppressive matters in the education system today. Grading and evaluation no longer have to pigeonhole students. Instead, the practice of assessment can be enriching and affirming to both educators and students alike. Students cannot be judged based on a three-hour test or a bubble sheet. Students want their academic work to mean something, and their hard work (or lack of hard work) should be measured authentically with transparency.

Finally, Student Choice!

Learner choice and voice during the assessment process are essential. Educators must provide a variety of opportunities for learners to develop skills in ways that meet their specific interests and needs. They need activities and tools that will help students to develop content-area knowledge and skills. As Renee Poth states, "Assessments should help students to be able to identify where they are on their learning journey and offer a variety of ways for students to show what they have learned and can do" (Poth, 2021, para. 3).

Summarizing the Main Points

- Most standardized tests measure strictly analytical intelligence, leaving out and ignoring practical and creative intelligence completely.
- Formative assessment is a crucial way for educators to check student understanding, and use these insights to guide future instruction.
- Authentic assessment is a true measure of intellectual ability. It requires students to demonstrate their deep understanding, higher-order thinking, and complex problem-solving through the performance of learning tasks.
- A rubric is a tool that communicates the expectations for a task by listing criteria, and each describes different levels of performance.
- Peer and self-assessment are critical assessment practices to assist in learner responsibility, metacognition, and agency.

Essential or Extension Questions

- Why must educators use both summative and formative assessments in their learning programs?
- How do authentic learning experiences and assessments better access the three types of intelligence: practical, analytical, and creative?
- What are the crucial elements of designing and using a rubric during the assessment process?
- Why is it of paramount importance to share the criteria of a rubric before beginning the instructional task?
- How can you infuse more reflection (both teacher and learner) into your learning and assessment practices?

References and Resources

Arter, J., & Chappuis, J. (2006). *Creating & recognizing quality rubrics.* Portland, OR: ETS.

Brookhart, S. (2013). *How to create and use rubrics for formative assessment and grading.* ASCD. Retrieved from www.ascd.org/publications/books/112001/chapters/What-Are-Rubrics-and-Why-Are-They-Important%C2%A2.aspx

Chick, N. (n.d.). *Metacognition.* Retrieved from https://cft.vanderbilt.edu/guides-sub-pages/metacognition/

Dewey, J. (1910). *How we think?* Boston: D.C. Heath and Company.

Dewey, J. (1916). *Democracy and education: An introduction to the philosophy of education.* New York: Macmillan.

Fluckiger, J. (2010). Single point rubric: A tool for responsible student self-assessment. *The Delta Kappa Gamma Bulletin, 76*(4), 18–25.

Hattie, J., & Timperley, H. (2007). The power of feedback. *Review of Educational Research, 77*(1), 81–112. doi:10.3102/003465430298487

Marshall, K. (2019). Pushing back on outmoded beliefs. *Teaching Channel.* https://www.teachingchannel.com/blog/pushing-back-on-outmoded-beliefs

Martin-Kniep, G. (2004). *Becoming a better teacher: Eight innovations that work.* Alexandria, VA: ASCD.

Mohan, N., Jukes, I., & Schaaf, R. (2021). *Literacy is still not enough: Modern fluencies for teaching, learning, and assessment.* Thousand Oaks, CA: Corwin.

National Governors Association Center for Best Practices & Council of Chief State School Officers. (2010). *Common core state standards for English language arts and literacy in history/social studies, science, and technical subjects.* Washington, DC: Authors.

Popham, W. J. (1997). What's wrong – and what's right – with rubrics. *Educational Leadership, 55*(2), 72–75.

Poth, R. (2021). Promoting student choice and voice in learning. *Getting Smart.* Retrieved from www.gettingsmart.com/2021/10/12/promoting-student-choice-and-voice-in-learning/

Sternberg, R. (1985). *Beyond IQ: A triarchic theory of intelligence.* Cambridge, MA: Cambridge University Press.

Tillema, H. (2010). Formative assessment in teacher education and teacher professional development. *International Encyclopedia of Education (Third Edition)*, 563–571. doi:10.1016/B978-0-08-044894-7.01639-0

The University of Exeter. (2019). *Chapter 10 – peer and self-assessment in student work: Principles and criteria*. Retrieved from http://as.exeter.ac.uk/academic-policy-standards/tqa-manual/lts/peerselfassessment/

Wallis, C. (2017). Is the U.S. education system producing a society of "smart fools"? *Scientific American*. Retrieved June 1, 2019, from www.scientificamerican.com/article/is-the-u-s-education-system-producing-a-society-of-ldquo-smart-fools-rdquo/?WT.mc_id=send-to-friend

Wiggins, G. (1989). A true test: Toward more authentic and equitable assessment. *Phi Delta Kappan, 70*(9), 703–713.

Zohar, A., & David, A. (2009). Paving a clear path in a thick forest: A conceptual analysis of a metacognitive component. *Metacognition Learning, 4*, 177–195.

8

The Best of Both Worlds

Providing Learner Empowerment in the Age of High-Stakes Learning

Time for a Change

Robert John Meehan wrote, "Learning should be viewed as a form of enthusiasm transferred to the student." Today's generations are experiencing a world that is increasingly out of step with traditional assumptions and approaches to teaching, learning, and assessment. The reality is that many children today do not learn the way teachers prefer to teach. The challenge is that some educators and decision-makers are unwilling to acknowledge there is a widening gap between the world we grew up in, the world we live in today, and the schools we have created. Schools are changing. The main issue is that the world is changing far faster.

Our role as educators is not just to stand up in front of our students and show them how smart we are. Rather, it is to help them discover how smart *they* are to assume increasing control and responsibility for their learning.

To be effective modern-day educators, we must grapple with the instinct to show and tell our learners everything. Learners have spent far too long being passive witnesses to their education. Remember, to survive and thrive in the unpredictable future, today's learners must grow into tomorrow's leaders. To prepare them for what lies ahead, they must wrest back control. The ultimate goal of education and the blueprint for learners should be for them to develop into self-directed, self-regulated, creative, independent, divergent thinkers and doers.

Hardware, Headware, Heartware

Schools and society, especially in the light of the ongoing pandemic, have seen technology as the great savior of the world. *Hardware* allows us to communicate, create, and collaborate. During the pandemic, it has provided a means for millions of learners to safely carry on their studies using online tools and curriculums. However, learning is far more about *headware* than it is about *hardware*. The content learners are exposed to will come and go, and they may or may not remember what they have been taught. Only the processes remain behind in times of radical change. Learning is all about *headware* – critical thinking, problem-solving, creativity, communication, and collaboration. However, for learner buy-in, they must also become explorers, navigators, dreamers, creators, and leaders throughout their learning process. This leads us to the final term – *heartware*. *Heartware* is all about the passion, ownership, empowerment, energy, commitment, engagement, and empathy learners experience as they navigate through their learning journeys.

So Where to Begin? It First Starts With This Realization

The secret to success for educators has very little to do with being good at shelling out content, lecturing, and completing paperwork and far more to do with creating an engaging and participatory learning environment that compels learners to *want* to be there. Today's generations learn best by personally experiencing learning that is physical, emotional, intellectual, and spiritual. Great educators provide experiences that create long-term memories and connections. Great teachers design learning experiences that put students in the driver's seat and then get out of the way.

This is not about *making* students learn; it's about getting students to *want* to learn. Without motivation and engagement, no learning will take place.

Answer these questions: Would learners choose to be in your classroom if they didn't have to be there? And if they don't want to be there, what do we need to change?

The Most Effective Learning App *Ever*!

The killer app and best one-to-one device in today's classroom is a great teacher – a teacher who has a love of learning; a teacher who has an appreciation of the aesthetic, the esoteric, the ethical, and the moral; a teacher who understands great educational theorists such as Papert, Montessori, Dewey, Freire, and Piaget; a teacher who knows how to empower kids to do amazing things.

Today's learners are not the same learners that our current schools were originally designed for over 130 years ago, and they are certainly not the learners that many of today's educators were trained to teach. Education continues to operate on assumptions about teaching, learning, and assessment that are targeted at students from another age and another world – one that has come and gone.

We want to make it clear that we are not advocating that educators throw out all of the traditional educational approaches. There is a place for traditional teaching and learning experiences. There is a place for using stand-and-deliver lectures, teaching basic skills, and memorization. After all, that is how you transmit culture; that is, how you transmit democracy; that is how you transmit traditions from one generation to the next. To be clear, educators have every right to expect learners to honor the traditional ways of learning. Make sure you heard us say that loud and clear.

But at the same time, we have to acknowledge that our world has changed – and continues to change at an accelerating rate. As a result, the needs of our learners, once they leave us, are fundamentally different. Instead of obedient, dependent citizens, the world requires self-directed, self-regulated, highly motivated, creative, independent, divergent thinkers and doers.

One final reminder. At the beginning of this book, we defined learner agency as

> the attitudes, motivations, and empowerment individuals have within a learning context as exhibited in the learner's ability to select a learning environment, a content or subject area, a learning approach, and a learning pace.

Educators have the ability to provide learners with flexible learning environments. Educators can incorporate many of the subjects and resources learners prefer in their learning experiences. Educators can alter instructional approaches and ways learners demonstrate their understanding. Educators can place more power in the hands and minds of those they teach.

As you finish this book, the fundamental question you should be asking yourself is this: "How have I modified my instructional assumptions and practices to empower my learners?" Nothing is stopping us from modifying the way we learn and how we teach. Substantial changes don't take place by trying to make massive alterations to current practice in short periods.

Substantial change occurs by taking a series of small steps that lead to big strides. Instead of trying to change everything at once, educators should begin by taking a series of baby steps – selecting one activity, one assignment, or one project to begin the process of empowering learners to assume the mantle of leadership for themselves. As we leave you to empower your learners by providing them with more agency, choice, and voice in your learning environment, we want to share with you these quotes to summarize our main messages throughout our combined musings. The traditional means for completing a book is to find a quote that creates an inspirational sendoff to the reader. To that end, we searched high and low to try and find just the perfect quote to end on. Unfortunately, we found far too many quotes that perfectly summarized our ideas and weren't able to agree on just one to narrow it down to. So we're handing it off to you and offering you the agency to determine which quote or quotes most inspire you to lead the learner agency movement.

- "Change is the law of life . . . those who look only to the past or the present are certain to miss the future" (John F. Kennedy).
- "The mind is a fire to be kindled, not a vessel to be filled" (Plutarch).
  Translation from the Loeb Classical Library, 1927.
- "Learning is not the product of teaching. Learning is the product of the activity of learners" (John Holt).
  Growing Without Schooling magazine #40 1977. Retrieved from www.goodreads.com/quotes/7159708-learning-is-not-the-product-of-teaching-learning-is-the.
- "Children have to be educated, but they have also to be left to educate themselves" (Ernest Dimnet).
- Attributed to Ernest Dimnet in Rhonda L. Clements, Leah Fiorentino (2004), *The Child's Right to Play: A Global Approach*, p. 111.
- "The great aim of education is not knowledge but action" (Herbert Spencer).
  A Mother's Advice to Her Son, 1726, p. 137.
- "I never teach my pupils, I only attempt to provide the conditions in which they can learn" (Albert Einstein).
  Cited in Walter & Marks, 1981, p. 1. Walter, G., & Marks, S. (1981). *Experiential learning and change*. New York: John Wiley and Sons.

- "A teacher is one who makes himself progressively unnecessary" (Thomas Carruthers).
  Cited in TeachThought, 2020 May 16. Retrieved from www.teachthought.com/pedagogy/great-best-quotes-about-teaching.
- "The difference between school and life? In school, you're taught a lesson and then given a test. In life, you're given a test that teaches you a lesson" (Tom Bodett).
  Quoted by Clark, 2007 August 17. Retrieved from www.newtownbee.com/08172007/the-difference-between-school-and-life-in-school-youre-taught-a-lesson-a/#:~:text=school%20and%20life%3F-,In%20school%2C%20you're%20taught%20a%20lesson,and%20then%20given%20a%20test.&text=In%20life%2C%20you%C3%A2%E2%82%AC%E2%84%A2,everything%20he%20learned%20in%20school.
- "The best teachers are those who show you where to look but don't tell you what to see" (Alexandra K. Trenfor).
  Quoted by Anderson, E. (2014, March 10). One way to make yourself much smarter, right now. *Forbes*. Retrieved from www.forbes.com/sites/erikaandersen/2014/03/10/one-way-to-make-yourself-much-smarter-right-now/?sh=767a6cbf3c5a.

The Digital Library

Collectively, to extend your professional and personal growth as an educator, we have amassed an expansive collection of articles, resources, and examples. The digital library is a treasure trove for educators to explore and carry on the mission of empowering learners with a voice and choice in schools. Think of this as an additional book at no cost.

Link: https://bit.ly/LEARNERVOICESTUDENTCHOICE

#LearnerChoice #StudentVoice

We understand far too well the limitations of a book as the primary outlet for professional development. Unlike the success of many one-hit wonders in the music industry, professional growth and skill development are not ideal using this approach. Cumulative, spaced repetition and the development of a community of support and practice are the keys to sustained professional development and substantial learning. Twitter, Instagram, and Facebook have become havens for educators to share ideas, resources, and support. We offer a way to connect and contribute.

On Twitter, please share ideas and ask questions using either the #LearnerChoice or #StudentVoice hashtags.

On Instagram, please share ideas and ask questions using either the #LearnerChoice or #StudentVoice hashtags.

Reference

Meehan, R. J. Retrieved from http://robertjohnmeehan.com/

For Product Safety Concerns and Information please contact our EU
representative GPSR@taylorandfrancis.com
Taylor & Francis Verlag GmbH, Kaufingerstraße 24, 80331 München, Germany

www.ingramcontent.com/pod-product-compliance
Lightning Source LLC
Chambersburg PA
CBHW052215300426
44115CB00011B/1698